STATE OF THE WORLD'S INDIGENOUS PEOPLES

INDIGENOUS PEOPLES' ACCESS TO HEALTH SERVICES

UNITED NATIONS

DESA

The Department of Economic and Social Affairs of the United Nations is a vital interface between global policies in the economic, social and environmental spheres and national action. The Department works in three main interlinked areas: (i) it compiles, generates and analyses a wide range of economic, social and environmental data and information on which Member States of the United Nations draw to review common problems and to take stock of policy options; (ii) it facilitates the negotiations of Member States in many intergovernmental bodies on joint course of action to address ongoing or emerging global challenges; and (iii) it advises interested Governments on ways and means of translating policy frameworks developed in United Nations conferences and summits into programmes at the country level and, through technical assistance, helps build national capacities.

Note

The views expressed in this publication do not necessarily reflect those of the United Nations. The designations employed and the presentation of the material in this publication do not imply the expression of any opinion whatsoever on the part of the Secretariat of the United Nations concerning the legal status of any country or territory or of its authorities, or concerning the delimitations of its frontiers.

The designations of country groups in the text and the tables are intended solely for statistical or analytical convenience and do not necessarily express a judgement about the stage reached by a particular country or area in the development process.

Mention of the names of firms and commercial products does not imply the endorsement of the United Nations.

Symbols of United Nations documents are composed of capital letters combined with figures.

ACKNOWLEDGEMENTS

The State of the World's Indigenous Peoples has been a collaborative effort of experts and organizations. The introduction was written by the secretariat of the Permanent Forum on Indigenous Issues within the Division for Social Policy and Development of the Department of Economic and Social Affairs. The thematic chapters were written by Ms. Oksana Buranbaeva, Dr. Myriam Conejo Maldonado, Dr. Ketil Lenert Hansen, Dr. Mukta S. Lama, Dr. Priscilla S. Migiro and Dr. Collin Tukuitonga. The Secretariat of the Permanent Forum on Indigenous Issues oversaw the preparation of the publication. Special acknowledgements go to the editor, Jeffrey Reading, translator Raul Molina, and also the UN Graphic Design Unit, Department of Public Information.

Ms. Shamshad Akhtar, Assistant-Secretary-General for Economic Development and Senior Advisor on Economic Development and Finance, of the Department of Economic and Social Affairs provided invaluable comments.

FOREWORD TO THE STATE OF THE WORLD'S INDIGENOUS PEOPLES

By Mr. Wu Hongbo, Under-Secretary-General for Economic and Social Affairs

Over the past two decades, international efforts have been made to improve the rights of indigenous peoples, to bring awareness to their issues, including their engagement in developing policy and programmes in order to improve their livelihoods. In the First Decade of the World's Indigenous People (1995-2004) the United Nations created the United Nations Permanent Forum on Indigenous Issues as well as the Special Rapporteur on the rights of indigenous peoples. During the Second Decade of the World's Indigenous People (2005-2015), there have been further initiatives such as the creation of Expert Mechanism on the Rights of Indigenous Peoples. The adoption of the United Nations Declaration on the Rights of Indigenous Peoples in September 2007 was a major step for the United Nations as the Declaration had been debated for over 20 years.

The United Nations Permanent Forum on Indigenous Issues is an advisory body to the Economic and Social Council with a mandate to discuss indigenous issues related to economic and social development, culture, the environment, education, health and human rights. At its twelfth session, the Permanent Forum on Indigenous Issues reviewed health as one of its mandated areas and stated the right to health materializes through the well-being of an individual as well as the social, emotional, spiritual and cultural well-being of the whole community.[1]

The United Nations Declaration on the Rights of Indigenous Peoples states that indigenous peoples have the right to be actively involved in developing and determining their health programmes; the right to their traditional medicines, maintain their health practices, and the equal right to the enjoyment of the highest attainable standard of physical and mental health. Unfortunately, indigenous peoples suffer higher rates of ill health and have dramatically shorter life expectancy than other groups living in the same countries. This inequity results in indigenous peoples suffering unacceptable health problems and they are more likely to experience disabilities and dying at a younger age than their non-indigenous counterparts.

Indigenous peoples' health status is severely affected by their living conditions, income levels, employment rates, access to safe water, sanitation, health services and food availability. Indigenous peoples are facing destruction to their lands, territories and resources, which are essential to their very survival. Other threats include climate change and environmental contamination (heavy metals, industrial gases and effluent wastes).

Indigenous peoples also experience major structural barriers in accessing health care. These include geographical isolation and poverty which results in not having the means to pay the high cost for transport or treatment. This is further compounded by discrimination, racism and a lack of cultural understanding and sensitivity. Many health systems do not reflect the social and cultural practices and beliefs of indigenous peoples.

---

[1] E/2013/43 p. 2.

At the same time, it is often difficult to obtain a global assessment of indigenous peoples' health status because of the lack of data. There has to be more work undertaken towards building on existing data collection systems to include data on indigenous peoples and their communities.

This publication sets out to examine the major challenges for indigenous peoples to obtain adequate access to and utilization of quality health care services. It provides an important background to many of the health issues that indigenous peoples are currently facing. Improving indigenous peoples' health remains a critical challenge for indigenous peoples, States and the United Nations.

Contents

INTRODUCTION

INTRODUCTION

At its first session, the United Nations Permanent Forum on Indigenous Issues requested the United Nations System produce such a report on the state of the world's indigenous peoples.[2] It was also suggested the report be a key advocacy tool for raising awareness on indigenous peoples' issues in general and in particular to raise the profile of the Permanent Forum. In addition, the report should be of value for deliberations within the Economic and Social Council, the General Assembly and other bodies of the UN system.

The first publication of *The State of the World's Indigenous Peoples* was published in 2009 and its major focus was on: Poverty and Well-being; Culture; Environment; Contemporary Education; Health; Human Rights and Emerging Issues. The report was well received, and, according to press reports, the publication revealed alarming statistics on indigenous peoples' poverty, health, education, employment, human rights, the environment and more. This was the first United Nations publication and provided much needed information on the status of indigenous peoples throughout the world.

The *State of the World's Indigenous Peoples* will remain a recurrent "flagship" publication produced by the United Nations. It is intended that publications such as this will deal with a broad spectrum of indigenous peoples' issues. It is hoped that such a publication, given its function of supporting the United Nations Permanent Forum, will also promote awareness of indigenous peoples' issues within the United Nations system, with States, academia and the broader public.

The current situation of indigenous peoples remains a concern within the United Nations. It has been estimated that the world's 370 million indigenous peoples reside in approximately 90 countries of the world.[3] They are among the world's most marginalized peoples, and are often isolated politically and socially within the countries where they reside by the geographical location of their communities, their separate histories, cultures, languages and traditions. They are often among the poorest peoples and the poverty gap between indigenous and non-indigenous groups is increasing in many countries around the world. This influences indigenous peoples' quality of life and their right to health.

Indigenous peoples' access to adequate health care remains one of the most challenging and complex areas. There is an urgent need to focus on health issues as well as alternative health care frameworks. As previously stated, health is one of the six mandated areas of the United Nations Permanent Forum on Indigenous Issues and is one of the focuses of the World Health Organization, which recognizes the right to health as a fundamental human right in its constitution. The United Nations Declaration on the Rights of Indigenous Peoples includes articles (21, 23, 24 and 29) that refer specifically to the right to health, including indigenous peoples' right to improving their economic and social conditions in the area of health, with particular attention to the needs of indigenous elders, women, youth, children and persons with disabilities. Further, indigenous peoples have the right to determine their health programmes and to administer these programmes through their own institutions, as well as maintain their traditional health practices.

---

[2] Permanent Forum on Indigenous Issues, Report on the First session (12-24 May 2002) E/2002/43.

[3] Harry Patrinos and Gillette Hall, Indigenous Peoples, Poverty and Development, 2010, p. 8.

Also, that States take effective measures to ensure that programmes for monitoring, maintaining and restoring the health of indigenous peoples, as developed and implemented by the peoples affected by such materials, are duly implemented.

Indigenous peoples face a myriad of obstacles when accessing public health systems. These include the lack of health facilities in indigenous communities and cultural differences with the health care providers such as differences in languages, illiteracy and lack of understanding of indigenous culture and traditional health care systems. There is also an absence of adequate health insurance or lack of economic capacity to pay for services. As a result, indigenous peoples often cannot afford health services even if it is available. Marginalization also means that indigenous peoples are reluctant or have difficulties in participating in non-indigenous processes or systems at the community, municipal, state and national levels.

There are also major concerns regarding the lack of data on indigenous peoples' health and social conditions. Not only is there a lack of disaggregated data based on ethnicity but also data related to the location of indigenous peoples' residence such as urban, rural or isolated areas. As a result, there is a lack of information, analysis and evaluation of programmes and services relating to indigenous peoples' health situation.

One of the important areas for health care for indigenous peoples lies in intercultural frameworks and models of care. Health care services need to be pluricultural in order to develop effective models of care and best practices so that such programmes and services are culturally and linguistically appropriate for indigenous peoples. Also, indigenous peoples must be able to participate in the design and implementation of comprehensive health plans, policies and programmes.

It has been estimated that over 80 per cent of the world's indigenous peoples live in Asia, Latin America and Africa,. However, there is still little information known about their health status and their levels of access to health services. Even in wealthy nations, most studies indicate an alarming health disadvantage for indigenous peoples. Historically, indigenous peoples have suffered the impact of colonization and assimilation policies as well as the imposition of foreign development models. Indigenous peoples continue to suffer discrimination in their own countries which has a major impact on their lives, in particular, their health. Indigenous peoples are not only a marginalized group with health problems, they are also highly aware of their situation, quite political and willing to work to towards improving their health and social status. Therefore, indigenous peoples have the right to determine their own policies, strategies and interventions in order to obtain the highest attainable standards of health and health services, as set out in the United Nations Declaration on the Rights of Indigenous Peoples.

The concept of indigenous peoples

There has been considerable debate devoted to the question of the definition or understanding of "indigenous peoples" however, no such definition has ever been adopted by any United Nations body, and the prevailing view today is that no formal universal definition is necessary for the recognition and protection of their rights.

One of the most cited descriptions of the concept of "indigenous" was outlined in the José R. Martínez Cobo's *Study on the Problem of Discrimination against Indigenous Populations.* After consideration of the issues involved, Martínez Cobo offered a working definition of "indigenous communities, peoples and nations". In doing so, he expressed a number of basic ideas forming the intellectual framework for this effort, including the right of indigenous peoples themselves to define what and who are indigenous peoples. The working definition is as follows:

> Indigenous communities, peoples and nations are those which, having a historical continuity with pre-invasion and pre-colonial societies that developed on their territories, consider themselves distinct from other sectors of the societies now prevailing on those territories, or parts of them. They form at present non-dominant sectors of society and are determined to preserve, develop and transmit to future generations their ancestral territories, and their ethnic identity, as the basis of their continued existence as peoples, in accordance with their own cultural patterns, social institutions and legal system.

This historical continuity may consist of the continuation, for an extended period reaching into the present of one or more of the following factors:

a. Occupation of ancestral lands, or at least of part of them.

b. Common ancestry with the original occupants of these lands.

c. Culture in general, or in specific manifestations (such as religion, living under a tribal system, membership of an indigenous community, dress, means of livelihood, lifestyle, etc.).

d. Language (whether used as the only language, as mother tongue, as the habitual means of communication at home or in the family, or as the main, preferred, habitual, general or normal language).

e. Residence in certain parts of the country, or in certain regions of the world.

f. Other relevant factors.

On an individual basis, an indigenous person is one who belongs to these indigenous populations through self-identification as indigenous (group consciousness) and is recognized and accepted by these populations as one of its members (acceptance by the group). This preserves for these communities the sovereign right and power to decide who belongs to them without external interference.[4]

During the many years of debate at the meetings of the Working Group on Indigenous Populations, observers from indigenous organizations developed a common position that rejected the idea of a formal definition of indigenous peoples at the international level to be adopted by States. Similarly, government delegations expressed the view that it was neither desirable nor necessary to elaborate a universal definition of indigenous peoples. Finally, at its fifteenth session, in 1997, the Working Group concluded that a definition of indigenous peoples at the global level was not possible at that time, and this did not prove necessary for the adoption of the Declaration on the Rights of Indigenous Peoples.[5] Instead of offering a definition, Article 33 of the United Nations

---

[4] Martínez Cobo (1986-1987), paras. 379-382.

[5] Working Group on Indigenous Populations (2006a) and (2006b), paras. 153-154.

Declaration on the Rights of Indigenous Peoples underlines the importance of self-identification, that indigenous peoples themselves define their own identity as indigenous.

Article 33

1. Indigenous peoples have the right to determine their own identity or membership in accordance with their customs and traditions. This does not impair the right of indigenous individuals to obtain citizenship of the States in which they live.

2. Indigenous peoples have the right to determine the structures and to select the membership of their institutions in accordance with their own procedures.

ILO Convention No. 169 also enshrines the importance of self-identification. Article 1 indicates that self-identification as indigenous or tribal shall be regarded as a fundamental criterion for determining the groups to which the provisions of this Convention apply. Furthermore, this same Article 1 contains a statement of coverage rather than a definition, indicating that the Convention applies to:

a. tribal peoples in independent countries whose social, cultural and economic conditions distinguish them from other sections of the national community and whose status is regulated wholly or partially by their own customs or traditions or by special laws or regulations;

b. peoples in independent countries who are regarded as indigenous on account of their descent from the populations which inhabited the country, or a geographical region to which the country belongs, at the time of conquest or colonization or the establishment of present state boundaries and who irrespective of their legal status, retain some or all of their own social, economic, cultural and political institutions.

The concept of indigenous peoples emerged from the colonial experience, whereby the aboriginal peoples of a given land were marginalized after being invaded by colonial powers, whose peoples are now dominant over the earlier occupants. These earlier definitions of indigenousness make sense when looking at the Americas, Russia, the Arctic and many parts of the Pacific. However, this definition makes less sense in most parts of Asia and Africa, where the colonial powers did not displace whole populations of peoples and replace them with settlers of European descent. Domination and displacement of peoples have, of course, not been exclusively practised by white settlers and colonialists; in many parts of Africa and Asia, dominant groups have suppressed marginalized groups and it is in response to this experience that the indigenous movement in these regions has reacted.

It is sometimes argued that all Africans are indigenous to Africa and that by separating Africans into indigenous and non-indigenous groups, separate classes of citizens are being created with different rights. The same argument is made in many parts of Asia or, alternatively, that there can be no indigenous peoples within a given country since there has been no large-scale Western settler colonialism and therefore there can be no distinction between the original inhabitants and newcomers. It is certainly true that Africans are indigenous to Africa and Asians are indigenous to Asia, in the context of European colonization. Nevertheless, indigenous identity is not exclusively determined by European colonization.

The Report of the Working Group of Experts on Indigenous Populations/Communities of the African Commission on Human and Peoples' Rights therefore emphasizes that the concept of indigenous must be understood in a wider context than only the colonial experience:

> The focus should be on more recent approaches focusing on self-definition as indigenous and distinctly different from other groups within a state; on a special attachment to and use of their traditional land whereby ancestral land and territory has a fundamental importance for their collective physical and cultural survival as peoples; on an experience of subjugation, marginalization, dispossession, exclusion or discrimination because these peoples have different cultures, ways of life or modes of production than the national hegemonic and dominant model.[6]

In the 60-year historical development of international law within the United Nations system, it is not uncommon that various terms have not been formally defined, the most vivid examples being the notions of "peoples" and "minorities". Yet the United Nations has recognized the right of peoples to self-determination and has adopted the Declaration on the Rights of Persons Belonging to National or Ethnic, Religious and Linguistic Minorities. The lack of formal definition of "peoples" or "minorities" has not been crucial to the Organization's successes or failures in those domains nor to the promotion, protection or monitoring of the rights accorded to these groups. Nor have other terms, such as "the family" or "terrorism" been defined, and yet the United Nations and Member States devote considerable action and efforts to these areas.

In conclusion, in the case of the concept of "indigenous peoples", the prevailing view today is that no formal universal definition of the term is necessary, given that a single definition will inevitably be either over- or underinclusive, making sense in some societies but not in others.

About this publication

The publication includes seven chapters that examine indigenous peoples' access to and utilization of quality health care services within the seven sociocultural regions of the Permanent Forum: Africa; Asia; Central and South America and the Caribbean; the Arctic; Central and Eastern Europe, Russian Federation, Central Asia and Transcaucasia; North America; and the Pacific.

Each of the authors provides an overview of health issues in their sociocultural regions as well the challenges that indigenous peoples face in trying to access and utilize health services.

The first chapter by Dr. Priscilla S. Migiro emphasizes the difficulties that indigenous peoples in Africa face in being recognized, firstly, as indigenous peoples and, secondly, accessing health services within the region's population of about 960 million people who already face health challenges with a high burden of communicable and emerging non-communicable diseases. Access to health care is not uniform across the continent, with variations from one country to the next and also within countries. National figures of morbidity and mortality often mask inequities within countries. Dr. Priscilla S. Migiro also focuses on the barriers to the enjoyment of the right to health, the lack of data on indigenous peoples' health status and the loss of land in which indigenous peoples depend for their livelihoods and traditional medicines.

---

[6]   Report of the African Commission's Working Group of Experts on Indigenous Populations/communities.

In the second chapter, Dr. Mukta S. Lama provides an overview and analysis of the situation of indigenous peoples in the Asian region. The Asian subregions include a multitude of indigenous groups who comprise 70 per cent of the estimated 350 million indigenous peoples worldwide. Indigenous peoples in Asia die younger, have higher rates of malnutrition and child mortality, and carry high burden of "diseases of the poor", namely undernutrition and infectious diseases. Dr. Lama points out that the health of indigenous peoples is often not considered a priority by national governments and as a result, health care needs remain unheard in health care planning with weak representation of indigenous peoples in the government system. Dr. Lama concludes that the exercise of right to self-determination is important in enabling indigenous peoples to revive and reclaim their cultural traditions and indigenous identity and self-esteem based on positive images that are crucial for their overall health and well-being. Such autonomy would also involve empowering indigenous peoples to preserve and develop their own solutions and plans to improve their health rather than imposing solutions upon them.

The third chapter by Dr. Ketil Lenert Hansen analyses the major health issues confronting Sami peoples in Norway, Finland, Sweden and Russia and the Inuit in Greenland. The chapter includes an analysis of the unique challenges faced by the indigenous peoples living in the far north due to their specific socioenvironmental location with an increased risk of health problems compared with the average national statistics. Dr. Ketil Lenert Hansen specifies the major constraints to delivering good quality health care in the North and at the same time outlines how traditional healing is being integrated within health services for indigenous peoples.

In the fourth chapter, Dr. Myriam Conejo Maldonado provides an overview and analysis of the situation of indigenous peoples in the Central and South America and the Caribbean region and illustrates the stark contrast in access to health services between the indigenous and non-indigenous populations. Indigenous peoples live in poverty and comprise 60 per cent of the poor in the region. Several countries in the region have included an intercultural approach to health in their development plans. However, sociocultural and linguistic barriers still exist, as well as barriers in terms of geographical location and lack of access to health care. Dr. Myriam Conejo Maldonado concludes that there must be a new approach to health services for indigenous peoples based on interculturality, human rights, and collective rights.

The fifth chapter on North America emphasizes the complex arrangements that the United States and Canada has with indigenous peoples in terms of health policies. To a large degree, jurisdictional conflict between state/provincial and federal governments impact on the accessibility and comprehensiveness of health services for indigenous peoples. The challenges for indigenous peoples in both Canada and the United States are to 1) take control of their own personal health to achieve balance in life; 2) assume authority and control over health and social services which impact their lives; and 3) design and implement a sustainable health system which meets their unique needs. The role of the federal and provincial governments is to work in partnership with indigenous peoples to design and implement health systems.

In chapter six, Dr. Collin Tukuitonga provides a background of the historical, political and cultural factors that have shaped events in Pacific countries that have influenced the health status of indigenous peoples. Dr. Collin Tukuitonga describes the current health situation; the social determinants of health, health service funding and delivery; and the initiatives that have been shown to be effective in improving indigenous peoples' access to all levels of health care. While there are number of initiatives under way in developed countries that are designed to improve access to health care services, there is limited information on the impact of these programmes. There are however, encouraging signs that health initiatives provided "by indigenous peoples for indigenous people" is improving access to services.

The seventh chapter by Ms. Oksana Buranbaeva outlines indigenous peoples' access to health in the Russian Federation. Russian federal legislation protects the "numerically small indigenous peoples" or "small-numbered indigenous peoples of Russia", defined as those who live in territories traditionally inhabited by their ancestors; maintain a traditional way of life and economic activity; number fewer than 50,000; and identify themselves as separate ethnic communities. Ms. Oksana Buranbaeva describes the situation and policies that the Soviet Union adopted vis-à-vis indigenous peoples which had both negative and positive consequences on indigenous peoples' current access to health services. Ms. Oksana Buranbaeva concludes that a comprehensive strategy is required in order to develop in partnerships and consultation with indigenous peoples that draw on the experiences of other Arctic countries to enhance access to indigenous peoples health services.

Overview of major international responses to indigenous peoples

1957 – ILO Convention 107 on Indigenous and Tribal Populations is adopted
(http://www.ilo.org/ilolex/english/convdisp1.htm)

1972 – The Study of the Problem of Discrimination against Indigenous Populations is launched (also known as the Martínez Cobo study)

1982 – The Working Group on Indigenous Populations is established by the United Nations
(http://www.ohchr.org/english/issues/indigenous/groups/groups-01.htm)

1984 – The Study of the Problem of Discrimination against Indigenous Populations is submitted to the UN

1985 – The Voluntary Fund for Indigenous Populations is created

1989 – ILO Convention No. 169 concerning Indigenous and Tribal Peoples in Independent States is adopted (http://www.ilo.org/ilolex/english/convdisp1.htm)

1992 – The Rio Earth Summit adopts the Convention on Biological Diversity
(http://www.biodiv.org/convention/default.shtml)

1993 – The World Conference on Human Rights recommends the establishment of a Permanent Forum on Indigenous Issues

1993 – International Year of the World's Indigenous People

1994 – The first International Decade for Indigenous People is launched (1994-2004)

1994 – The Voluntary Fund to support small-scale projects during the Decade is created

1998 – First Roundtable on Intellectual Property and Indigenous Peoples organized by the World Intellectual Property Organization - WIPO (http://www.wipo.int)

2000 – Establishment of the United Nations Permanent Forum on Indigenous Issues (UNPFII)
(http://www.un.org/esa/socdev/unpfii/index).

2001 – The mechanism of a Special Rapporteur on the Human Rights and Fundamental Freedoms of Indigenous People is established by the Commission on Human Rights (http://www.ohchr.org/english/issues/indigenous/rapporteur/).

2002 – A Voluntary Fund for Indigenous and Local Communities is established by the Convention on Biological Diversity (http://www.cbd.int).

2003 – A Voluntary Fund is established by the United Nations to support the Permanent Forum.

2005 – The Second International Decade for Indigenous People is launched (2005-2015), including a fund to support small-scale projects.

2005 – A Voluntary Fund for Indigenous and Local Communities is created by World Intellectual Property Rights.

2007 – The UN Declaration on the Rights of Indigenous Peoples is adopted by the UN General Assembly (http://www.un.org/esa/socdev/unpfii/en/declaration.html).

2007 – The new Expert Mechanism on the Rights of Indigenous Peoples is established by the Human Rights Council.

2014 – High Level Plenary Meeting of the United Nations General Assembly also known as the World Conference on Indigenous Peoples.

Chapter One
Access to Health Services by Indigenous Peoples in the African Region

Dr. Priscilla Santau Migiro

CHAPTER ONE

ACCESS TO HEALTH SERVICES BY INDIGENOUS PEOPLES IN THE AFRICAN REGION

DR. PRISCILLA SANTAU MIGIRO[7]

Introduction

Definition of indigenous peoples in the African region

A strict definition of indigenous peoples is neither necessary nor desirable. It is much more relevant and constructive to try to outline the major characteristics, which can help us identify who are the indigenous peoples and communities of Africa.

> The approach that has been advocated by the African Commission's Working Group of Experts on Indigenous Populations/Communities includes the following overall characteristics of groups identifying themselves as indigenous peoples:
>
> ≡ Their cultures and ways of life differ considerably from the dominant society;
>
> ≡ Their cultures are under threat, in some cases to the extent of extinction;
>
> ≡ The survival of their particular way of life depends on access and rights to their traditional lands, territories and natural resources;
>
> ≡ They suffer from discrimination as they are regarded as less developed and less advanced than the more dominant sectors of society;
>
> ≡ They often live in inaccessible regions, often geographically isolated and suffer from various forms of marginalization, both politically and socially.
>
> ≡ They are subject to domination and exploitation within the national political and economic structures that are commonly designed to reflect the interests and activities of the national majority.

---

[7]   Dr. Migiro is a Masaai woman from Kenya. She received her undergraduate degree in medicine and postgraduate qualifications in Paediatrics and Child Health from the University of Nairobi. She has worked in various capacities in the Ministry of Health and in private health sector. Since 2004, Dr. Migiro has worked in the ministry's headquarters where she worked her way to become the Head of the Division of Child and Adolescent Health, where she has been involved in development of policies, strategies and guidelines in child survival and development. Since June 2012, Dr. Migiro has worked in the Department of Health Promotion involved in development of policies, strategies and guidelines of health promotion.

Discrimination, domination and marginalization violates indigenous peoples human rights as peoples/communities, threatens the continuation of their cultures and ways of life and prevents them from genuinely participating in decisions on their own future and forms of development.[8]

Africa's population of about 960 million people already faces health challenges with a high burden of communicable and emerging non-communicable diseases. Access to health is not uniform across the continent, from one country to the next nor within countries. National figures of morbidity and mortality often mask inequities within countries. The vulnerable populations include the poor, the hard to reach, women and children, persons with disabilities and the marginalized.

Indigenous peoples often live in remote and hard-to-reach areas, and many are less educated, few in number and culturally different from their more populous neighbours. They face additional challenges of access to health services. This constitutes a violation of the African Charter such as:

- The right of equal access to the public services of one's country (Article 13 (2))
- The right to education (Article 17(1))
- The right to medical care and attention (Article 16(2)).[9]

Further, they are also discriminated against by health service providers and considered to be "backward". This can be seen from the view of a President of an African country who said, "How can you have a stone-age creature continuing to exist in the time of computers? If the Bushmen want to survive, they must change, otherwise, like the dodo they will perish".[10]

Indigenous Africans and the Millennium Development Goals (MDG)

The Millennium Declaration, signed by 147 Heads of State and Government in September 2000, and the Millennium Development Goals have provided an opportunity for a renewed focus on indigenous peoples in the international development debate. The report of the Fourth Session of the United Nations Permanent Forum on Indigenous Issues, stated that "Indigenous peoples have the right to benefit from the Millennium Development Goals and from other goals and aspirations contained in the Millennium Declaration to the same extent as all others".[11] However, by failing to ground the goals in an approach that upholds indigenous peoples' individual and collective rights, the MDGs fall short in addressing the health disparities that persist between indigenous peoples and other poor, marginalized groups. By advancing the dominant paradigms of health and development rather than an approach based on individual and collective human rights, the MDGs also promote projects that are potentially detrimental to indigenous peoples by violating their rights to their collective lands, territories and natural resources.

---

[8] Report of the African Commission's Working Group of Experts on Indigenous Populations/Communities by the African Commission on Human and Peoples' Rights and the International Working Group on Indigenous Affairs (2005).

[9] African Charter on Human and Peoples' Rights: OAU Doc. CAB/LEG/67/3 rev. 5, 21 I.L.M. 58 (1982), entered into force 21 October 1986).

[10] Suzman, J .,An Introduction to Regional Assessment of the San in Southern Africa.2001, Legal Assistance Centre, Windhoek. Namibia.

[11] E/2005/43 United Nations Permanent Forum on Indigenous Issues, Report of the Fourth Session (2005).

Moreover, because the cultures and world views of indigenous peoples are not taken into account in the formulation of the MDGs, the goals do not consider indigenous peoples' concept of health, which extends beyond the physical and mental well-being of an individual to the spiritual balance and well-being of the community as a whole. To improve the health situation of indigenous peoples, there must thus be a fundamental shift in the concept of health so that it incorporates the cultures and world views of indigenous peoples as central to the design and management of state health systems.[12]

Reports from countries reviewing progress on MDGs have shown that data on indigenous peoples are missing in national monitoring and reporting. The reviews also reveal that there is no clear mechanism identified to include indigenous peoples in the design, implementation and monitoring of policies designed to achieve the MDGs.[13]

An analysis of the health situation of indigenous peoples in the African region

Maybury-Lewis[14] estimates that there are over 14.2 million self-identifying indigenous peoples in the African region. The African Charter on Human and Peoples' Rights (ACHPR)[15] report lists some of the best known indigenous peoples whom they divide into two groups, hunter-gatherers and pastoralists. The report gives 11 examples of hunter-gatherers in 13 countries and 23 examples of pastoralists in 22 countries. These indigenous peoples often occupy hard-to-reach areas with poor infrastructure and harsh terrain. To further compound the problem is the lack of recognition of indigenous peoples by African states. This means that disaggregated data on indigenous peoples' health status are hard to find. In fact, because indigenous peoples are essentially invisible in the data collection of many international agencies and in most national censuses, the disparities in their health situation as compared to other groups continues to be obscured.[16] For example, in Kenya, demographic and health surveys have been undertaken every five years since 1989, excluding the hard-to-reach areas of North-Eastern Kenya because of the terrain. It is only the last two surveys of 2003 and 2008-2009 that these areas were included. The reason given for this omission is that those districts account for less than 4 per cent of Kenya's population.[17] These areas are occupied by nomadic pastoralists and hunter gatherers, all of whom have poor health indicators which, as a vulnerable minority, should justify their inclusion instead of exclusion.

Indigenous peoples of Central Africa

The indigenous people in central Africa have often been collectively identified as "Pygmy". Due to the fact the term "Pygmy" carries negative connotations due to its association with the assumption of inferior status, there is now a policy in some central African countries to officially designate such groups as indigenous peoples or *populations autochtones*.

---

[12]   State of the World's Indigenous Peoples, United Nations publication (2009)

[13]   Ibid.

[14]   Maybury-Lewis D. 2002. Indigenous peoples, ethnic groups and the state. Needham, Massachusetts: Allyn & Baker.

[15]   Report of the African Commission's Working Group of Experts on Indigenous Populations/Communities by the African Commission on Human and Peoples' Rights and the International Working Group on Indigenous Affairs (2005).

[16]   State of the World's Indigenous Peoples, United Nations publication (2009).

[17]   Kenya Demographic and Health Service 1989, 1993, 1998: National Council for Population and Development, Central Bureau of Statistics.

Indigenous peoples in Central Africa number between 300,000 to 500,000 peoples. They consist of at least 15 distinct ethnolinguistic groups including the Gyeli, Kola, Baka, Aka, Bongo, Efe, Mbuti, western Twa, and eastern Twa. They live in ten central African countries: Angola, Burundi, Cameroon, Central African Republic, Democratic Republic of Congo, Equatorial Guinea, Gabon, Republic of Congo, Uganda and Rwanda.

In general, access to health services is a challenge due to regional overpopulation, poor infrastructure and indequate personnel. For indigenous peoples, this is even worse as they live in remote areas. In his report following a vist to the Republic of Congo, Professor James Anaya, the Special Rapporteur on the Rights of Indigenous Peoples noted there is inadequate cultural adaptation to the delivery of health services, which appears to create a barrier to the enjoyment of the right to health by indigenous peoples that goes beyond proximity to the health facility. He noted that while the government had taken important steps to improve indigenous health, more needs to be done so that there is equal access to health services especially in remote areas.[19] Indigenous peoples also reported the challenges they face in accessing health services even where they are free, such as maternal and child health. Lack of money to pay for prescription drugs and obstetric services are significant blocks, creating difficulties and barriers. Most villages do not have health facilities, so they are forced to rely on those located in majority Bantu villages which often discriminate against indigenous peoples.[20]

Mr. Jean Dominique Dambo, the leader of the indigenous people in Dzaka, a village near Ouesso, the main town in the Sangha region in northern Congo said, "It is difficult; we don't have a health centre, no school, even though we are near the capital". He further stated, "Over there, not far from our village, the people are getting free treated mosquito nets and other goods while we are not informed about it; I am sure they forgot about us". He also confirmed that recent health campaigns by the government targeting mothers and children in Ouesso excluding indigenous peoples in the area.   Indigenous peoples rely heavily on traditional medicines. This however poses another challenge. The growing inaccessibility to forests and lack of support by the government is seriously eroding their knowledge and skills in the area of traditional medicine.

A study carried out by the Ministry of Health and the United Nations Populations Fund (UNFPA) in 2012 indicated that indigenous women are virtually excluded from reproductive health services. According to the study, while 94 per cent of the Congolese women access antenatal care, only 37 per cent of the indigenous women have access to such services.[23] As a result of this study, the

[18]   Jackson, D. Implementation on International Commitments on Traditional Forest Related Knowledge: Indigenous peoples' experiences in Central Africa.

[19]   A/HRC/18/35/Add.5.

[20]   A/HRC/18/35/Add.5.

[21]   http://www.irinnews.org/report/79995/congo-we-remain-marginalised-indigenous-people-say, 2013

[22]   Report of the Country Visit of the Working Group on Indigenous Populations/Communities to the Republic of Congo, 15-24 March 2010.

[23]   http://www.irinnews.org/report/97574/in-congo-few-pygmy-women-have-access-to-reproductive-health-services.

Working Group on Indigenous Populations/Communities made the following recommendations to governments in regards to health:

1. Provide well-equipped health centres stocked with adequate medicines and endowed with qualified staff within the communities where indigenous peoples live;

2. Provide training for health personnel from indigenous communities in terms of supervision and capacity building for traditional birth attendants;

3. Develop targeted sensitization campaigns and initiate community actions to ensure that the indigenous populations familiarize themselves with: immunization, antenatal and postnatal controls, HIV/AIDS screening; monitoring of chronic parasitic diseases among indigenous communities.[24]

The Batwa of Uganda

The Batwa are also a vulnerable population. They have limited access to education, a high rate of alcoholism and poor medical care. They have high child mortality rates and low life expectancy. As with other indigenous peoples in the African region, there is also a lack of data on their health status and published research data are rare.[25] Their situation is made worse by loss of land which they depend on for medicines. Women are also at high risk of getting HIV because of interaction with neighbouring communities, at risk of rape and having to exchange sex for necessities. Access to testing and care and treatment is a challenge, as they have to pay for services, and health workers do not treat them well.[26] Coordinated action is needed by all sectors to improve the health of the Batwa peoples. In order for this to happen, the following were recommended:

≡ Acknowledge the rights of the Batwa as indigenous peoples;

≡ Increase Batwa participation in developing policies and programs;

≡ Enforce equal opportunity policies.

Kenya

In Kenya, health facilities are often located in urban centres with almost no mobile health facilities to cater for nomadic pastoralists and communities in far-flung regions in the north and semi-arid areas where infrastructure is non-existent. The cost of accessing medical and health facilities in Kenya is also costly and often beyond the reach of many indigenous communities, who may not have the means to travel long distances to purchase certain prescribed drugs that are unavailable in public health facilities. The fact that there are almost no health facilities in close proximity to most indigenous peoples living in North-Eastern Kenya and remote parts of the Coast province and Rift Valley means that they have to walk long distances even during an emergency, which results in poor health outcomes.

---

[24] Report of the Country Visit of the Working Group on Indigenous Populations/Communities to the Republic of Congo, 15-24 March 2010.

[25] Social Determinants of Health for Uganda's Indigenous Batwa: Sherilee Harper: Backgrounder No 32, June 2012.

[26] State of the World's Minorities and Indigenous Peoples. 2013. Minority Rights International. p. 68.

A report undertaken for the Ministry of Public Health indicated that the IlChamus people, for example, spend an average of 600 Kenyan shillings ($7) on transport expenses to take pregnant women in labour for delivery at Marigat district hospital, while the Waata community in Madogo of Tana River spends an average of 2,000 Kenyan shillings ($24) on transport hire to take their sick to the provincial hospital in Garissa. It has been reported that most deliveries are conducted at home because of these challenges.[27] This report included only marginalized peoples and omitted other groups like the Maasai of southern Kenya.

Other factors identified as barriers to health services included:

- Health facilities, where available, are sometimes not operational due to staff shortages;
- Lack of essential drugs and supplies;
- Beliefs in the effectiveness of traditional herbs which are free in the villages, while health services require payment;
- Lack of awareness of the services available, especially because of low education levels;
- Deliveries occur at home mainly because of the long distances to facilities including the need to adhere to traditional practices performed at birth. For example, some communities do not like male health workers assisting women to deliver babies.
- Lack of their own indigenous health staff;
- Language barrier between health workers and indigenous peoples;
- Resistance to family planning services by women because of perceived negative side effects and lack of support from the men. They feel the need to have many children because of their populations are small. This is explained by an Ogiek community member:

> "Why are we being asked to practice family planning so that other people from outside the community can come and occupy our land? We do not want to be continuously referred to as minorities".

At the Katilu health centre in Turkana south, a community member said:

"Men in our community do not allow women to deliver in the clinic because they want to perform traditional rituals and apply herbs. The umbilical cord of the male baby is cut using a common spear in the community, while that of the female baby is cut using a common knife in the community. They only allow women to go to the hospital two weeks prior to the time of delivery".

Tanzania

The indigenous peoples of the United Republic of Tanzania include the Maasai, the Barbaig (Datoga), Akie, Taturu and Hadzabe. The former two groups are predominantly pastoralists, whereas the latter comprise forest-dwelling hunter-gatherers. The groups collectively practice pastoralism and hunting-gathering. The Maasai are the most populous, numbering about 450,000. The

---

[27] Nyambedha, E.O., Final Report for Development of Vulnerable and Marginalized Peoples Plans (VMPPS): Ministry of Public Health and Sanitation, Kenya, 2013.

Akie number about 5,200, while the Hadzabe population number between 1,000 and 3,000. The concept of indigenous peoples is not acknowledged in Tanzania, but the government "recognizes the vulnerability of some of the marginalized communities".[28] The delivery of health services in the areas occupied by indigenous peoples is difficult. This is because of poor infrastructure and also that the communities are sparse and migratory. They have to depend on services provided by non-governmental organizations, faith-based organizations and other agencies.

A study on the differences in health between the Datoga/Barabaig and their neighbours indicated how patterns of health are linked to wider issues of marginalization. The marginalization of the Datoga/Barabaig includes the lack of access to their traditional homelands where their lands are being acquired by the government and private interests for non-pastoral commercial use such as parks, private ranches and commercial wheat estates. Communal lands are being fenced off resulting in the Datoga/Barabaig being evicted from their traditional lands. The loss of their pasture lands has resulted in the decimation of their herds. The large-scale prairie-type farming has also resulted in the destruction of trees and other vegetation, affecting rain patterns and soil erosion. In some areas, water is extremely scarce. The relationship between the Datoga/Barabaig and the surrounding community has been one of hostility and antagonism. Incidences of abuse of human rights, the beating and arrest of pastoralists and confiscation of cattle on the pretext of trespass have been common.[29] Not surprisingly, the Datoga/Barabaig are at a greater risk of anaemia, maternal mortality and tuberculosis. Infant mortality is also high among the Datoga (20 per cent), while fertility is lower than in neighbouring groups, and pastoral Datoga children show early growth faltering and little catch-up growth when compared to neighbouring groups.[30] The pastoralists are also vulnerable to HIV/AIDS due to negative cultural practices and low levels of literacy. The negative cultural practices are FGM, early sexual debut and early marriages for girls and the low social status of women.

Botswana

The indigenous peoples of Botswana are collecticvely called the Basarwa, Bakgalagadi or San and are hunter-gatherers. In his report the Special Rapporteur on the Rights of Indigenous Peoples noted that the government of Botswana has made efforts to address the situation of indigenous peoples through the Remote Area Development Policy of 1975, which has been revised over time in line with new developments.[31]

In the revised programme the Government "shall adopt a community-led development approach which aims to promote participatory processes and community participation in issues affecting their own development". The new policy also acknowledges the need for affirmative measures for the benefit of communities that have faced intractable disadvantages, either for logistical reasons or because of long standing historical prejudice and subjugation by the dominant groups". Such measures will be adopted across a variety of sectors to improve access to education, health, employment and economic development opportunities, and to develop sociopolitical institu-

---

[28] Country Technical Note on Indigenous Peoples' Issues: United Republic of Tanzania. Submitted by IWGIA, June 2012.

[29] Isa G. Schivji, Globalisation and Popular Resistance (2002) p. 9 .www.caledonia.org.uk/papers/Globalisation%20 and%20Popular%20Resistance.doc.

[30] Alyson G. Young, Young Child Health among Eyasi Datoga: Socioeconomic Marginalization, Local Biology, and Infant Resilience with the Mother Infant Dyad (2008), p. 66.

[31] A/HRC/15/37/Add.2.

tions.[32] The government of Botswana has expressed concern over the difficulties faced by providing a health care system that incorporates and respects both Western and traditional medicines. In recognition of these challenges the Special Rapporteur on the Rights of Indigenous Peoples highlighted the need to enhance the understanding of and respect for traditional medicine, which continues to be practiced among indigenous communities but remains largely excluded from the government health system.

Namibia

The San, the Himba (Ovatue, Ovatjimba and Ovazemba) satisfy the criteria for indigenous peoples. The loss of their lands, destitution, cultural breakdown and high poverty levels have made the San the only ethnic group in Namibia whose health status has declined since independence. Having lost their original source of food, they now depend entirely on government food aid. The health problems are due mainly to poverty and marginalization. Most of the population has poor access to health facilities. More than 80 per cent of them live more than 80 kilometres from any sort of health facilities. These facilities are expensive, and mobile outreach services are irregular and often ill-equipped to deal with complicated problems. In some cases the staff of the mobile units cannot speak any of the San languages, giving rise to the likely risk of miscommunication and wrong diagnoses.[33]

Namibia has a high prevalence of HIV/AIDS, and the San are particularly vulnerable due to lack of information, low standard of living and the unavailability of adequate treatment. The Special Rapporteur on the Rights of Indigenous Peoples recommended measures to mitigate these negative effects. These included educating indigenous communities on health issues, which should be done in all languages in the communities concerned, allocating adequate resources to indigenous peoples' health services, including them in medical insurance programmes, capacity-building, collaboration and coordination, as well as funding organizations that are working towards the eradication of diseases.[34]

South Africa

The Khoi/San peoples of South Africa are among the poorest and most marginalized populations. There is lack of access to safe water and also high levels of domestic violence. The Special Rapporteur on the Rights of Indigenous Peoples also noted that although HIV prevalence was high in the country, there were no figures for indigenous peoples, and therefore HIV/AIDS should be considered a serious threat. The Special Rapporteur also made the following recommendations:

≡ The possibility of establishing a fully equipped clinic in Platfontein to serve the area;

≡ Health services should target the specifically marginalized indigenous communities;

≡ Introduction of drinking water to indigenous communities should be considered a priority in the development plans in the areas where services either do not exist or is insufficient.[35]

---

[32] A/HRC/15/37/Add.2.

[33] Country Report of Research Project by ILO and ACHPR on the Constitution of and legislative protection of rights of indigenous peoples.

[34] Country Report of Research Project by ILO and ACHPR on the Constitution of and legislative protection of rights of indigenous peoples.

[35] E/.CN.4/2006/78/Add.2.

The pastoralists of North and West Africa

The nomadic pastoralists of the Sahel are geographically and socially marginalized, inhabiting large regions unsuitable for agriculture and infrastructural development. Human survival in communities in these environments would be virtually impossible without livestock that provides for basic needs. To pastoralists the well-being of their livestock is important as it is the source of their livelihoods and a basis for recognition and respect.[36] The close contact between human and animals and consumption of raw milk contributes to zoonoses like anthrax, Q fever, brucellosis and echinococcosis.[37] A paper by A. Sheik-Mohamed and J.P. Velema summarized evidence on the health status of nomadic populations and provided an assessment on the best ways for the provision of health care.[38] The authors noted that nomadic peoples had poor access to health services, were prone to infectious diseases (STIs, guinea worm, leishmaniasis, trachoma, tuberculosis, brucellosis) and had higher rates of maternal and childhood mortality. On the other hand, viral infections and intestinal parasites were not so common. In the case of helminths, the migratory lifestyle of the pastoralists minimizes such infections as they move from accumulated dirt and rubbish. For viral infections, serological surveys on measles undertaken on the Tuareg peoples in Niger showed that 64.5 per cent of children five years of age were seronegative.[39] This situation not only makes them susceptible, but it is also an indication that they have not been vaccinated. Other possible strategies for nomadic pastoralists include moving from areas where there are health epidemics and avoiding areas which are infested by vectors like mosquitoes and ticks. Their mobility can also bring disease to an area or cause them to acquire diseases to which they have no immunity. Obstacles to health service delivery included:

1. Conventional health systems do not reach nomadic pastoralists;

2. Health services are usually in the hands of settled populations who do not relate well to nomadic pastoralists;

3. Settled populations tend to look down on nomadic pastoralists as uneducated and primitive;

4. There are prohibitive costs for providing health care.

The provision of health care includes:

≡ Mobile primary health care services that are capable of moving with the nomadic pastoralists;

≡ Due to the fact that community participation is important in primary health care programs, it was found that involving nomadic pastoralists was difficult because of their

---

[36] Schelling E., Wyss K., Diguimbaye C. et al. (2008) "Towards integrated and adapted health services for nomadic pastoralists and their animals: a north-south partnership" in Handbook of Transdisciplinary Research. A Proposition by the Swiss Academies of Arts and Sciences (eds G Hirsch Hadorn, H Hoffmann-Reim, S Biber-Klemm, W Grossenbacher, D Joye, C Pohl Springer, Heidelberg, pp. 277-291.

[37] Schelling E., Diguimbaye C., Daoud S. et al. (2003), "Brucellosis and Q-fever seroprevalences of nomadic pastoralists and their livestock in Chad". Preventive Veterinary Medicine 61, pp. 279-293.

[38] A. Sheik-Mohamed and J.P. Velema, "Health Care for Nomads in Sub-Saharan Africa", Tropical Medicine and International Health; Vol 4 No 10, pp. 695-707, October 1999.

[39] Measles in a West African Nomadic Community, Loutan, L. and Paillard, S., Bulletin of the World Health Organization, Vol. 70, No. 6 1992.

mistrust of government. Therefore, the provision of essential drugs and supplies was considered more helpful;

≣ Having nomadic pastoralist community health workers who can be trained to provide a mix of essential services, obtain regular medical supplies and refer complicated cases is likely to be more affordable and sustainable in the long run.

HIV/AIDS and indigenous peoples in the African region

As of December 2012, there were 22 million people living with HIV in sub-Saharan Africa.[40] As most indigenous peoples live in remote regions, they may be protected by their isolation from HIV/AIDS and have lower prevalence rates than their neighbours. For example, in Botswana in 2002 it was found that while the adult prevalence for HIV was 35.3 per cent, it was 21.4 per cent for the San in Ganzi. However, with settled lifestyles more and more San are exposed to HIV. An increase of HIV/AIDS was also noted among the indigenous peoples of Cameroon and this was attributed to the influx of labourers working in the commercial logging industry. In Kenya, the HIV prevalence in North-Eastern Kenya was less than 0.5 per cent in 2007 compared to the national figure of 7.2 per cent,[41] and rose to 1 per cent in 2008-2009 while the national prevalence decreased to 6.3 per cent.[42] The current national prevalence is at 5.6 per cent. This area of North-Eastern Kenya was omitted during the study due to the outbreak of conflict in the region.

In Tanzania, there is awareness that indigenous peoples like the Maasai pastoralists are at increased risk of HIV by nature of their lifestyle.[43] At the same time, data are difficult to find. The community also has low literacy and there are the usual challenges of language barriers. Some cultural practices like FGM, early marriages, polygamy and multiple sexual partners also make women in this community more vulnerable to the infection. The provision of HIV testing, treatment and care services is made difficult by the harsh terrain, long distances to facilities and low literacy levels. Most of these areas are served by faith-based organizations.

The above information highlights the plight of indigenous peoples in the African region. The situation globally may not be very different; however, there has been some attention at this level to look more closely at HIV/AIDS and indigenous peoples. For example, United Nations Permanent Forum theme for the 2009 International Day of the World's Indigenous Peoples on 9 August 2009 was "Indigenous Peoples and HIV/AIDS". In his message, the Secretary-General of the United Nations emphasized that it was essential that "indigenous peoples have access to the information and infrastructure necessary for detection, treatment and protection". He noted that indigenous peoples "tend to suffer from the low standards of health", which is perpetuating the gap in many countries between the recognition of their rights and the actual situation on the ground. He called on governments and civil society "to act with urgency and determination to close this implementation gap, in full partnership with indigenous peoples".[44]

---

[40] http://www.afro.who.int/en/rdo/speeches/3732-message-of-the-who-regional-director-for-africa-dr-luis-g-sambo-on-the-occasion-of-world-aids-day-2012.html.

[41] National AIDS and STI Control Programme, Ministry of Health, Kenya. July 2008. Kenya AIDS Indicator Survey, 2007. Nairobi, Kenya.

[42] Kenya National Bureau of Statistics (KNBS) and ICF Macro. 2010. Kenya Demographic and Health Survey, 2008-2009. Calverton, Maryland: KNBS and ICF Macro.

[43] Hilde Basstanie and Rafael Ole Moono Ngorongoro District HIV/AIDS Programme Formulation Report, 2004.

[44] http://www.unaids.org/en/Resources/PressCentre/Featurestories/2009/August/20090811IntDayWorldsIndigenous/.

Indigenous peoples face a higher vulnerability to HIV due to a range of factors including stigmatization, structural racism and discrimination and individual/community disempowerment. Health Canada in collaboration with UNAIDS and Public Health Agency Canada hosted an International policy dialogue on HIV/AIDS and indigenous peoples. This dialogue provided a platform to discuss the impact of HIV/AIDS on indigenous peoples and to explore a way forward in terms of research, policy and program development.

Report findings of the dialogue included:

- ≡ Relationship between HIV/AIDS and indigenous peoples has not received due international attention despite them being vulnerable;

- ≡ It clearly identified patterns of transmission for indigenous men and women including a higher proportion of new HIV diagnoses among indigenous peoples;

- ≡ It noted high rates of HIV transmission among indigenous women, particularly in developing countries;

- ≡ It noted a younger age of HIV infection of indigenous peoples compared with the non-indigenous population in some countries.

As a result of the above, the participants:

- ≡ Called for the identification of indigenous peoples as a priority group;

- ≡ Called for countries to develop national strategies for HIV and indigenous peoples;

- ≡ Advocated for AIDS service organizations to develop culturally appropriate services for indigenous peoples in partnership with indigenous communities' representatives;

- ≡ Noted how indigenous people are often invisible in reported statistics;

- ≡ Discussed how best to leverage international policy instruments, such as the UN Declaration on the Rights of indigenous peoples (UNDRIP) and ILO Convention 169;

- ≡ Welcomed the creation of the International indigenous peoples Working Group on HIV/AIDS (IIHAWG).

Traditional medicine

Traditional medicine is the sum total of knowledge, skills and practices based on the theories, beliefs and experiences used by indigenous peoples or different cultures to maintain health and prevent, diagnose and improve or treat physical and mental illness.[45]

Africans have relied on traditional medicine for generations before the advent of western medicine. The art was passed from generation to generation and sometimes from father to son. In Africa the cause of disease is not perceived in the same way as western medicine. Causes of illness and death are rooted in beliefs of witchcraft, sorcery and superhuman forces.[46]

---

[45] WHO 2002, Traditional Medicine Strategy 2002-2005.

[46] Rödlach, A. (2006). Witches, Westerners, and HIV: AIDS and Cultures of Blame in Africa. Walnut Creek: Left Coast Press pp. 101-104.

In the present day, indigenous Africans rely on traditional medicine and practitioners as they have done for generations. Compared to western medicine practitioners, traditional medicine practitioners are more readily available, less expensive and more acceptable. It is estimated that in Malawi 80 per cent of the 12 million people make use of traditional medicine for their needs.[47] In 2000, there were approximately 4500 traditional healers in Zimbabwe and only 1400 doctors.[48] Generally, in sub-Saharan Africa the ratio of traditional healers to the population is 1:500, while doctors trained in western medicine it is 1:40,000.[49] As indigenous peoples have always lived in harmony with their environment and learned the important plants which can be used as medicines, they resort to this method of healing before seeking treatment in orthodox medicine. For a long time there has been little effort to understand traditional medicine as it was considered to be shrouded in mystery. Some governments tried to suppress indigenous medicine, which then went underground and continued to thrive.[50] Most African countries have the tolerant model of health system where western medicine is practiced but other forms are tolerated.[51] The World Health Organization estimates that up to 80 per cent of people in the African region use traditional medicine and that the widespread use is due to its affordability.[52] Moreover, it is popular because it is firmly embedded in the wider belief system. Traditional medicine is also said to be more effective in the treatment of psychic and psychosomatic conditions. This is because the healers have knowledge of the patient's background while conserving African culture.[53]

Some African countries have made efforts to integrate traditional medicine into the health system. There are countries where traditional medicine practitioners have been registered and have associations. In South Africa, for instance, traditional healers are recognized and regulated by law.[54] However, caution is required in advocating for blanket use of traditional medicine because further research is needed to ascertain the efficacy of certain medicinal plants and treatments used.

Effects of sedentarization on indigenous peoples

The world is changing rapidly, and the lifestyles of indigenous peoples are also changing and will continue to change. This means that their previously active lifestyle and dietary habits will change. While indigenous peoples have a higher burden of infectious diseases, non-communicable diseases are also emerging. Living in settled areas with higher population densities predisposes them to infectious diseases. Increased population density in settled areas facilitates the transmission of density-dependent diseases such as malaria. At the same time, pathogenic organisms may be

---

[47] Peltzer 1988, "The role of faith healers in primary mental health care: A South African perspective", Curare:11.207-210).

[48] UNAIDS (2000). Report of the Inter-regional Workshop on Intellectual Property Rights in the Context of Traditional Medicine, Bangkok, Thailand.

[49] Richter, 2004, PEP for rape survivors in South Africa: Reflecting on the process to get to government policy: International Conference on AIDS.

[50] Green, E.C., Engaging indigenous African healers in the prevention of AIDS and STDs in Anthropology in Public Health: Bridging differences in culture and society, Edited by Robert A Hahn, Oxford University Press Inc. New York 1999.

[51] WHO 2002, Traditional Medicine Strategy 2002-2005; Anfom ,E.E 1986: Traditional Medicine in Ghana; J.B. Danquoh memorial lectures.

[52] WHO 2002, Traditional Medicine Strategy 2002-2005.

[53] Steinglass M., "It Takes a Village Healer - Anthropologists Believe Traditional Medicines Can Remedy Africa's AIDS Crisis. Are They Right?" Lingua Franca April 2002, p. 32.

[54] E/CN.4/2006/78/Add.2 of 15/12/05.

introduced by the number of people moving into, and establishing themselves in settled areas. Further, the intrusion of people into previously unsettled areas may also expose them to new disease hazards.[55] Barkey found that settled Turkana men reported severe complaints and higher rates of infectious diseases than the nomads, including a significantly higher frequency of cold with cough, eye infection, and chest infection than the nomads. They also had higher body mass index.[56]

Children of pastoralists also experience malnutrition when they live in settlements as their diets change from dairy products to starches and sugars. Comparing settled and nomadic Rendille children in Kenya and Nathan found that sedentary children under six years had significantly higher levels of malnutrition and anaemia than nomadic children.[57] This was attributed to the consumption of three times more milk by the nomadic children. Indigenous peoples need to be made aware of the consequences of change in lifestyle and what they need to do to mitigate the negative effects.

Best practices in delivering health services

This section provides examples of best practices and innovations that have been used to reach indigenous peoples in remote regions.

Outreach services

Mobile outreach clinics or strategically placed health posts have been used to reach remote areas. The challenge has been for these entities to provide services on a regular basis and the fact that they may not be able to deal with emergencies. They are also expensive and difficult to sustain. In many instances, staff do not speak indigenous languages, therefore creating another barrier.

Providing a culturally sensitive health service

Indigenous peoples in the African region, apart from having poor access to quality health services, also find the available services are not friendly. At most times the health workers look down upon them as "backward and primitive" peoples. Indigenous peoples also have the problem of language barriers and therefore use health facilities only when their conditions are advanced. As previously stated, cultural sensitivity is important if available health services are to be utilized. Also taking into account traditional knowledge which indigenous communities have relied on for thousands of years is extremely important. In South Africa, Ngomane et al. found that pregnant women in rural districts delayed visiting clinics, preferring instead to be looked after by traditional healers in order to protect their unborn infants from harm.[58] They also shied away from delivery in hospitals because of the harsh treatment they received from the nurses.

---

[55]   Sheik-Mohamed, A., Velema, J.P. "Where Health Has no access; the nomadic populations of sub-Saharan Africa" Tropical Medicine and International Health, Vol. 4 No pp. 695-707, Oct 1999.

[56]   Barkey, N.L., Campbell, B.C. and Leslie, P.W. (2001), "A Comparison of Health Complaints of Settled and Nomadic Turkana Men". Medical Anthropology Quarterly, 15: 391-408. doi: 10.1525/maq.2001.15.3.391.

[57]   Nathan M., Fratkin E., Roth E. "Sedentism and child health among Rendille pastoralists of Northern Kenya", Social Science and Medicine Vol 43, Issue 4, August 1996. http://www.sciencedirect.com/science/article/pii/0277953695004289.

[58]   Ngomane, S., Mulaudzi, F.M., "Indigenous beliefs and practices that influence the delayed attendance of antenatal clinics by women in the Bohlabelo district in Limpopo, South Africa". Midwifery (2010), doi:10.1016/j.midw.2010.11.002.

According to Ngomane et al., indigenous women made the following comments about their treatment in the hospital:

- ≡ "The kneeling position is not allowed in hospital and nurses give you instructions and won't listen to you".
- ≡ "If you air your views or your opinion, they laugh at you and ridicule you".
- ≡ "They make you feel small and useless".
- ≡ "The nurses give you instructions and will not listen to you".

The women also indicated that their rationale for going to clinics and hospitals is often motivated by fear of complications or maternal death and complications that could cause them to lose their infants:

- ≡ "I came to the clinic to put my name on their books, in case I have a difficult delivery".
- ≡ "My sister was saved by the hospital as the baby was delivered by an operation".

It is important that there is dialogue between the community and the health sector. The similarities and differences between the two must be identified in order to reach consensus on issues pertaining to improved antenatal attendance. This will create a feeling of empowerment and awareness in the community, which will assist members of the community to utilize their resources and antenatal care services optimally.

Innovation in delivery of health services

When studies of Chadian pastoralists and their livestock revealed that the vaccination status was higher in the animals than in children[59,60] authorities decided to conduct joint campaigns bringing together veterinarians and public health workers. These campaigns not only demonstrated the feasibility of working across sectors, but were also 15 per cent cheaper than separate campaigns. For such efforts to succeed however there is need for community participation at all stages and multi-stakeholder engagement.

Other innovations which are being used by countries are maternity shelters in remote areas. These shelters are in the hospital compound and encourage pregnant women to come and stay there towards the end of their pregnancies. For example, one such shelter is found in Garissa in the North-Eastern part of Kenya. In this area, the maternal mortality rates in 2003 were estimated between 1,000-1,300 per 100,000 live births against a national figure of 410 per 100,000 live births.[61]

---

[59] Zinsstag J., Schelling E., Daoud S. et al. (2002) "Serum retinol of Chadian nomadic pastoralist women in relation to their livestocks' milk retinol and beta-carotene content", International Journal for Vitamin and Nutrition Research 72, 221-228.

[60] Schelling E., Diguimbaye C., Daoud S. et al. (2003) "Brucellosis and Q-fever seroprevalences of nomadic pastoralists and their livestock in Chad". Preventive Veterinary Medicine 61, 279-293.

[61] Central Bureau of Statistics (CBS) [Kenya], Ministry of Health (MOH) [Kenya], and ORC Macro. 2004. Kenya Demographic and Health Survey 2003. Calverton, Maryland: CBS, MOH, and ORC Macro.

The use of maternal homes was also introduced in Eritrea in 2007 to reduce maternal mortality in remote areas. This led to a 56 per cent increase in facility deliveries and no maternal deaths in the 20 months since the introduction of the concept.[63]

The Kenya Ministry of Health also has a strategy to deliver services to the household through the Community Strategy.[64] In this strategy community health workers are trained in various maternal, newborn and child health services and deployed in the community. It is envisaged that they will be able to provide integrated community case management of pneumonia, diarrhoea, malaria and malnutrition starting in hard-to-reach, underresourced areas.

Another innovative way of delivering services is the concept of the tuberculosis (TB) Manyatta. This was devised by Dr. Tonelli,[65] a Catholic nun working in a remote district in North-Eastern Kenya in 1976. The pastoralists living there had a high default rate for TB treatment. As a result, she urged them to construct small dwellings next to the health facility where the patient could receive observed treatment for four months, supported by a family member. As this concept was very successful, TB Manyattas were set up in remote areas for nomadic pastoralists.[66] In Namibia, the treatment of TB for the San has been improved by educating family members on TB treatment.[67] South Africa and Rwanda have also started health insurance for their populations, and it is hoped this will trickle down to indigenous peoples.

Addressing the data gaps

Information on the health status of indigenous peoples in the African region is not adequate. Health systems in many African countries have challenges in collecting, collating and analysing data for their populations.

---

[62] http://www.unicef.org/infobycountry/Kenya 62635.html.

[63] http://www.unicef.org/esaro/5479_maternal_newborn_health.html.

[64] Taking the Essential Package of Health to the Community: A Strategy for the Delivery of Level One Services: MOH, Kenya 2006.

[65] http://annalenatrust.org/index.php?option=com_content&view=article&id=46&Itemid=53.

[66] WHO: A Brief Hisory of Tuberculosis Control in Kenya: 2008 sourced from http://whqlibdoc.who.int/publications/2009/9789241596923_eng.pdf.

[67] State of the World's Minorities and Indigenous Peoples 2013, Events of 2012, Minorities Rights Groups International.

This challenge becomes more evident in data for indigenous peoples because:

≡ Indigenous peoples have not yet been fully recognized in many States as such, therefore, no provision has been made to collect data. For example, the concept of indigenous peoples is not acknowledged in Tanzania but the government "recognizes the vulnerability of some of the marginalized communities".[68]

≡ Indigenous peoples in the African region are usually lumped together as marginalized groups. This lack of recognition makes it difficult to take bold steps to put strategies in place to collect disaggregated data according to ethnicity.

≡ States may also be hesitant to collect ethnic-specific data as a way to discourage tribalism and promote national unity and cohesiveness.

≡ Indigenous peoples often live in remote and hard-to-reach areas where collecting data is considered difficult and expensive and since the population is small, it will not have a major impact on the overall results. An example of this is Kenya, where three demographic and health surveys in 1989, 1993 and 1998, omitted northern Kenya, which is inhabited by nomadic pastoralists because the population was less than 4 per cent. The 2003 demographic survey indicated that the national under-five mortality rate was 115 per 1,000 live births, while it was 163 per 1,000 in North-Eastern Kenya.[69]

≡ Challenges in data collection included language barriers between data collectors and respondents.

≡ As most of indigenous African communities have low literacy levels, the data are collected by people who do not speak the language or understand the culture. Therefore, obtaining accurate demographic data is difficult. Among the Maasai community obtaining accurate data on maternal and infant deaths is a challenge, as they may never be reported. Further, among the Maasai it is difficult to know which woman has never had a child because the practice is for every married woman to be called the mother of a child. Therefore, in cases where a woman has no child, she is given one by a family member to raise as her own.

≡ Another significant gap is the lack of adequate research on indigenous peoples' health issues in the African region.

During the International consultation of indigenous peoples' health between 23 and 26 November 1999 the objective was amongst others to provide key elements for the development of World Health Organization policies, strategies and recommendations for the protection of and promotion of the right to health of indigenous peoples. The following recommendations were made to WHO;

≡ Promote the systematic collection and reporting of statistics disaggregated by ethnicity by member states. This will require the development of working criteria or definitions of ethnicity and the development of indicators that are able to measure what constitutes a positive health outcome in indigenous peoples' terms.

≡ Develop, in close consultation with the informal advisory group, a comprehensive research agenda which places emphasis on the broad determinants of health.[70]

---

[68] Country technical notes on Indigenous peoples issues, United Republic of Tanzania June 2012 and submitted by IWGIA

[69] Central Bureau of Statistics (CBS) [Kenya], Ministry of Health (MOH) [Kenya], and ORC Macro. 2004. Kenya Demographic and Health Survey 2003. Calverton, Maryland: CBS, MOH, and ORC Macro.

[70] WHO/HSD/00.1.

It is clear that there are significant data gaps in the health of indigenous peoples in the African region. These can be addressed at the very outset by states recognizing indigenous peoples. This can then set the stage for strengthening health systems in data collection, disaggregating data according to ethnicity, and empowering the communities themselves by increasing access to education. Having indigenous peoples collecting data will increase accuracy of the data.

Affirmative action and training of indigenous health care workers

Indigenous peoples often live in rural and remote areas where access to health services is reduced or simply not available. At the same time, where there are health facilities, staff are not able to communicate in indigenous languages, creating a further barrier. Training health workers from indigenous communities could address this challenge. At the same time, many of these communities have poor access to education, which makes it harder to target students for medical training colleges. Improving education and affirmative action for bright indigenous students to undertake bridging courses in order to enter training institutions is a possible solution. Another strategy is to have more rural-based training schools and tuition support for indigenous students. Increasing the proportion of medical students who come from rural backgrounds provides positive rural learning experiences in medical school. Further, specific rural residency/vocational training programmes will increase the number of graduating physicians who possess interest, knowledge and skills for rural practice. Recruiting and retaining physicians in rural practice requires attention to the environment, health system, financial constraints and other factors.[71] Another strategy to attract and retain health care workers in rural and remote areas is to improve the working environment in these areas. A study undertaken in Zambia indicated that nurses considered satisfactory accommodation, access to continued education and motivation to work as important non-monetary incentives for working in remote areas.[72]

Development of responsive health policies

The foundation of having best practices in delivering health care to indigenous peoples is for states to embrace multicultural health systems. The World Health Organization asserts that all people have the right to health. During the fiftieth anniversary celebration of the Universal Declaration on Human Rights on 8 December 1998 in Paris, the WHO Director General Dr. Gro Harlem Brundtland said:

> "It is no coincidence that the idea to establish a world health organization emerged from the same process that identified the universal value of human rights. The WHO constitution states the enjoyment of the highest attainable standard of health is one of the fundamental rights of every human being without distinction of race, religion, and political beliefs, economic or social condition".

In most state health systems cultures and views of indigenous peoples are ignored or dismissed as health systems are based exclusively on western medicine. This approach marginalizes indige-

---

[71] Bulletin of the World Health Organization 2010;88:395-396. doi: 10.2471/BLT.09.073072.

[72] http://wiredspace.wits.ac.za/handle/10539/9082.

nous peoples, denying them access to basic health services and devaluing their traditional health systems. Most health systems can be defined as monocultural, multicultural or intercultural.[73]

Monocultural: This is based on the concept of society being homogenous and privilege the dominant national culture over all other cultures. Though there maybe some acknowledgement of ethnic or linguistic or cultural diversity, it is not reflected in policies and resource allocation. Further, data collection does not take into account any ethnic or cultural differences.

Multicultural: This system welcomes and promotes different cultures in society. It is still insufficient if it fails to ensure equality among cultures.

Intercultural: This goes beyond mere recognition to seeking exchange and reciprocity in a mutual relationship, as well as in solidarity among the different ways of life.

There are four fundamental prerequisites that must be present in order for an intercultural health system to exist. These are:

1. Fundamental respect for human rights as codified in international human rights instruments and international law.

2. Recognition of indigenous peoples because if states do not acknowledge the existence of indigenous peoples, it is not possible to develop policies that respond to their health capacities and needs. Often indigenous peoples are included in broader categories such as "vulnerable groups" or "the poor", obscuring the particularities of their situation. Furthermore, this recognition entails the structural reforms necessary to exercise self-determination, which in the case of health, corresponds to supporting the development of indigenous health systems while also ensuring full and effective participation in the health services offered by the state.

3. Political will, since the mere existence of policies aimed at improving the health of indigenous peoples is insufficient if they are not successfully implemented.

4. Conscious decision on the part of the national society to engage in an exchange and sharing of knowledge, values and customs which, if practiced on a daily basis, would overcome monoculturalist structures.

Taking into account the above prerequisites in view of the African situation, challenges are evident because many countries have not ratified ILO 169 Convention.[74]

Conclusion

Indigenous peoples of Africa have inadequate access to health services. This is due to the lack of recognition of indigenous peoples rights and the fact that health indicators are poor, education levels are low and access to other social services is lacking. The general lack of data is also a concern that makes it difficult to address the problems and target solutions. Loss of their lands

---

[73] Chapter 5, State of the World's Indigenous Peoples, United Nations, 2009.

[74] ILO 168 sourced from:
http://www.ilo.org/wcmsp5/groups/public/---ed_norm/---normes/documents/publication/wcms_100897.pdf.

has made indigenous peoples vulnerable as they cannot access the healing medicines and traditional food as they did in the past. Improving indigenous peoples' situation needs their active participation in the design and implementation of health services. Legal recognition by states will help to pave the way for documenting and tackling the current challenges in health care. Adopting targeted intervention and conducting research will also go towards meeting the health care challenges, including the need to increase the level of accessible and responsive health services, document and preserve traditional medicine practices which are effective, improve education status and train indigenous health workers. Indigenous peoples' resource and knowledge must not be discarded, otherwise Africa will be poorer.

References

African Charter on Human and Peoples' Rights, OAU Doc. CAB/LEG/67/3 rev. 5, 21 I.L.M. 58 (1982), entered into force 21 October 1986.

Barkey, N.L., Campbell, B. C. and Leslie, P. W. (2001), A Comparison of Health Complaints of Settled and Nomadic Turkana Men. Medical Anthropology Quarterly, doi: 10.1525/maq.2001.15.3.391

Basstanie, Hilde and Rafael Ole Moono Ngorongoro District HIV/AIDS Programme Formulation Report (2004).

Bulletin of the World Health Organization 2010;88:395-396. doi: 10.2471/BLT.09.073072.

Central Bureau of Statistics (CBS) [Kenya], Ministry of Health (MOH) [Kenya], and ORC Macro. 2004. Kenya Demographic and Health Survey 2003. Calverton, Maryland: CBS, MOH, and ORC Macro.

Country Technical Note on Indigenous People Issues. United Republic of Tanzania; submitted by IWGIA. June 2012.

Isa G. Schivji, Globalisation and Popular Resistance (2002).

Country Report of Research Project by ILO and ACHPR on the Constitution of and legislative protection of rights of Indigenous peoples.

Green, E.C: "Engaging indigenous African healers in the prevention of AIDS and STDs" in

Anthropology in Public Health: Bridging differences in culture and society Edited by Robert A Hahn, Oxford University Press Inc., New York, 1999.

Jackson, D. Implementation on International Commitments on Traditional Forest Related Knowledge: Indigenous peoples' experiences in Central Africa.

Kenya National Bureau of Statistics (KNBS) and ICF Macro. 2010. Kenya Demographic and Health Survey 2008-2009. Calverton, Maryland: KNBS and ICF Macro.

Luongo, 2006, Witches, Westerners and HIV/AIDS and Cultures of Blame in Africa: Magic, Ritual and Witchcraft 3(1).

Maybury-Lewis, D., Indigenous Peoples, Ethnic Groups and State, 2002, Needham Massachusetts, Allyn & Baker.

National AIDS and STI Control Programme, Ministry of Health, Kenya. July 2008 Kenya AIDS Indicator Survey 2007, Nairobi, Kenya.

Nyambedha, E.O., Final Report for Development of Vulnerable and Marginalized Peoples Plans (VMPPS): Ministry of Public Health and Sanitation, Kenya 2013.

Ngomane, S., Mulaudzi, F.M., Indigenous beliefs and practices that influence the delayed attendance of antenatal clinics by women in the Bohlabelo district in Limpopo, South Africa. Midwifery (2010), doi:10.1016/j.midw.2010.11.002.

Peltzer, 1988, "The Role of Faith Healers in Primary Mental Health Care: A South African perspective".

Report of the African Commission's Working Group of Experts on Indigenous Populations/Communities, 2005 ACHPR and IWGIA.

Report on the Fourth Session of the UN Permanent Forum on Indigenous Issues, UN Doc. E/C.19/2005/9, 2005.

Report of the Country Visit of the Working Group on Indigenous Populations/Communities to the Republic of Congo, 15-24 March, 2010.

Report of the International Consultation on the Health of Indigenous peoples, WHO/HSD/00.1 2000.

Report of the Special Rapporteur on the rights of Indigenous peoples, James Anaya: Addendum; The situation of the Indigenous peoples in Botswana 2 June 2010. A/HRC/15/37/Add.2.

Report of the Special Rapporteur on the rights of Indigenous peoples, James Anaya; Addendum: The situation of the Indigenous peoples in the Republic of the Congo, 11 July 2011.

Report of the Special Rapporteur on the situation of human rights and fundamental freedoms of Indigenous peoples, Rodolfo Stavenhagen: Addendum; Mission to South Africa, 15 December 2005 E/.CN.4/2006/78/Add.2.

Richter 2004 "PEP for rape survivors in South Africa: Reflecting on the process to get to government policy", International Conference on AIDS.

Schelling E., Wyss K., Diguimbaye C. et al., (2008), "Towards integrated and adapted health services for nomadic pastoralists and their animals: a north-south partnership" in Handbook of Transdisciplinary Research. A Proposition by the Swiss Academies of Arts and Sciences (eds G Hirsch Hadorn, H. Hoffmann-Reim, S. Biber-Klemm, W. Grossenbacher, D. Joye, C. Pohl Springer, Heidelberg.

Schelling E., Diguimbaye C., Daoud S. et al., (2003), Brucellosis and Q-fever seroprevalences of nomadic pastoralists and their livestock in Chad. Preventive Veterinary Medicine 61.

Sheik-Mohamed, A. and J.P. Velema: Health Care for Nomads in sub-Saharan Africa, Tropical Medicine and International Health, Vol 4 No 10, October 1999.

Sheik-Mohamed, A., Velema, J.P., Where health has no access; the nomadic populations of sub-Saharan Africa, Tropical Medicine and International Health, Vol. 4 No. 10 Oct 1999.

Social Determinants of Health for Uganda's Indigenous Batwa Sherilee Harper: Backgrounder No 32, June 2012.

State of the World's Indigenous Peoples, United Nations, New York, 2009.

State of the World's Minorities and Indigenous peoples, 2013, Minority Rights International.

Steinglass M (2002). It Takes a Village Healer—Anthropologists Believe Traditional Medicines Can Remedy Africa's AIDS Crisis. Are They Right? Lingua Franca April 2002.

Suzman, J An Introduction to Regional Assessment of the San in Southern Africa (2001) Legal Assistance Centre, Windhoek, Namibia.

Taking the Essential Package of Health to the Community: A Strategy for the Delivery of Level One Services: MOH, Kenya, 2006.

UNAIDS (2000). Report of the Inter-regional Workshop on Intellectual Property Rights in the Context of Traditional Medicine, Bangkok, Thailand.

Young, Alyson G. Young Child Health among Eyasi Datoa: Socioeconomic Marginalization, Local Biology, and Infant Resilience with the Mother Infant Dyad (2008).

World Health Organization 2002: Traditional Medicine Strategy 2002-2005.

World Health Organization, A brief History of Tuberculosis control in Kenya: 2008 sourced from: http://whqlibdoc.who.int/publications/2009/9789241596923_eng.pdf.

Zinsstag J, Schelling E, Daoud S et al. (2002) Serum retinol of Chadian nomadic pastoralist women in relation to their livestocks' milk retinol and beta-carotene content. International Journal for Vitamin and Nutrition Research 72, 221-228.

http://www.afro.who.int/en/rdo/speeches/3732-message-of-the-who-regional-director-for-africa-dr-luis-g-sambo-on-the-occasion-of-world-aids-day-2012.html.

http://www.unaids.org/en/Resources/PressCentre/Featurestories/2009/August/20090811IntDayWorldsIndigenous/.

http://www.sciencedirect.com/science/article/pii/0277953695004289.

http://www.unicef.org/infobycountry/Kenya 62635.html.

http://www.unicef.org/esaro/5479_maternal_newborn_health.html.

http://annalenatrust.org/index.php?option=com_content&view=article&id=46&Itemid=53.

http://wiredspace.wits.ac.za/handle/10539/9082.

http://www.ilo.org/wcmsp5/groups/public/---ed_norm/-normes/documents/publication/wcms_100897.pdf.

http://www.irinnews.org/report/79995/congo-we-remain-marginalised-indigenous-people-say, 2013.

http://www.irinnews.org/report/97574/in-congo-few-pygmy-women-have-access-to-reproductive-health-services.

www.caledonia.org.uk/papers/Globalisation%20and%20Popular%20Resistance.doc.

Chapter Two
Access to Health Services by Indigenous Peoples in Asia

Dr. Mukta Lama

Chapter Two

Access to Health Services by Indigenous Peoples in Asia

Dr. Mukta Lama

Introduction

Indigenous peoples living in Asia have limited access to appropriate health care services. As a consequence of this and other health determinants, they suffer the worst health of identifiable groups in the Asian region. Indigenous peoples in Asia die younger, have higher rates of malnutrition, child mortality, and carry high burden of "diseases of the poor" namely undernutrition and infectious diseases. A number of explanations account for the disparities in access to health services experienced by the indigenous peoples. The health of indigenous peoples is often not a priority of the national governments, thus health care needs remain unheard in health care planning with no or weak representation of the indigenous peoples in the government system. The general health care services in most cases do not arrive in the remote regions of the country where most indigenous peoples live, and even when they do arrive, they are often not appropriate to address the needs of indigenous peoples and often do not accommodate the belief systems and processes for improving health and well-being. There is an urgent need to address disparity and deficits in indigenous health in Asia, which is a challenge for democratic governance in the region.

The UN Special Rapporteur on the right to health noted that the right to health and right to survive are two of the most basic human rights. This is aligned with the provision of International Covenant on Economic, Social and Cultural Rights (ICESCR), in which Article 12 recognizes "the right of everyone to the enjoyment of the highest attainable standard of physical and mental health". Further, the General Comment No. 14 of the UN Committee on Economic, Social and Cultural Rights, elaborates that the right to health, "is the right to the enjoyment of a variety of facilities, goods, services and conditions necessary for the realization of the highest attainable standard of health.... [The right includes both] timely and appropriate health care ... [and] the underlying determinants of health, including access to safe and potable water, and adequate sanitation, an adequate supply of safe food, nutrition and housing, healthy occupational and environmental conditions, and access to health-related education and information, including on sexual and reproductive health". In this context, morbidity and mortality of children and poor health of indigenous peoples is a matter of pressing social justice inequality for which governments and other actors must be held accountable. Despite the impressive improvements in poverty reduction and social development in a number of Asian countries over the past decades, the persistence problems of poor indigenous health remain a major issue in the Asian region.

One of the major challenges in addressing the issue of indigenous health deficit is the invisibility or obscured visibility of the issue from the national discourse in many states. Little is known in the rest of the world about their struggle for equality and their profound disparities in health status and/or access to health services. The majority of countries in the Asian region do not have any structural capacity for collecting health information disaggregated for indigenous peoples from within the larger non-indigenous populations. Some governments intentionally avoid collecting the disaggregated data by indigenous ethnicity in their effort to portray national unity or discourage differentiation within their citizenry. Many Asian countries lack capacity to acknowledge the relevancy of indigenous-specific data in part due to competition for resources and lack of incentives for institutions to support the creation of an evidence base for an indigenous peoples' health information system. The United Nations has repeatedly called for nation states to gather baseline disaggregated information specific to indigenous peoples, and in some situations this is gradually beginning to occur. Nevertheless, in Asia, unlike other parts of the world like the Americas and Australia, an additional complexity, coined the "Asian controversy", relates to the definition of precisely who is indigenous. Deprived of clear client identification of membership in indigenous population groups and/or tribes, the task of collecting data and the subsequent use in planning, implementing and monitoring health initiatives are not simply possible.

In practice, different countries with specific historic and contextual relationships to the state and the dominant population, indigenous peoples in Asia have been identified and referred to by different names such as "minority nationalities", "schedule tribes", "ethnic minorities", "hill tribes", "cultural communities", "adivasi", "janajati", and others. Some of the Asian states officially recognize the term "indigenous peoples" to identify those people who have distinct cultural tradition and history. Countries such as Philippines, Taiwan, Malaysia, Nepal and, more recently, Japan have embraced the term following the United Nations Declaration on Rights of the Indigenous Peoples (UNDRIP) and ILO Convention No. 169 on Indigenous and Tribal Peoples. While countries such as China, India and Bangladesh, for example, resist the recognition due to contentions in the definition, they have adopted various affirmative action and special measures for the peoples by adopting specific labels in their specific country context.[75]

Notwithstanding the diverse country-specific stance in formally recognizing the category "indigenous peoples", the majority of the Asian countries engage with the distinct group of populations in their legal, administrative and political uses ranging from the purpose of affirmative action to assimilation and discrimination. China for example, in its 2000 census enumerates 55 officially recognized terms for minority nationalities or *minzu* who reside in five autonomous geographic regions. For instance, the identification of China's *minzu* emphasizes the social, cultural, economic conditions, customs, traditions, language and geographic concentrations that distinguish indigenous peoples from other sections of national community.[76] Despite not officially adopting the term "indigenous", identification of China's minority nationalities largely corresponds to the definition developed by ILO Convention No. 169 and the World Bank.[77] China's case echoes that in other countries in Asia, including, for example, India, Malaysia and other countries. Scholars have debated both for and against the adoption of the term but they appear to agree that the definition in the Asian setting should be broad enough to encompass the plurality of indigenous groups in question with respect to their historic and country-specific contexts. The category "indigenous peoples", supplemented by the assertion of the peoples who wish to self-identify themselves by

[75] Kingsbury 1998; Erni 2008.

[76] Minority Affairs Editorial Department. Working Handbook of Minority Nationalities [CHN: Minzu Gongzuo Shouce]. Kunming (CHN): Yunnan People's Publishing House; 1985.

[77] Chee-Beng 2008; Li 2008.

the term has increasingly become a social reality in Asia,[78] thus is the term "indigenous" is being used interchangeably with the other more specific terminology contained in this chapter.

Who are indigenous peoples in Asia?

Asia includes a vast geographically diverse area of about 12 million square kilometres that is culturally and ecologically divided into five subregions. The distribution of indigenous peoples into very different geographic subregions and the degree of engagement in indigenous issues by the various nations' actors and the differences within the concerned indigenous peoples themselves differs substantially. For example, the knowledge about indigenous peoples in different countries within subregions varies greatly. Five subregions are conventionally categorized as western, south-eastern, southern eastern and central Asian subregion.

The following table shows the distribution of countries with the subregions:

Table 1: Subregions and countries in Asia

Central Asia
Kazakhstan, Kyrgyzstan, Tajikistan, Turkmenistan, Uzbekistan
Eastern Asia
China, Taiwan, Democratic People's Republic of Korea, Japan, Mongolia, Republic of Korea
Southern Asia
Afghanistan, Bangladesh, Bhutan, India, Iran (Islamic Republic of), Maldives, Nepal, Pakistan, Sri Lanka
South-Eastern Asia
Brunei Darussalam, Cambodia, Indonesia, Lao People's Democratic Republic, Malaysia, Myanmar, Philippines, Singapore, Thailand, Timor-Leste, Viet Nam
Western Asia
Armenia, Azerbaijan, Bahrain, Cyprus, Georgia, Iraq, Israel, Jordan, Kuwait, Lebanon, Oman, Qatar, Saudi Arabia, State of Palestine, Syrian Arab Republic, Turkey, United Arab Emirates, Yemen

Source: DESA.

The Asian subregions are culturally diverse in their ecology, geography and physical features. The regions include a multitude of indigenous groups who comprise 70 per cent of the estimated 350 million indigenous peoples worldwide. As mentioned earlier in the report, comprehensive data on the demographic status of the indigenous peoples in the Asian region are incomplete or not available. Information on indigenous peoples in Central and Western Asia, in particular, is so scarce it is very difficult to draw even a rough profile of the population. The data available within subregions

---

[78] Baviskar 2007; Hathaway 2010.

on the population of indigenous peoples are also limited for various reasons. An estimate offered by the International Working Group on Indigenous Affairs (IWGIA) in 2008 with a subsequent edition by Hall and Patrinos (2012) is an often cited source for understanding the distribution of the indigenous peoples is in the subregions of Asian continent. The following figure shows the approximate distribution of the population in the four subregions:

Figure 1: Indigenous Population in Asia (million)

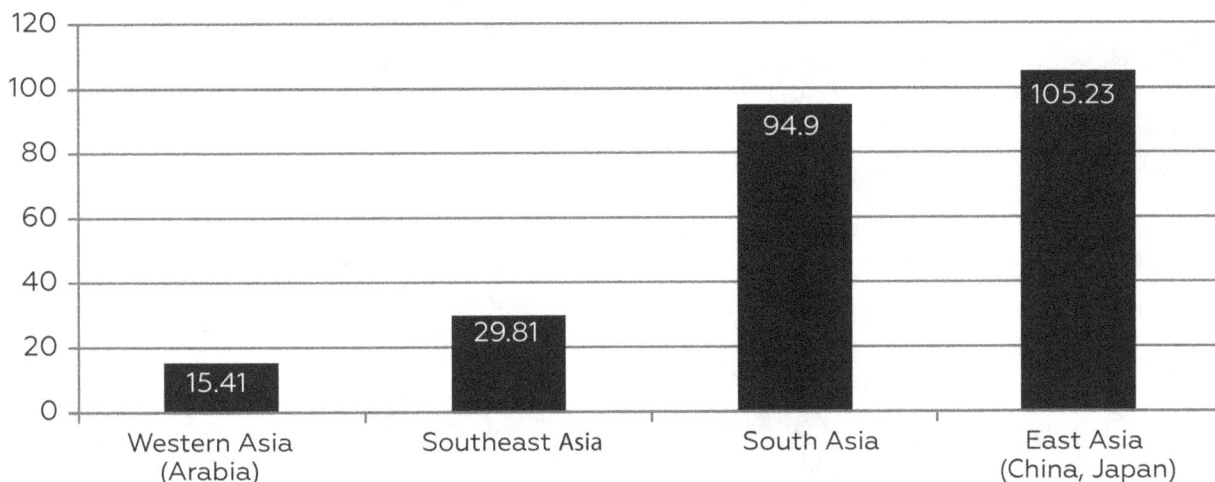

Source: Compiled from IWGIA (2008) in Hall and Patrinos (2012).

China has largest share of indigenous population in the world estimated to be about 105 million indigenous peoples. In Japan, according to Figure 1, there are some 230,000 indigenous peoples. There are 84.3 million indigenous peoples in India which makes India the second largest in terms of the absolute concentration of indigenous peoples. As the above figure shows, the South Asian region as a whole includes an indigenous population of 95 million peoples. The share of indigenous population in South-East Asia is about 30 million while western Asia has only about 15 million.

Despite the official data, assimilation to promote commonality by absorption into the dominant communities and within the States where indigenous peoples live, the reality is that indigenous societies themselves are conspicuous by their immense plurality. Within indigenous societies, there is vast diversity in terms of language, customs, dress, tradition and social and political organization. There is no reliable information available to determine the exact number of cultural or linguistic groups within the indigenous communities in different countries. A rough estimate shows that South Asia alone may have more than 750 groups identified, although not all are recognized as so. For example, the Indian Constitution enlists 461 ethnic groups as Scheduled Tribes, but studies estimate more than 635 groups exist in the country.

An important point is that for countries like India where the constitution has guaranteed certain rights as Schedule Tribes, this translates into better information on socioeconomic and health situation than other countries which have no such policies. But even in the Indian situation the number of groups recognized formally may differ substantially from the number of groups that actually exists or are self-defined by the groups themselves as being indigenous. The government of Nepal recognized 59 groups as indigenous nationalities, but is in the process of revising the list to include other self-defined indigenous groups. A similar scenario is also true for other South Asian counties. Although the names of each specific group are difficult to list with the current state of the information collected and access to it, the following table gives an idea of the major groups until relatively better data can be collected on the subcontinent:

Table 2: Names of indigenous groups in South Asia

Country	Commonly referred names	Major indigenous groups	Approximate population
Bangladesh	Tribal, upajati, indigenous hill tribe, Jumma, indigenous hill men, aboriginal tribes	Bawm, Chak, Chakma, Khumi, Khyang, Lushai, Marma, Mro, Pangkhua, Tanchangya Tripura and others collectively known as Jumma and Adivasi in plain, including Santal, Banais, Bhuiyas, Bhumijies, Dalus, Garos, Gonds, Hadis, Hajangs, Hos, Kharias, Kharwars, Kochs, Koras, Maghs (Bakarganj District), Mal Paharias, Oraons, Maches, Mundas, Santhals, Sauria Paharias, Turis and others	1.7-3.7 million (1.2-2.5 per cent)
Bhutan		Sarchops, Khengs, Adivasi, Birmi, Brokpa, Doya, Lepcha, Toktop and others	Approximately 10 per cent of the total population
India	Scheduled Tribes or Adivasi (original inhabitants);	461 groups recognized; major groups include Gond, Oraon, Khond, Bhil, Mina, Onge, Jarawa, Nagas and others	84.3 million, they comprise 8.2 per cent of the total population
Nepal	Indigenous Nationalities (Adivasi Janajati)	Magar, Tharu, Tamang, Newar, Rai, Gurung, Limbu and others	8.4 million people, or 37.19 per cent of the total population
Pakistan		Pashtun, Sindhis, Baluchs, Kihals and Mors, Buzdar, Kailasha and others	Not available
Sri Lanka		Vyadha ("huntsmen/archers") or Vadda	1,229 and 4,510 people,

Source: IWGIA 2008.

Table 3 shows major groups in the East and South-Eastern regions of Asia. In South-East Asia the Ethnic Minority Classification Project carried out from 1953 to 1979 in China identified 55 ethnic minority groups but there were more than 400 names of nationalities registered officially with the government during early post-liberation years For example, the Philippines have three major groups, but within them are various other indigenous groups. The same pattern is true for several other countries in South-Eastern Asia.

Table 3: Indigenous peoples in East and South-East Asia

Country	Commonly referred names	Major indigenous groups	Approximate population
China	Minority nationality, *minzu*	55 groups recognized, which include Zhuang, Manchu, Hui, Miao, Uygur, Yi, Tujia, Mongolian, Tibetan, Bouyei, Dong, Yao, Korean, Bai, Hani, Li, Kazakh, Dai, She, Lisu, Gelao, Lahu, Dongxiang, Wa, Shui, Naxi, Qiang, Tu, Xibe, Mulam, Kirgiz, Daur, Jingpo, Salar, Bulang, Maonan, Tajik, Pumi, Achang, Nu, Ewenki, Jing, Jino, De'ang, Uzbek, Russian, Yugur, Bonan, Menba, Oroqin, Drung, Tatar, Hezhen, Gaoshan, Lhoba (not all may self-identify as indigenous)	105,226,114 (8.47 per cent of the total population of China)
Japan	Indigenous peoples	Ainu, Okinawans or Ryukyuan	Ainu (28,782), Ryukuans (1.3 million)
Philippines	Indigenous peoples and indigenous cultural communities;	Major seven collective names include Mindanao Lumad, Cordillera Peoples; Caraballo Tribes, Mangyan, Negrito/Aeta, Palawan hill tribes and Visayan	12-15 million (10-20 per cent of the total population)
Cambodia	chuncheat daoem pheak tech, which means literally "minority original ethnicity".	17 groups recognized; major groups include Brao, Chong or Khmer Daoem, Jarai, Kachak, Kanchruk, Kavet, Khaonh, Kraol, Kreung, Kui, Lun, Mil (Mel), Por (Poar, Pear), Phnong (Punong), Rhade (Ede), R'ong, S'och (Saoch), Stieng, Suoy, Thmon, Tumpuon.	101,000 (1 per cent of the total population of Cambodia)
Indonesia	masyarakat adat (communities governed by custom)	Masyarakat adat communities, including groups such as the Dayak Benuaq, the Orang Tengger and the Orang Badui	30-40 million estimate
Lao	Ethnic minorities and non-ethnic Lao	49 groups officially recognized, speakers of Mon-Khmer, Sino-Tibetan and Hmong-lu Mien language families	
Malaysia	Aborigines and natives	Orang Asli (original peoples) of peninsular Malaysia, the Bukitans, Bisayahs, Dusuns, Sea Dayaks, Land Dayaks groups of Sarawak and the natives of Sabah	12 per cent of the total population of Malaysia

Country	Commonly referred names	Major indigenous groups	Approximate population
Myanmar	Ethnic nation-alities, national races	Shan, Karen, Rakhine, Karenni, Chin, Kachin, Kayah, Mon	32 per cent of the total popu-lation
Thailand	Chao-Khao or hill tribes	Chao-Khao or hill tribes include Hmong, Karen, Lisu, Mien, Akha, Lahu, Lua, Thin and Khamu; indigenous fisher communities chao-ley, and hunter gath-ers group Mani people	923,257 (not in-cluding people in south and north)
Viet Nam	Ethnic minorities (dan toc thieu so, dan toc it nguoi)	53 groups identified including Tay, Thai, Nung, Hmong, Dao and Khmer	14 per cent of the total population

Source: IWGIA 2008.

Colonialism, especially of European origin is regarded as less applicable to Asia in defining the context of indigenous peoples' history. The past and present dispossession of the land and re-sources, as well as loss of political autonomy and culture of the indigenous groups in Asia, how-ever, is comparable to the situation in white settler colonies.

Indigenous peoples in Asia are subject to political domination, cultural discrimination, economic exploitation and dispossession in the hands of the dominant national society as equal to their counterparts in settler colonies in the past. Discrimination against indigenous peoples, based on language, race, culture and identity, is rampant across the Asian states. Indigenous activists in Asia often term this phenomenon of dispossession and domination a process of internal col-onization, to a large extent distinct to the Asian situation. They carry and suffer from negative impact and trauma induced by past and continuing discrimination. The harm such discrimination inflicts upon the physical and mental health of the indigenous children, women and men are least researched and often remain most invisible or misrecognized.

Indigenous health status

Identification of groups as indigenous peoples is paramount to the knowledge development about the status of the indigenous peoples' health. Measuring indigenous health that takes into consideration the indigenous concept of health is an even more complex task. The current data available on the indigenous status tend to be framed by generic biomedical measurement and illness. While this may partially capture the status of indigenous health, understanding of indige-nous health requires a broader approach. The description of the indigenous concept of health that goes beyond the biomedical approach is given by the World Health Organization's Committee on Indigenous Health (1999):[79]

---

[79] Committee on Indigenous Health, The Geneva Declaration on the Health and Survival of Indigenous Peoples, WHO, Geneva, WHO/HSD/00.1 (1999).

Indigenous peoples' concept of health and survival is both a collective and an individual intergenerational continuum encompassing a holistic perspective incorporating four distinct shared dimensions of life. These dimensions are the spiritual, the intellectual, physical, and emotional. Linking these four fundamental dimensions, health and survival manifests itself on multiple levels where the past, present, and future coexist simultaneously.

The above description clearly shows the need for broader approach to collecting information to document the present health status of indigenous peoples to contribute to the development of appropriate strategies and programmes. Baseline data on a broad range of health indicators are urgently needed to compare health indicators, and improve health standards by developing health goals between different groups of indigenous and non-indigenous peoples, as well as to study what interventions can improve the health of indigenous peoples over time.

Current health information, even when available, does not generate a comprehensive picture for the Asian region as a whole nor does it permit comparisons among indigenous peoples and between them and their non-indigenous mainstream counterparts. This section presents some basic indicators available from government and academic sources to highlight the health status of indigenous peoples in Asia.

The most commonly used health indicators in the National Census and Demographic and Health Surveys carried by the governments are infant mortality, mortality of children aged 0-5 years, child nutrition, incidence or prevalence of diseases and their risk factors, and life expectancy at birth. As has been indicated earlier, the scope for comparison across the country is limited as variations in the approach taken by the specific countries exist.

Health-related Millennium Development Goals include: 1) eradicate extreme hunger and poverty; 2) reduce child mortality; 3) improve maternal health; and 4) combat HIV/AIDS, malaria and other diseases. Data produced for measuring the progress of the MDGs unfortunately do not require disaggregation by ethnicity and are geared towards the aggregate national average. This data capture problem has made the situation of indigenous peoples' invisible and gives the impression of a distorted picture, where the nested and unseen data that could describe the most vulnerable minorities of indigenous peoples are getting worse, while the non-indigenous majority may be improving. This is important because the remedy needs to be targeted to alleviate the greatest needs especially if they are the poorest minorities with little power and influence.

In the design of population-based studies this is an easy detail to fix, because in many cases data are limited simply due to absence of an ethnicity or language variable. Even when the health data are generated by ethnicity omission of the variable in analysis means no disaggregated profiles specific to indigenous peoples or minorities as a whole.

The quality of data collected is clinically orientated towards statistical markers that give no indication of broader issues of physical wellness or social well-being. Indicators that use mortality rates measure the worst outcomes causing death thus mask co-morbidity. More comprehensive indicators and indices of health and wellness, the presence or absence of disease or risk factors, and long-term outcomes need to be developed with due consideration of the interaction with indigenous concepts of health and how to improve it.

Narrowing the indigenous to mainstream population health gap is a particular concern as some of the countries in Asia especially China, India and Viet Nam have achieved considerable progress in health including that of indigenous peoples. Epidemiologic and biostatistics evidence on indigenous health based on a review of the literature clearly shows that there is a systematic gap across the Asian states. The clear message coming from these data is that if the indigenous health gap is left unattended, then the disparities gap will expand. Hence, in the coming decades, the Asian indigenous peoples will experience even poorer health due to lower education and employment in a vicious cycle created by extreme poverty.

The case of China can be illustrative of the health situation of the indigenous peoples. An analysis of the trends in infant/child mortality and life expectancy in indigenous populations in Yunnan using the population census of the China from 1953 through 2000 and data obtained from Yunnan Provincial Health Department shows that the minority nationalities have lower rates in key health indicators. For example, the weighted average life expectancy at birth in 2000 for minority nationalities was 64.5 whereas the total Chinese population was 71.4. The variance between the majority Han population and minority nationalities within autonomous provinces where minority population are concentrated, however, is slightly less. For example, life expectancy of the Han population in Yunnan was 68.8, which shows a difference between Han and minority nationalities of only about 4.4 years.[80] Although a considerable heterogeneity between the different minority populations is to be noted, the pattern of data on the life expectancy can give an important indication of the poor situation of the population concerned.

Figure 2: Gap in life expectancy: comparing indigenous and non-indigenous populations, with states in order of 2009 HDI rating

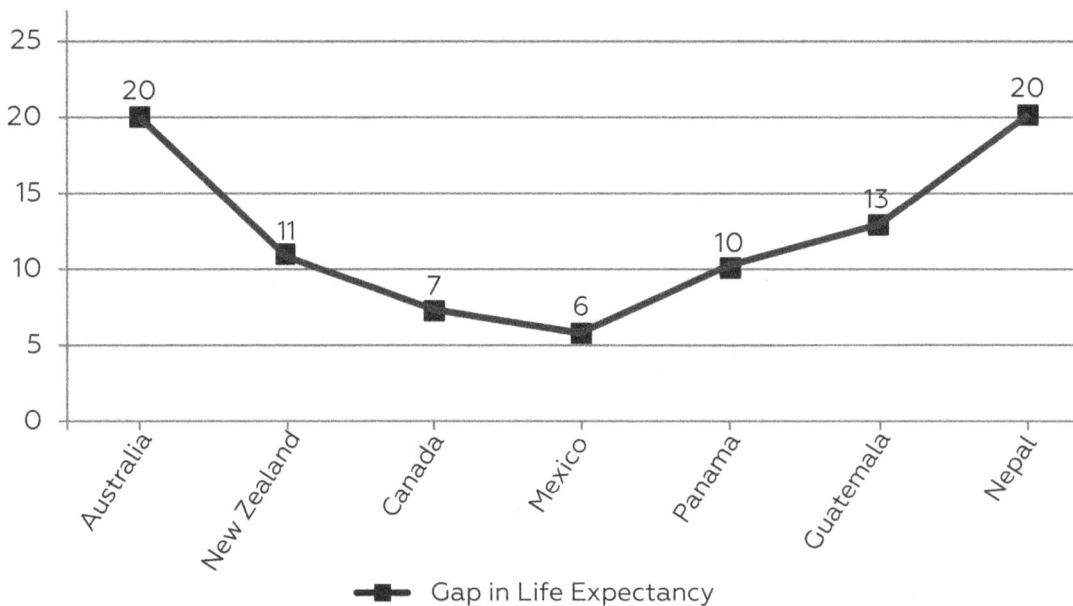

Source: MacIntosh, 2012:76.

Life expectancy is one of the key indicators of Human Development Index (HDI). Available data show a remarkable gap in life expectancy between indigenous and non-indigenous populations living within the same state. Comparing high-income to low- and middle-income counties shows that the gap for indigenous peoples is observed in diverse nations. While Australia had the high-

---

[80] Li, 2008.

est recorded gap in life expectancy--20 years--between indigenous and non-indigenous, it was comparable to that of low-income Nepal, as shown in Figure 3.[81] Nepal falls at 157th in HDI ranking.

Comparison between indigenous and non-indigenous groups in different countries depicts similar picture on infant and child mortality rate. Analysis of the health data made above by Jianghong Li (2008) for China, for example, shows that the weighted average mortality rate under age 1 for the sample minority nationalities was 77.8 deaths per 1,000 live births versus 53.6 for the Han Chinese in 2000. India shows a similar picture according to the 2005-2006 National Family Health Survey (NFHS-3) which provides estimates of important indicators on family welfare, maternal and child health, and nutrition according to social groups. Infant mortality rate for the Scheduled Tribe (ST) was recorded to be 62.1 against the rate of 57.0 per 1,000 live births for the total population in India.[82] The data also show that the highest morality rates are concentrated in the regions with indigenous populations, especially in rural areas. Similar to Yunnan in China, where a higher rate of the infant mortality exists, in India infant mortality is concentrated in the regions of Madhya Pradesh and Arunachal Pradesh, where significant indigenous population live. The pattern is clear; for provinces where indigenous peoples are in higher concentration, the mortality rates are correspondingly higher.

Figure 3: Infant mortality rate: indigenous versus mainstream by country (per 1,000 births)

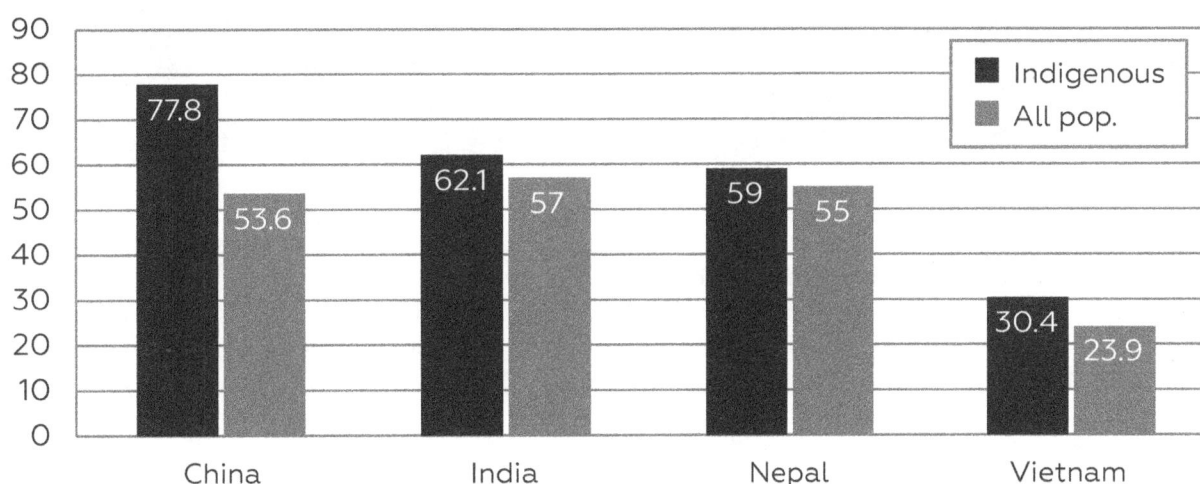

Sources: Li 2008, Mohindra and Labonté 2010, Bennett and Dahal 2008, Dang 2012.

Nepal and Viet Nam display a similar picture. For example, according to NDHS , in 2006 the infant mortality average in Nepal for indigenous peoples was 55 deaths per 1,000 live births while the national average was 59.[83] Viet Nam appears to be doing better in terms of reducing the infant mortality rate, but it has not been successful in reducing the disparity between its vulnerable ethnic minorities and the majority population. Viet Nam for example, has 30.4 infant deaths per 1,000 live births for ethnic minorities while national average is only 23.9.[84] The table above shows a comparative scenario on the infant mortality of the four different Asian countries.

---

[81] Cunningham, 2009; MacIntosh, 2013.

[82] Ministry of Tribal Affairs 2010.

[83] Bennett, Dahal, et al. 2008.

[84] Dang, 2012.

The case for child mortality and under-five mortality is also very similar in terms of the disparity between indigenous and non-indigenous populations in the Asian countries. Given the highly variable information availability we have information on the indicators for only few countries. In South Asia, for example, Nepal provides a glimpse of the situation in all three aspects of child mortality based on the further analysis of the national data. For India, Mohindra and Labonté (2010) have analysed the time trend information from the National Family and Health Survey (NFHS-1), 1992-1993; NFHS-2, 1998-1999; NFHS-3, 2005-2006. Bennett and Dahal (2008) did same for Nepal using the data set generated from National Demographic and Health Survey 2006. We draw from analysis of VHLSS by Dang (2012) for Viet Nam on the mortality rates. The following table shows the comparative picture of three countries in Asia disaggregated for indigenous population compared to the total population of the country.

Table 4: Infant, child and under-five mortality in selected Asian countries

Mortality	Nepal NDHS, 2006		India, NFHS 2005-2006		Viet Nam, VHLSS 2006	
	Indigenous nationality	All pop.	Scheduled Tribe	All pop.	Ethnic minority	Ethnic majority
Infant mortality	59	55	62.1	57	30	23
Child mortality	22	13	95.7	74.3	NA	NA
Under-five mortality.	80	68	35.8	18.4	41	28

Source: Bennett and Dahal, et al. 2008; Mohindra and Labonté 2010; and Dang 2012.

Data on child mortality are sparse in other countries that do not disaggregate by ethnicity. In the countries where data are collected using the geographic area as unit of analysis, proxy indicators are the means to generate some understanding of indigenous health to see the difference between the remote regions where indigenous peoples predominantly live compared with the other provinces with fewer indigenous peoples. In Pakistan, for example, Balochistan in the North-West Frontier Province (NWFP) and Federally Administered Tribal Areas (FATA) are the predominantly tribal areas. They are also the least developed provinces and have highest levels of infant mortality rate from 70 to 129 per 1,000 live births. Unfortunately, the majority of infant deaths were caused by preventable causes such as diarrhoea, respiratory infection, tetanus and others.[85] Thus, improving living conditions and access to health services would result in rapid improvements for child health in these regions.

Minority Rights Group International (MRG) Report 2013 shows that Baluchistan also experience highest level of maternal mortality ratio with 758 per 100,000 live births. This is indeed a shocking figure when the national maternal mortality rate has declined from 400 per 100,000 in 2004-2005 to 276 in 2006-2007. If Pakistan is to meet the MDG target of reducing the maternal mortality to 140 per 100,000 also for its tribal population, it will certainly require substantial restructuring of the state policies and programmes. We do not have access to official figures on maternal mortality in Myanmar, but research estimates reveal that the maternal mortality rate for the indigenous peoples is "triple that of the country as a whole, making this statistically among

---

[85] Walker, 2013.

the most dangerous places in the world to be a pregnant woman".[86] It is estimated that "one third of these deaths occur due to postpartum haemorrhage, a condition that can be prevented with the provision of basic health care services".[87]

Child nutrition is another major indicator used to assess the health status of the population. The available data reveal that a number of Asian countries have shown improvement in child nutrition over the last two decades. Astonishingly, despite such improvements, changes in the nutritional status of the children in indigenous communities are much slower in pace than their non-indigenous counterparts. A study by Ouyang and Pinstrup-Andersen (2012:1456) on health inequality between ethnic minorities and the Han populations in China states, "Health and nutrition status in terms of height-for-age and weight-for-age actually improved for both the Han group and the minority group, but the improvement is much smaller for the minorities, and hence the growing health gap". Another study conducted in China has made similar conclusions and suggested that stunting, wasting and being underweight were distinct indicators of the nutritional status of children and chronic growth retardation is the major type of child protein-energy malnutrition in poor rural minority areas of Yunnan Province, China.[88]

In Cambodia, more than 20 per cent of indigenous children under five children suffer from mal-nutrition and 52 per cent are classified as underweight and stunted in growth (Health Unlimited 2002). The country has a small population of indigenous peoples, approximately 100,000 with most concentrated in two provinces in one of the world's poorest countries with low human development index (UNDP 2004). The prevalence of malnutrition in Indonesia is similarly high at 24.6 per cent of children under five years old as of 2000. Indigenous Adat populations suffer greater risk of child mortality. Human development levels among the Philippines indigenous groups in region of Cordillera and specifically Manabo households vary, showing that the Manabo households had a much higher rate of under-five mortality at 96 deaths per 1,000 live births, which is higher than national average of 42 per 1,000.[89]

In Bangladesh indigenous peoples are largely concentrated in Chittagong Hill Tract (CHT) where approximately 600,000 indigenous Jumma peoples live. CHT, being one of the country's most deprived areas, suffers particularly extreme rates of ill health. Immunization coverage in CHT is recorded to be considerably low, with full immunization coverage by age 12 months at 51 per cent compared to 71 per cent overall in Bangladesh.[90]

The case of India corroborates the findings in China and other Asian countries and shows that nu-tritional status of the Scheduled Tribes (ST) children falls behind the national average compared with the mainstream or dominant communities. The mortality rate of ST children is worse and im-provement is slower than for other communities in the country. Adequate nutrition and access to vaccination are key determinants in child growth and mortality, thus both are depicted in Figure 4 and Figure 5, which show time trends in the child nutrition status and access to vaccination over the period from 1992-1993 to 2005-2006 in India:

---

[86]   Walker 2013:145.

[87]   http://www.unpo.org/article/11087#sthash.Zc7ut7Jr.dpuf.

[88]   Li, Guo et al., 1999.

[89]   Macdonald, 2012.

[90]   Minsitry of Health and Family Welfare, 2011.

Figure 4: Scheduled Tribe, malnutrition and vaccination, India

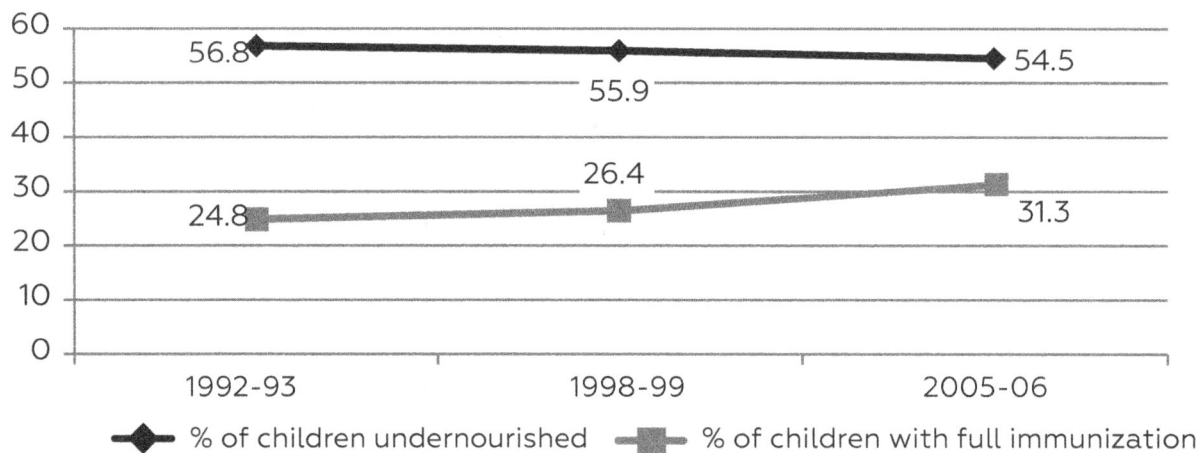

Total population, malnutrition and vaccination, India

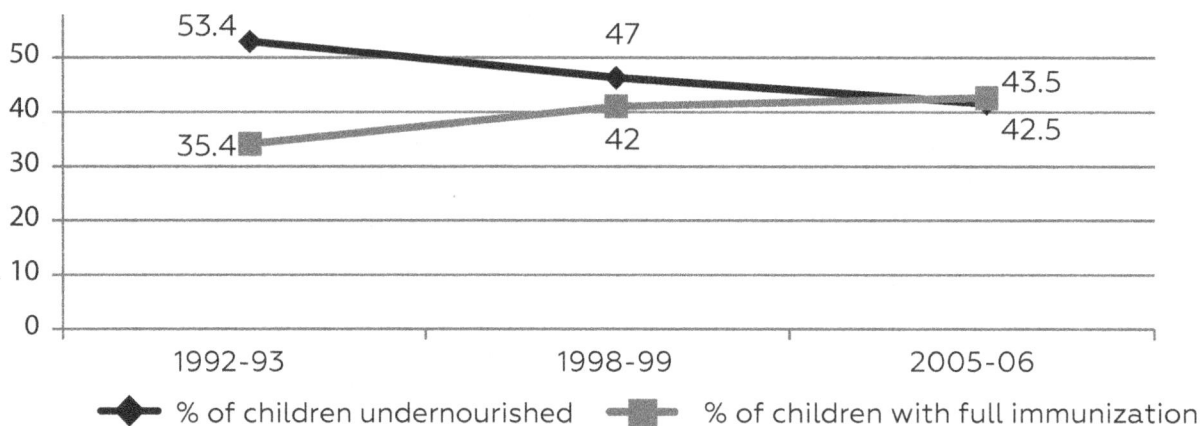

Source: Statistical Profile of Schedule Tribes in India 2010, Ministry of Tribal Affairs.

Immunization coverage is generally assessed using two indicators: breadth or coverage (percentage receiving any basic vaccination) and intensity or quality of coverage (percentage receiving all basic vaccinations). Analysis of NFHS data in India suggests that there have been substantial improvements between 1992 and 2005, especially among Scheduled Tribes.[91] However, a disaggregated analysis reveals that, despite the gains made, immunization rates among STs remained consistently below those recorded for other groups including the Scheduled Castes and Other Backward Classes (OBCs), for all types of vaccinations. This is attributed to the extremely poor immunization policy and coverage for ST children on the part of the government service delivery. The following table shows the vaccination coverage of ethnic minorities in Viet Nam:

---

[91] Das and Hall, 2012.

Figure 5: Children with full vaccination, Viet Nam 2002 (per cent)

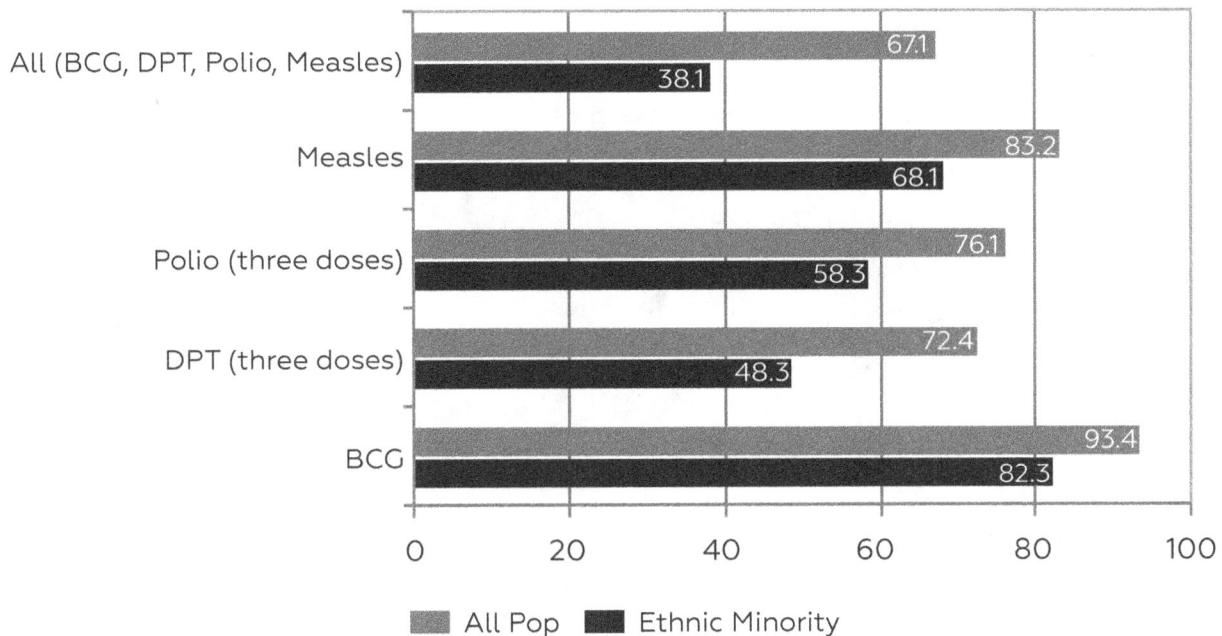

Source: Dang, 2012.

Access to vaccination in other Asian countries also shows that there have been improvements in the coverage, but the available data show that the ethnic minorities remain below the national average. The situation calls for proactive health policies of the government to reach indigenous peoples in the regions where they live. The disparity in access to vaccinations by the children in Viet Nam illustrates how indigenous peoples are constantly falling behind the dominant communities. As figure 5 shows the percentage of indigenous children who have received full immunization is 38.1 while the national average is 67.1 per cent.

Diseases and determinants of the health of indigenous peoples

Nutritional deficiency of indigenous peoples caused by the massive changes induced through colonization and state intervention in their ways of living has resulted in higher rate and complex form of disease patterns of indigenous peoples. Colonization, market expansion and state interventions have blocked indigenous peoples' access to their forest, river and other natural resources. The traditional ways of farming, food-gathering, hunting, or fishing places and practices has been destroyed and indigenous peoples become increasingly dependent upon the outside world for foods that are unfamiliar and low in nutrient quality. A study on determinants and disease patterns of indigenous peoples describes the nutritional deficiencies of indigenous peoples in the following words:

> Besides hunger and general inadequacy of food and dietary energy (calories), specific deficiencies of various nutrients are widespread. Examples are iron deficiency, which can be caused by dietary inadequacy or secondary to blood loss, intestinal parasites, or malaria;

hypothyroidism, shortness of iodine affects hundreds of millions of people; poor vitamin intake (e.g., vitamins A and D, folic acid); and heavy metals, such as zinc. These deficiencies and any underlying causes, including poverty and inadequate food, should be corrected to reach satisfactory outcomes for those affected.[92]

Table 5: Major health problems of indigenous peoples

- ≡ High infant and young child mortality
- ≡ High maternal morbidity and mortality
- ≡ Heavy infectious disease burdens
- ≡ Malnutrition and retarded growth
- ≡ Shortened life expectancy at birth
- ≡ Diseases and deaths associated with cigarette smoking
- ≡ Social problems, illnesses and deaths linked to misuse of alcohol and other drugs
- ≡ Accidents, poisonings, interpersonal violence, homicide and suicide
- ≡ Obesity, diabetes, hypertension, cardiovascular disease and chronic renal disease (lifestyle diseases)
- ≡ Diseases caused by environmental contamination (e.g., heavy metals, industrial gases, and effluent wastes) and infectious diseases caused by faecal contamination

Source: Gracey and King 2009:66.

Contemporary indigenous health issues in Asia are strikingly similar in many aspects to problems of indigenous peoples worldwide. Although the gap is gradually being narrowed in health status of indigenous and non-indigenous populations substantially over the last few decades in the region, there is a significant burden of disease for the indigenous population as compared to general population. The studies show that indigenous peoples in Asia "bear a triple burden of persisting infectious diseases, increasing chronic conditions, and a growing recognition of injuries and violence".[93] It further states that incomplete demographic transitions, greater risks of communicable diseases including HIV and AIDS, massive unplanned urbanization and a host of social determinants of health compound these problems. Thus poor health is caused by a number of factors: a high level of undernourishment, poor hygiene and sanitation, overcrowded living space, lack of clean drinking water, environmental contaminations and a high degree of poverty. In analysing the disease patterns of the indigenous peoples across the globe, Gracey and King (2009) summarized the major health problem of the indigenous peoples as per table above:

Generalization across the indigenous peoples in Asia with regard to their health status may be problematic as the extent of the disparities varies between the indigenous and non-indigenous population, as well as within the indigenous groups. There are also specific historical and local contextual factors in different Asia countries that affect the health of the indigenous peoples in particular location. For example, studies show that there is prevalence of malaria in particular parts of the Bangladesh, India and Indonesia affecting certain indigenous groups more than oth-

---

[92] Gracey and King, 2009:66.

[93] Rakić, 2008:728.

ers. Similarly, the problem of sexually transmitted diseases associated with the trafficking of girls and migration may be of higher severity in Thailand, Myanmar, India, Nepal and Indonesia.[94]

Conflict related injuries are also an important factor that comes into purview when describing indigenous health. Lao People's Democratic Republic for example still suffers from landmine explosion that takes lives of more than 100 people each year. Philippines and Myanmar are equally affected by conflict and related injuries which, among the indigenous peoples are a considerable problem. Indigenous peoples are also less prepared for the disaster related health problems such as the devastating typhoon experienced recently in Philippines.

The health deficit for indigenous women is greater than their male counterparts. The health discrepancy faced by the indigenous peoples of Peninsular Malaysia's diverse indigenous peoples, collectively known as Orang Asli, is an illustrative example for such situation. A report by the Women's Aid Organisation (WAO) which examined Malaysia's progress on gender equality pointed out that Orang Asli women have a lower life expectancy than men. They run a greater risk of malnutrition and have high rates of post-partum haemorrhage and puerperal sepsis. In a number of countries in Asia, indigenous women face the highest level of vulnerability of violence in conflict situations, trafficking and sexually transmitted diseases in addition to other burdens of disease.

Asia experiences higher incidents of infectious diseases such as tuberculosis and rheumatic fever which are quite uncommon among non-indigenous peoples. The indigenous populations are also suffering increasingly from the lifestyle diseases including obesity, heart diseases, cancer, type 2 diabetes, as well as physical, social and mental disorders.[95] Such disorders are often linked to misuse of alcohol and of other drugs which result from identity loss, disorientations in the collective cultural life world and indigenous identities.[96] Inaccessibility to proper health care services, inadequate clinical care and health promotion, and poor disease prevention services on the part of the State aggravate this situation because preventable conditions are not adequately addressed by the health care delivery systems.

Indigenous peoples' access to health services

Lack of access to adequate and culturally appropriate health care services is one of the primary experiences of the indigenous peoples in Asia and a key reason for indigenous health deficit. Compared to their non-indigenous counterparts, indigenous peoples have limited health care infrastructure and ability to utilize existing health services. Data coming from various countries on the group difference with respect to access indicate that indigenous groups, especially indigenous females, are most likely to report being in bad health, have the highest incidence of temporary health problems and are less likely to receive or seek treatment when ill. The systematic character of the health gap is related to the lack of general state capacity to provide health services to indigenous peoples. Restructuring of the existing preventive and curative health care services are at the heart of the indigenous peoples right to health and well-being.

---

[94] Macdonald, 2012.

[95] Anderson and White, 2008

[96] King, Smith, et al., 2009.

There are several other factors that impede indigenous access to health services besides the state capacity and willingness to provide necessary support for improving indigenous health. Unfortunately, only limited disaggregated information is available on utilization of existing health care services for indigenous peoples. One exception and a key indicator for assessing the utilization of the health care services by the population has been the visit of pregnant women to a health facility prior, during and after delivery. The data generated from national surveys in selected Asian countries show that a considerable disparity exist between the indigenous and non-indigenous population on access and utilization of such maternal-child services. For example, in China 73 per cent of the pregnant women in non-autonomous prefectures had antenatal examination but only 51 per cent of the mothers from autonomous prefectures with larger population of minority nationality made such visits.[97]

Other countries depict similar picture on health care service to mothers. Viet Nam shows that ethnic minority people are 16 per cent less likely to visit hospital when they are ill.[98] In Bangladesh, districts in Chittagong Hill Tracts (CHT), where the majority of Bangladeshi indigenous peoples live, antenatal care visits, assistance during delivery by medically trained personnel and post-natal care for mothers were lower than that of national figures. For example, the Khagrachhari district in CHT has recorded rate of 30 per cent antenatal, and 6.6 per cent post natal care visits which is lower than national average of 47.6 and 16.1 per cent, respectively.[99] Further analysis of demographic and health information for a 2005-2006 survey in Nepal shows that 34 per cent of mothers from indigenous nationalities receive antenatal care from a skilled birth attendants as compared to 44 per cent for average population. The disparity appears wider still when comparing access to antenatal care with hill Brahman community, where 76 per cent of mothers receive such assistance. The Indian situation is not very different as the only one third of women belonging to Scheduled Tribes receive antenatal care as compared to the population average of about one half (49 per cent) for the mainstream. It even indicates the worst case scenario as the proportion of Scheduled Tribe women to have received such care actually declined from 35 per cent in 1998 to 32 per cent in 2006 (Das and Hall 2012).

Another measure to assess the access of health institutions and facilities by the population has also been through identifying the place of birth or delivery. Asian countries have varying records of delivery, but on the whole, the majority of indigenous mothers tend to give birth in their homes. In India for example, only about 29 per cent of mothers from the indigenous population had delivery in the health facilities indirectly, which means that some 71 per cent give birth in their own homes without any assistance from skilled birth attendants. The situation of the non-ST communities was better than of the STs, with 49 per cent of the mothers having access to health facilities for delivery. The following table shows the place of delivery in India for indigenous and non-indigenous population:

---

[97] Li, 2008.

[98] Dang, 2012.

[99] Ministry of Health and Family Welfare, 2004.

Figure 6: Place of delivery (access to health institutions and facilities), India

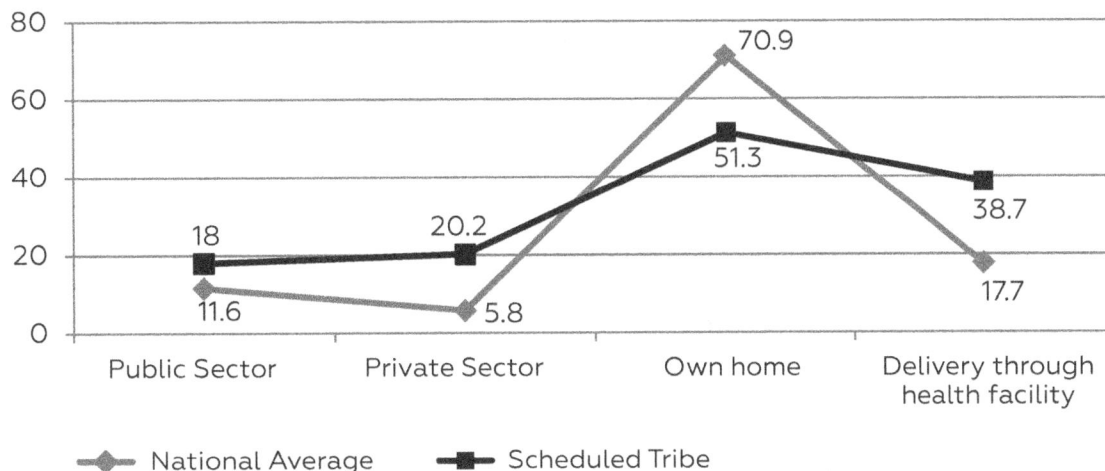

Source: Das, 2012.

Indigenous peoples' access to health services utilization information

Whereas some countries in Asia are improving indigenous access to health information, in general most countries are substantially lagging behind due to multiple reasons. Viet Nam, for example shows that knowledge about HIV/AIDS among never-married women is recorded to be at the rate of about 95 percent. There is, however, difference in knowledge about HIV/AIDS for different ethnic groups. Women belonging to ethnic minority groups are 12 per cent less likely to ever hear about the HIV/AIDS, and 18 per cent less likely have correct perception about it and significantly less likely to know about correct ways about how they could prevent themselves from contracting HIV/AIDS. In India, 60.9 per cent of mainstream population has heard about HIV/AIDS, compared to only 38.6 per cent of women from Scheduled Tribes who have received such information. The situations of Bangladesh and Nepal are also similar as 46 per cent of the population has ever heard of HIV/AIDS and only 13 per cent of women have complete information on transmission of the disease in Bangladesh. Disparity between the indigenous and non-indigenous peoples in Nepal with regard to knowledge about HIV/AIDS remains a cause of concern as the only 60 per cent of women among the indigenous peoples living in southern plains of Nepal known as Tarai have heard about HIV/AIDS compared to national average of 73 per cent. Indigenous women lack direct links and access to public information and mass media, and most importantly it is not communicated in their mother tongue.

There are several reasons that indigenous peoples in Asian countries have limited access to health care services and information. The first and often-cited reason is the distance to the health facilities. As most indigenous peoples in Asia live in remote parts of the country where government has not invested in the health infrastructure, thus leaving the majority of indigenous populations to rely on the traditional medicines and methods for health care. Nor has there been effort in recognizing and promoting the complementary indigenous knowledge and practices on health care and well-being. As the following figure shows, even when health care infrastructure does exist, the availability of drugs and quality health advice is lacking for indigenous groups.

Figure 7: Problems in accessing medical advice or treatment (per cent), India

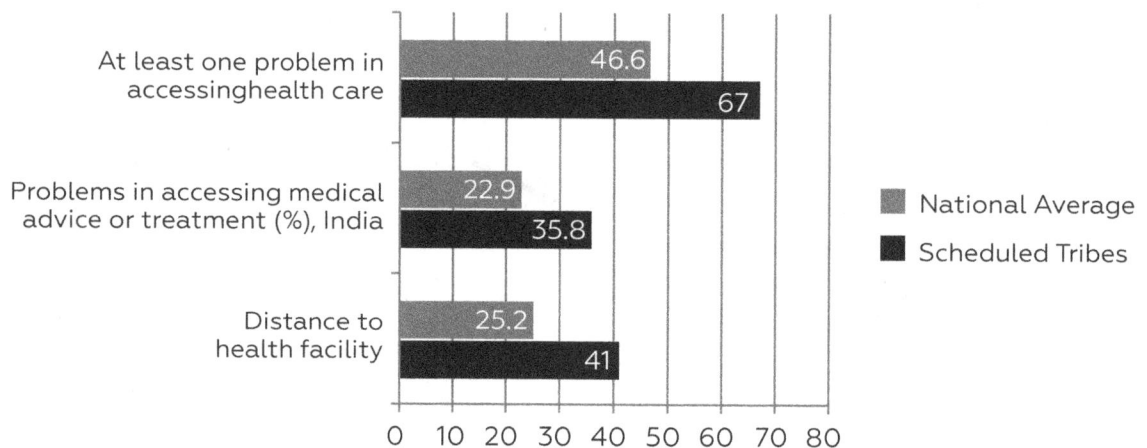

Source: Statistical Profile of Schedule Tribes in India 2010, Ministry of Tribal Affairs.

Reducing language barriers is critical for improving indigenous peoples' access to health care, and other services provided by the State. In the majority of the Asian countries, language of the dominant communities is being adopted as official language. Unfortunately, indigenous population often cannot speak a language other than their own mother tongue except in the condition of cultural assimilation. Thailand is a representative case in Asia. More than 100,000 indigenous peoples in Thailand officially referred to as hill tribes had no access to the public health system. The National Commission on Human Rights of Thailand noted that for the hill tribes who have not yet received legal status, the public health service is elusive. Referring to the question of linguistic barriers, the Committee on the Elimination of Racial Discrimination in its concluding observations stated that "the Committee is concerned about the inadequate access to social welfare and public services by certain ethnic groups because of language barriers and the limited availability of such services where these groups live".[100]

A great number of indigenous peoples have attributed their inability to access health services to affordability. In Nepal for example, 43 per cent of indigenous women have reported that they are unable to receive the health care services due to lack of money. Despite the fact that poverty has been drastically reduced in Asian countries over the past few decades, including for indigenous peoples, available data show that indigenous peoples have a higher poverty rate in the region. The exception is China, where the poverty gap between indigenous and non-indigenous population is stable, while the poverty gap is widening in most Asian countries.[101]

Finally, access to health care services by indigenous peoples is hampered by lack of representation of the indigenous peoples in the health management system. There are very few health professional and workers trained from among the indigenous populations who can be involved in management of health care. The investment in the training of indigenous persons in the health

---

[100] Walker, 2013:161.

[101] Hall and Patrinos, 2012.

work force is substantially behind in almost all countries. Indigenous representation and participation in decision-making with regards to health policies, planning and evaluation at the national level and their right to participate in decision-making in local health facility management are critical to improving indigenous access to health services.

Indigenous health and post-2015 development framework

The above analysis of the available data from different Asian countries on the health status of the indigenous peoples shows a systematic deficit in the indigenous health and access to health services from the government. Indigenous peoples seems to fall behind in all major health indicators employed by the existing mainstream health policies and programmes even when the state has made significant progress in economic growth and social development. Irrespective of the HDI of the country and growth rate, indigenous peoples have a lower rate of life expectancy, higher infant and child mortality, poorer maternal health outcomes and lower levels of access to health services provided by the government, including development of and access to information on indigenous health and health services. Persistent and ever-growing inequality between indigenous and non-indigenous peoples living in the same State is intertwined with the question of human rights violation.

The health deficit and persistent social inequalities result from the combined effects of social determinants of health and the indigenous specific factors related to colonization and history. The WHO Commission on Social Determinants of Health and the 1986 Ottawa Charter for Health Promotion (WHO 1986) identified income, education, employment, living conditions, social support and access to health services as the key social determinants of poor health.[102] These factors certainly apply to the indigenous peoples, as poverty and other disadvantages are disproportionately concentrated in the indigenous areas alongside a generic lack of government support. The general socioeconomic factors of indigenous health inequalities arise from historically and culturally specific factors particular to the peoples affected. Thus Indigenous health is affected by the colonial and intergenerational dispossession, structure of racial discrimination, loss of identity, culture, language and land, as well as spiritual, emotional and mental disconnectedness.[103]

The Millennium Development Goals (MDGs) have achieved a significant progress towards reduction of poverty, child death, infectious diseases such as malaria, tuberculosis and HIV/AIDS and increase in school enrolment and employment over the past. While the MDGs are making a real difference in people's lives, the changes for the indigenous peoples, however, have not been equal to their non-indigenous counterparts. The MDGs have some major deficiencies with regard to indigenous peoples. The first is that MDGs rely on national aggregate results and remains blind to the need of social groups such as indigenous peoples with specific conditions of disadvantages. The progress in the national average technically can be attained without any improvements in the minority indigenous peoples' health situation or can even be accomplished at the cost of ethnic minority by diverting programs though priority investing of resources in easily accessible (urban and semi-urban) areas where higher populations are concentrated, thus driving statistics on improvement at the national level. Such a situation can only begin to be addressed by improvement on the lack of disaggregated data for indigenous peoples. The lack of data seriously hampers the State's ability to plan and monitor

---

[102] Nettleton, Napolitano, et al. 2007.

[103] Cunningham, 2009.

the progress on MDGs with visibility of the specific ethnic groups. The second critique of the MDGs has been its lack of reference to the principles of human rights for attaining these goals.

Another major weakness of the conventional approach, including that of the MDGs, has been to target general health application population health initiatives where the exclusive focus has been on non-indigenous notions of health primarily consisting of biomedical perspectives on disease and treatment. The mainstream health strategies have not yet taken into consideration the relational and holistic concept of indigenous health that defines health and well-being in broader terms than the absence of disease and physical health. Indigenous health embraces spiritual, emotional and mental aspects together with physical health in their understanding of well-being and health. The indigenous concept of health also goes beyond the individual and considers the collectivity and harmonious relationship with other members of the community and nature as intricate part of the well-being.

The United Nations is currently engaged in the process of devising a new global development plan for the post-2015 period, when the MDG program will conclude. There is a wide range of agreement that the new global development framework that will replace the MDG should situate inequality and human rights central to it strategy. Such an approach is crucial not only because inequality has negative impact on growth and creates tension between communities but also undermines democracy. Indigenous peoples have called for post-2015 framework to be based on a foundation of human rights. This is highly relevant as the right to life is broadly interpreted as not just protection from arbitrary killing, but also as creating material conditions where food, clean water, and medicine are available to all. With regard to indigenous peoples, ILO Convention No. 169 on Indigenous and Tribal Peoples, which has been key reference for indigenous peoples worldwide, recognizes the health related rights specifically in Article 25.[104] This provision complements with the similar health rights affirmed in UNDRIP 2007, Article 21 (1) which recognizes the rights of indigenous peoples to the improvement of their economic and social conditions "in the areas of education... housing, sanitation, health and social security".

The report of the High Level Panel on the Post-2015 Development Agenda recommended five big transformative shifts; one of them is stated as "Leave no one behind". This recommendation recognizes the issue of inequality and discrimination as central ones and calls for further work on the MDG achievements. It states that; "We must keep faith with the original promise of the MDGs, and now finish the job. ... We should ensure that no person—regardless of ethnicity, gender, geography, disability, race or other status—is denied universal human rights and basic economic opportunities". This indicates the necessity to emphasize the task of removing both direct and indirect discrimination faced by the affected communities for achieving equity in health. As elsewhere, indigenous peoples in Asia face direct discrimination as manifested in a range of spheres, from

---

[104] ILO C 169, Article 25 1) governments shall ensure that adequate health services are made available to the peoples concerned, or shall provide them with resources to allow them to design and deliver such services under their own responsibility and control, so that they may enjoy the highest attainable standard of physical and mental health; 2) health services shall, to the extent possible, be community-based. These services shall be planned and administrated in co-operation with the peoples concerned and take into account their economic, geographic, social and cultural conditions as well as their traditional preventive care, healing practices and medicines; 3) the health care system shall give preference to the training and employment of local community health workers, and focus on primary health care while maintaining strong links with other levels of health care services; and 4) the provision of such health services shall be coordinated with other social, economic and cultural measures in the country.

access to health facilities and the delivery of health services. They are also adversely affected by the underlying determinants of health, such as access to safe drinking water, sanitation, adequate housing and nutrition. Additionally, health practitioners may give lower-quality diagnoses, medication and care and may even show neglect towards those discriminated against. Indirect discrimination that indigenous peoples experience may on the surface appear neutral, but it has the effect of discrimination. One prime example of indirect discrimination includes providing health information and services only in the dominant language or in accordance with dominant cultural practices, which results in the de facto exclusion of indigenous peoples.

The report also calls for a "data revolution" to improve the quality of statistics and information available to citizens. In the Asian region, as in other parts of the world, indigenous peoples have spoken clearly on this issue stating that such a data revolution should include the collecting disaggregated information on key indicators for both baseline and progress tracking. A number of Asian countries have already begun collecting the information disaggregated to create profiles for specific to indigenous peoples on key health indicators such as life expectancy, child mortality and others. The post-2015 framework should intensify the task and collect quantitative data on different types of health facilities, locations and their users disaggregated by ethnicity. Similarly, disaggregated data on health practitioners, patient-health worker ratios, staff recruitment would be crucial in planning inclusion of the indigenous professionals into the health workforce. Finally, quantitative and qualitative data on the burden of preventable and treatable disease, disability and premature death and their determinants among indigenous peoples should also include in such a data revolution envisioned in post-2015 development framework. This would be in line with the High Level Panel's call for designing "goals that focus on reaching excluded groups by making sure we track progress at all levels of income, and by providing social protection to help people build resilience to life's uncertainties".

Conclusion

Several common health problems that indigenous peoples share with other excluded populations may be addressed through general health initiatives. Indigenous peoples however, further, face distinct set of complex issues that require initiatives specific to indigenous peoples. Indigenous peoples, for example, suffer from political marginalization and loss of autonomy. In order to reverse the effect of colonization and political marginalization the recognition of indigenous peoples' right to self-determination is regarded as an appropriate mechanism. Through the exercise of the right to self-determination, indigenous peoples can revive and reclaim their cultural traditions and indigenous identity and self-esteem based on a positive image that is crucial for overall health and well-being of the people. Such autonomy would also involve empowering indigenous peoples to preserve and develop their own solutions and plans to improve their health rather than imposing solutions upon them. Article 24.1 of the UNDRIP is illustrative of such an autonomy. It states, "Indigenous peoples have the right to their traditional medicines and maintain their health practices, including the conservation of their vital medicinal plants, animals and minerals".

The dispossession that indigenous peoples suffered from both through colonial and contemporary processes of dispossession has left a legacy of impoverished indigenous communities which has resulted in a detrimental effect on indigenous peoples' health. The process has displaced them from their lands and alienated them from their natural resources. The land and territory for indigenous peoples is deeply linked to their identity, culture, spirituality and overall health of the community.

Indigenous language is also central to identity, cultural expressions and collective living. It is especially important as a fundamental cultural expression of indigenous knowledge on health, medicine and spirituality and thus for well-being. Indigenous languages, however, are being lost rapidly and with them is the loss of valuable knowledge on medicinal plants, healing and indigenous identity. The post-2015 development agenda should consider revitalization of the indigenous languages as an important strategy connected to disease prevention and health promotion.

Finally, improving equity in health for indigenous peoples is linked to fulfilling their right to participate in decision-making. The participation of the population in all health-related decisions from community, national and international levels is an important dimension of the human right to health. Consultation processes have began for the post-2015 development agenda and has offered important opportunity for participation of the indigenous peoples in formulating a new global partnership for eradicating poverty and transform economies through sustainable development to promote improved indigenous health and well-being to levels comparable to non-indigenous groups.

References

Anderson, I. and J. White (2008). Populations at Special Health Risk; Indigenous Populations. International encyclopedia of public health. K. Heggenhougen and S. R. Quah. Amsterdam; London, Elsevier.

Baviskar, A. (2007). Indian Indigeneities: Adivasi Engagements with Hindu Nationalism in India. Indigenous experience today. M. d. l. Cadena and O. Starn. Oxford, Berg. Wenner-Gren International Symposium series: 275-303.

Bennett, L., D. R. Dahal, et al. (2008). Caste, Ethnic and Regional Identity in Nepal: Further Analysis of the 2006 Nepal Demographic and Health Survey. Calverton, Maryland, USA, Macro International Inc.

Chee-Beng, T. (2008). The Concept of Indigenous Peoples and Its Application in China. The concept of indigenous peoples in Asia : a resource book. C. Erni. Copenhagen ; Chiang Mai, IWGIA and Indigenous Peoples Pact Foundation: 241-256.

Cunningham, M. (2009). Health. State of the world's indigenous peoples. U. N. D. o. E. a. S. Affairs. New York, United Nations: 155-187.

Dang, H.-A. (2012). Viet Nam: A Widening Poverty Gap for Ethnic Minorities. Indigenous peoples, poverty, and development. G. Hall and H. A. Patrinos. New York, Cambridge University Press.

Das, M. B. and G. Hall (2012). India: The Scheduled Tribes. Indigenous peoples, poverty, and development. G. Hall and H. A. Patrinos. New York, Cambridge University Press.

Erni, C. (2008). The concept of indigenous peoples in Asia : a resource book. Copenhagen ; Chiang Mai, IWGIA and Indigenous Peoples Pact Foundation.

Gracey, M. and M. King (2009). "Indigenous health part 1: determinants and disease patterns". The Lancet 374(65-75).

Hall, G. and H. A. Patrinos (2012). Indigenous peoples, poverty, and development. New York, Cambridge University Press.

Hathaway, M. (2010). "The emergence of Indigeneity: Public intellectuals and an indigenous space in Southwest China". Cultural Anthropology 25(2): 301-333.

International Work Group for Indigenous Affairs (IWGIA) (2008). The Indigenous World 2008. Edison, NJ, Transaction Publishers.

King, M., A. Smith, et al. (2009). "Indigenous Health Part 2: The Underlying Causes of the Health Gap". The Lancet 374: 76-85.

Kingsbury, B. (1998). ""Indigenous Peoples" in International Law: A Constructivist Approach to the Asian Controversy". The American Journal of International Law 92(3): 414-457.

Li, J. (2008). "Trends in infant/child mortality and life expectancy in indigenous population in Yunnan Province, China". Australian and New Zealand Journal of Public Health 32(3): 216-223.

Li, Y., G. Guo, et al. (1999). "Prevalance and coorelates of malnutrition among children in rurual minority area of China". Pediatrics International 41(549-556).

Macdonald, K. (2012). Indigenous Peoples and Development Goals: A Global Snapshot. Indigenous peoples, poverty, and development. G. Hall and H. A. Patrinos. New York, Cambridge University Press.

MacIntosh, C. (2013). "The Role of Law in Ameliorating Global Inequalities in Indiegnous Health". Journal of Law, Medicine and Ethics Spring: 74-88.

Ministry of Health and Family Welfare, G. o. t. P. s. R. o. B. (2004). Social Assessment and Tribal Health Nutrition and Population Plan for the HNP Sector Program (2005 to 2010).

Ministry of Tribal Affairs, G. o. I. (2010). Statistical Profile of Scheduled Tribes in India 2010.

Minsitry of Health and Family Welfare, G. o. t. P. s. R. o. B. (2011). Tribal/Ethnic Health Population and Nutrition Plan for the Health, Population and Nutrition Sector Development Program (HPNSDP) 2011 to 2016.

Mohindra, K. and R. Labonté (2010). "A systematic review of population health interventions and Scheduled Tribes in India". BMC Public Health 10(438): 1-10.

Nettleton, C., D. A. Napolitano, et al. (2007). An overview of current knowledge of the social determinants of indigenous health (Commission on Social Determinants of Health, Working Paper). Geneva, World Health Organization.

Ouyang, Y. and P. Pinstrup-Andersen (2012). "Health Inequality between ethnic Minority and Han Populations in China". World Development 40(7): 1452-1468.

Rakić, J. G. (2008). Indigenous Health, Asian. Encyclopedia of Public Health. W. Kirch, Springer: 727-728.

Walker, B., Ed. (2013). State of the World's Minorities and Indigenous Peoples 2013. London, Minority Rights Group International.

WHO (1986). The Ottawa Charter for Health Promotion.
http://www.who.int/healthpromotion/conferences/previous/ottawa/en/
(Accessed December 20, 2013).

CHAPTER THREE

ACCESS TO HEALTH SERVICES BY INDIGENOUS PEOPLES IN THE ARCTIC REGION

KETIL LENERT HANSEN, PHD

CHAPTER THREE

ACCESS TO HEALTH SERVICES BY INDIGENOUS PEOPLES IN THE ARCTIC REGION

KETIL LENERT HANSEN, PHD[105]

Introduction

The focus in this chapter is on access and utilization of quality health care services for the indigenous peoples from the northern regions of Fennoscandia and the Inuit (the Kalaallit) in Greenland.

Indigenous peoples in many parts of the world are described as among the most vulnerable minority groups, with the poorest health status; they receive a poorer quality of care than their majority peers. Indigenous peoples struggle to access health services in relation to their needs and face health service disparities when compared to the majority population.[106] These disparities are superimposed on the higher cost and logistics of communications, transportation and rapidly changing extreme weather related to delivering timely health care to people living in northern, often remote communities.

"One of the major constraints to delivering good quality health care in the North has been the allocation of financial and human resources. Another of particular significance is a problem related to communication and transportation infrastructure that links regional and peripheral facilities with central or national referral centres. In addition, the harsh climatic conditions and the special needs of the indigenous populations pose significant challenges".

In several circumpolar northern countries, health professional shortages and service delivery challenges exist. Many patients live in rural areas, often remote and isolated, thus far away from the health care service providers. Consequently people living in these locations face long journeys and high costs to obtain health care.[108] Childbirth in Greenland is an example of the challenge of obtaining health care support in the North. Women are required to leave their local communities during pregnancy, as a consequence of new policies and guidelines in Greenland.[109]

---

[105] Ketil Lenert Hansen, who has a Ph.D. in public health, is a researcher at the Arctic University of Norway.

[106] MRG, 2013, p. 188.

[107] Ikaheimo, 2010, p. 414.

[108] Vuori, Kylanen and Tritter, 2010, p. 513.

[109] R. A. Montgomery-Andersen, Willen and Borup, 2010, pp. 301-303.

Several health and living condition indicators demonstrate that indigenous peoples living in the far northern countries face increased risks for health problems compared to mainstream national population statistics. Indigenous peoples in the north tend to have higher rates of chronic conditions and disease including but not limited to hypertension, obesity and type 2 diabetes.[110]

Discrimination is associated with poorer physical and mental health and health services inequity. It is important to understand the historical context of indigenous peoples' rapid social and cultural change and how current health conditions are thought to emanate from colonization affecting the health status of indigenous peoples in the past and present.[111] Too often those issues are not taken into account when designing health interventions.

This chapter will focus on the health care challenges for indigenous peoples living in the Arctic and how indigenous peoples face these challenges. The particular focus is on the Sami living in Norway, Sweden, Finland and Russia and the Inuit in Greenland.

Indigenous and total populations in Norway, Sweden, Finland, Russia and Greenland

In Northern Norway (Nordland, Troms and Finmark) the total population is 470,000[112] (2011). In Northern Sweden (Norrbotten, Västerbotten) the total population is 520,000.[113] In Finland (Oulu, Lappi) the total population is 650,000, and in the Komi Republic (Russian Federation) the total population is 1,050,000. In Greenland the total population is 56,000, including 50,000 born in Greenland, (2013).[114] In sum, the total population estimation for the four countries is 2,750,000.

The Sami include several subgroups stratified according to geographical location and dialect. The size of the Sami population is approximately 70,000-100,000, but estimates vary in accordance with criteria used such as genetic heritage,[115] mother tongue and the personal sense of ethnicity.[116] The largest proportion of Sami is believed to reside in Norway (60,000), followed by Sweden (36,000) and Finland (10,000), with the lowest proportion residing on the Russian Kola Peninsula (2,000).[117] Accurate population estimates are difficult to assess because there are no current standards for routinely measuring demographic numbers to indicate the scope and magnitude of the Sami population, due to a lack of information on race and ethnicity in indicators contained within public registers. Sami population estimates may be far less than true population counts. For example, based on numbers from several register data, there are about 40,000-50,000 Sami in Sweden alone.[118]

The Sami are the indigenous peoples living in the Nordic countries and they reside in the northern regions of Fennoscandia in what today comprises the northern areas of Norway, Sweden, Finland

[110] P. M. D. Bjerregaard and Young, 2008, pp. 3-17.

[111] Marrone, 2007, p. 189.

[112] K. Young, 2008, p. 27.

[113] K. Young, 2008.

[114] T. K. Young, Rawat, and Dallmann, 2012, p. 27.

[115] Slaastad, 2012, pp. 3-78.

[116] Ketil Lenert Hansen, 2011, pp. 19-22.

[117] Slaastad, 2012, pp. 3-78.

[118] Sven Hassler, Sjölander and Ericsson, 2004, pp. 384-388.

and Russia's Kola Peninsula, as depicted on Map 1.[119] They belong to the Finno-Ugric language group. The Sami language consists of several dialects and distinct written languages.

The Kildin (Kola) Sami population was 1,991 persons in the 2002 Russian Census, 89 per cent of whom resided in Murmansk Oblast. According to the 2002 Census, about 38 per cent of Sami live in towns and cities, a higher proportion than the average 28 per cent for indigenous peoples of northern Russia. The number of Sami over the age of 60 years has reduced sharply as a result of high mortality rate particularly among Sami males. A low birth rate and a high death rate among the Kola Sami may lead to a sharp population decline in the near future.[120]

Map 1: Greenland and Sápmi. Home of the Sami, stretches over four countries: Norway, Sweden, Finland and Russia's Kola Peninsula. Sami flags are superimposed over the regions where Sami live.

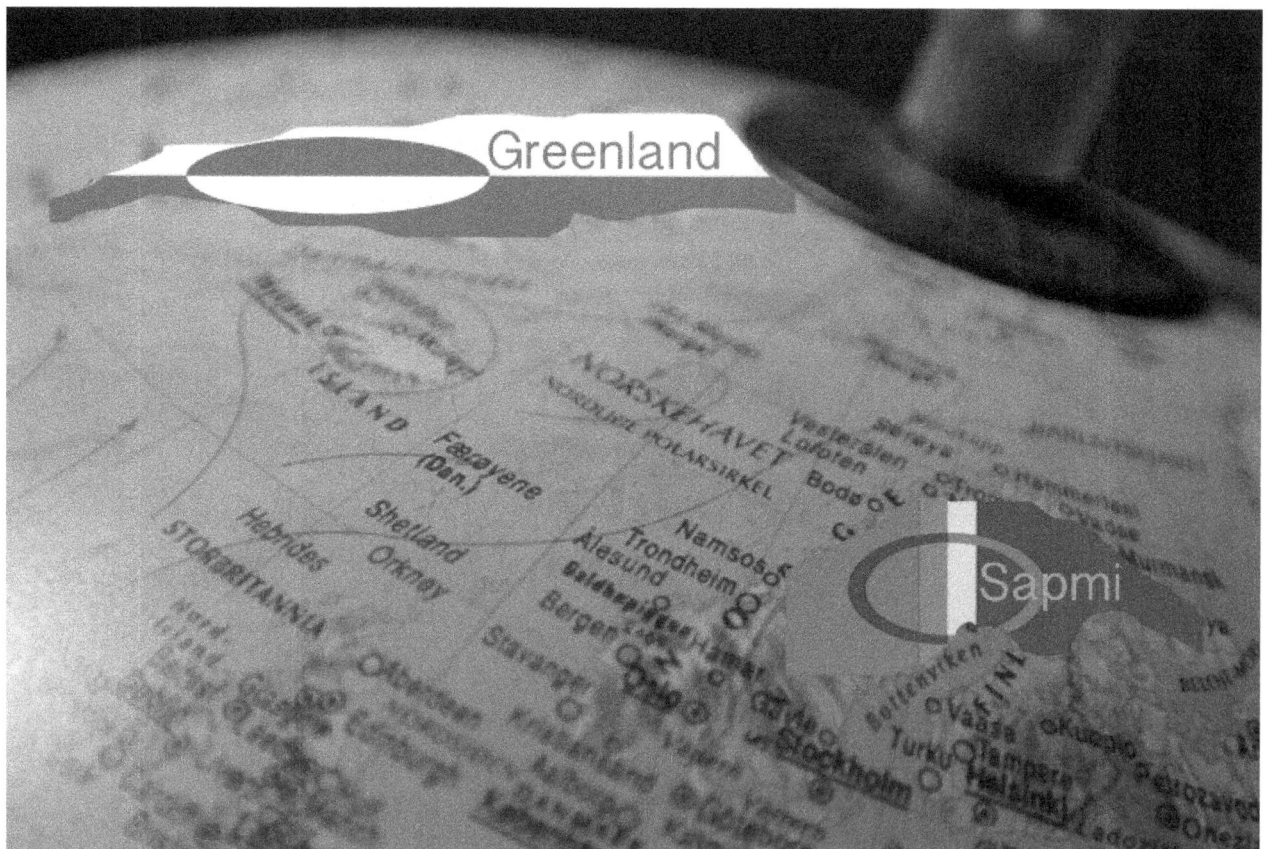

Illustration: Ketil Lenert Hansen.

---

[119] Kulonen, Pulkkinen and Seurujärvi-Kari, 2005.

[120] Kozlov in P. M. D. Bjerregaard and Young, 2008, pp. 163-165.

The Beginnings of political transformation for Sami peoples

During the last three decades, Sami society has undergone an ethnic and cultural revival.[121] Their political situation has also improved. In Norway, Sweden and Finland the Sami have been recognized as the original inhabitants of northern Scandinavia.[122] However, it is only the Norwegian Government that has ratified the ILO-Convention No. 169 in recognition of the Sami as indigenous peoples. The National Sami Parliament has been established in each of the three countries.[123] However, these parliaments often do not have the strength, national legislative authority and social structures of an extensive bureaucracy to adequately articulate the international rights and needs of the Sami.[124]

Sami are engaged in a variety of livelihoods, including farming, fishing, trapping and sheep and reindeer breeding and herding. Although considered as "traditional" and a cultural marker of the Sami, reindeer herding was of relatively recent vintage, developed during the sixteenth century. In both Norway and Sweden, but not in Finland; semi-nomadic reindeer herding is, by law, an occupation strictly reserved for the Sami. Data from 2009 found that only a minority (3,010 individuals) of the Sami in Norway; were actively engaged in reindeer herding with slightly more men than women.[125] Many Sami live in the large urban cities, especially: Tromsø, Umeå, Rovaniemi, Stockholm and Oslo, and are involved in all the modern professions, occupations, and trades.[126]

Today the challenges facing the Sami peoples consists of conserving traditional knowledge, values and culture traits, while adapting to the local communities and indeed a world that continues to change. Many Sami people find themselves in a transitional state where it is important to adapt to a changing new world without losing sight of the values of the Sami traditional world view.[127]

In Greenland, about 90 per cent of the population is Inuit and the remainder are mainly Danish.[128] The 17 small towns and 60 villages in the country are isolated from one another and can be reached only by boat or plane. The majority of the approximately 56,000 inhabitants live on the south and central west coast. The largest town is the capital, called Nuuk, which has 15,000 inhabitants. Around 20 per cent of the population lives in villages with between 300 and 500 inhabitants.

The Inuit culture is distinct, although influenced by relations with Danish, European and other cultures and societies around the globe. Language and diet are central markers of Greenlandic culture. A majority of the population speaks Kalaallisut (West Greenlandic), which has led to its status as the official "Greenlandic" language. Hunting and fishing have always been an important aspect of the Greenland Inuit culture, and most Greenlanders still hunt at least part-time to supplement their diet. Today, local food makes up approximately 20 per cent of the diets; the spectrum of food items is much narrower, usually consisting of meat and blubber of marine mammals (seals in particular), birds, fish, caribou and musk.[129] Greenland's economy since World War Two

[121] P. Pedersen, Høgmo and Solbakk, 2012.

[122] Kulonen, et al., 2005.

[123] Sjolander, 2011, pp. 1-2.

[124] Sjolander, 2011, p. 2.

[125] Slaastad, 2012.

[126] P. Pedersen, et al., 2012.

[127] P. M. D. Bjerregaard and Young, 2008, p. 15.

[128] Niclasen and Mulvad, 2010.

[129] P. M. D. Bjerregaard and Young, 2008, p. 30.

has increasingly become dependent upon commercial fishing, which represents 90 per cent of the region's export income. The economy is however dependent upon subsidies from Denmark which amounts to approximately 50 per cent of public spending in Greenland.[130]

The influence of colonialism

The Sami people in Sápmi and the Inuit in Greenland have a common history with colonization. Greenlandic social anthropologist Aviâja Egede Lynge has stated: "We have always been taught that we were one of the best colonies in the world. No slavery, no killing … so why, then should we have had a reason to de-colonize? And why should we have a reason to ask questions about 250 years of colonial presence?"[131] Today, Greenland has achieved greater self-determination with the home rule, however, Greenlanders still feel ruled by Denmark. Despite the fact that the members of the home rule government are native Greenlanders, most leading positions are still in the hands of the Danish population who have strong influences on decision-making processes.

In Norway, the process of assimilation, frequently referred to as "Norwegianization", lasted from 1850 to approximately 1980. According to the Land Act of 1902, property could be transferred only to Norwegian citizens (i.e., persons able to speak, read and write Norwegian), and proficiency in the Norwegian language continued to be a criterion for buying or leasing state land until the 1940s. For almost a century, the Sami language was prohibited in Norwegian schools, from 1860 to 1959. Residential schools were important arenas for the assimilation of Sami children into the dominant cultures assisted by individual experiences of stigmatization and discrimination.[132]

Although the overt policies of assimilation may be a thing of the past in terms of Nordic society and politics, the negative consequences have been projected into the present and, indeed, will inform relations in the future. It takes time to fundamentally change general frameworks in politics, legislation and ordinances, as well as myths and attitudes, to appropriately redress and reclaim Sami culture, language, traditions and social needs; including equitable access to health care, education and employment and other determinants of health. Many people remain influenced by past assimilation policies despite the official legislation and policies having been reversed. Simply put, "being different" is often the source of discrimination and harassment, and, as a minority population, the Samis and Inuit are particularly vulnerable. Studies conducted abroad reveal discrimination against indigenous peoples tends to be closely associated with health issues. Discrimination has been found to be associated with negative mental and physical health outcomes, negative health behaviours and increased mortality.[133] Centuries of colonial contact have irrevocably damaged the cultural traditions and practices of indigenous Sami and Inuit populations, and have also had a lasting, negative impact on generations of Sami and Inuit youth.

---

[130] Niclasen and Mulvad, 2010, p. 438.

[131] Lynge, 2006. http://www.rethinking-nordic-colonialism.org/files/pdf/ACT2/ESSAYS/Lynge.pdf.

[132] Minde, 2005, p. 6.

[133] Williams and Mohammed, 2009, pp. 20-47.

The right to health care for indigenous peoples

Everyone has the right to access health facilities, goods and services without discrimination.[134] This means non-discrimination both in access to health care and in enjoyment of the underlying determinates of health. One key contextual barrier for indigenous peoples to access health care is the continuing impact of colonization. Even though the health status of indigenous peoples has improved in the last decades, significant health disparities continue to exist, for example, increasing rates of diabetes, cardiovascular diseases and cancers among the Inuit in Greenland.[135]

In countries where indigenous peoples were significantly impacted by colonization, it is important to understand the cultural and biological consequences of colonization and how these have affected the health status of indigenous peoples historically and currently.[136] One possible way to approach this issue is to investigate present differences in health care access and utilization between the indigenous peoples and the majority populations. This may assist in the effort to understand how ethnic, cultural and racial factors influence access and utilization. Specifically, this could be a way to study barriers to health care such as communication, cultural sensitivity, socioeconomic status, trust in the health care system and the level of satisfaction by the indigenous peoples who use the services.

Health status of Sami peoples

Past research on Sami peoples' health has revealed a uniquely positive situation compared to other indigenous peoples of the circumpolar regions of Greenland and Arctic Russia.[137] Life expectancy and mortality rates of the Norwegian and Swedish Sami and their non-Sami neighbours were quite similar.[138] Many of the health problems that indigenous peoples in the circumpolar region and elsewhere face are not as prevalent among the Sami, such as dramatic elevated risk for diabetes, cardiovascular disease, lung cancer and various infectious diseases. There are generally small differences in risk for the major diseases and causes of death.[139] At the same time, the knowledge of the health conditions of the Sami is not available, particularly regarding the condition of Russian Sami. However, the situation has improved over the last few years. An increasing number of articles on Sami health have been published in the Scandinavian countries, particularly in Norway and Sweden where a number of specific health problems have been identified. For example, among the Swedish reindeer-herding men a significantly higher risk of fatal accidents, work-related stress and suicide have been identified.[140] The increased risk of suicide among Sami men is also found in Norway and Finland.[141] The health problems of the Sami peoples are thought to be associated with discrimination and marginalization and lack of knowledge of the Sami identity and culture.[142] Several studies consider discrimination as an

---

[134] ICESCR and International Convention on the Elimination of all forms of Racial Discrimination, ICERD, Article 5.e. iv.

[135] P. M. D. Bjerregaard and Young, 2008, pp. 31-34.

[136] Marrone, 2007, p. 189.

[137] Ketil Lenert Hansen, 2011, p. 54.

[138] Brustad, Pettersen, Melhus and Lund, 2009; S. Hassler, Johansson, Sjolander, Gronberg and Damber, 2005.

[139] Hassler in P. M. D. Bjerregaard and Young, 2008, pp. 158-161.

[140] S. Hassler, et al., 2005; Kaiser, Sjolander, Liljegren, Jacobsson and Renberg, 2010.

[141] Silviken, Haldorsen and Kvernmo, 2006; Soininen and Pukkola, 2008.

[142] Sjolander, 2011, p. 9.

important risk factor for poor health. The Sami people in Scandinavia, as the Inuit in Greenland, have a long history of suffering discrimination and racism. A large proportion of Norwegian Sami peoples experience discrimination based on their background.[143] There are also similar findings among the Sami youth in the Nordic countries.[144] Furthermore, the results demonstrate that discrimination is associated with inferior self-perceived health and psychological distress,[145] which is supported by several other studies across multiple population groups in a wide range of cultural and national contexts,[146] including indigenous communities in the circumpolar north.[147] These findings suggest that perceived discrimination is an important emerging risk factor leading to negative health outcomes.

Among the most vulnerable groups in Russia are the indigenous peoples. There is no unified system of health monitoring of indigenous peoples, although some general trends show significantly lower than average health outcomes compared the majority Russian population. According to the 2002 Census the average life expectancy of Russian indigenous peoples was 15 years below the Russian average.[148] Among the Sami in Russia, smoking and alcohol use are very common. In a survey of 15-to 18-year-old Sami in Lovozero in the Kola Peninsula, 59 per cent identified as regular or episodic smokers. Girls tended to smoke more heavily than boys. Alcohol consumption in Murmansk Oblast was among the worst in Russia. A survey found that half of Sami teens, ages 15 to 18 years old, reported having used alcohol.[149] Studies demonstrate that alcohol abuse in the Russian north is linked to a range of social and economic factors.[150] Also the isolation of the parents from their children, who are away at boarding schools, and the stressful, effect of "modernization" are among the factors that often lead to alcohol dependency. The steady growth of suicides and violent behaviour among the indigenous peoples in the Russian north is another alarming trend. Suicide rates are up to four times the Russian average. Also a significantly higher level of emotional distress and psychological tension are found in indigenous children, and the prevalence of these conditions is increasing.[151]

Health status in the Inuit population in Greenland

Life expectancy in Greenland at the beginning of the twenty-first century was at the level of countries like India, Mongolia and Russia. Suicide and tobacco-related diseases are the main reasons for the low life expectancy in Greenland.[152] Infant mortality was around 10 per 1,000 in 2000-2004, compared to 4.2 per 1,000 in Norway in 2004.

The causes of mortality and morbidity in Greenland are all higher than Denmark and other Nordic countries. This includes a high infant mortality rate, high death rate due to unnatural causes, like

---

[143] Ketil Lenert Hansen, 2011; K. L. Hansen, Melhus, Hogmo and Lund, 2008.

[144] Omma, 2013; Turi, 2011.

[145] K. L. Hansen, Melhus and Lund, 2010; K. L. Hansen and Sorlie, 2012.

[146] Williams and Mohammed, 2009.

[147] P. M. D. Bjerregaard and Young, 2008.

[148] MRG, 2013, p. 186.

[149] Kozlov in P. M. D. Bjerregaard and Young, 2008, p. 162.

[150] P. M. D. Bjerregaard and Young, 2008, pp. 95-99.

[151] MRG), 2013, pp. 188-189.

[152] Bjerregaard and Stensgaard 2008 Greenland in P. M. D. Bjerregaard and Young, 2008, pp. 31-34.

suicides and accidents, which result in the life expectancy to be lower. Greenland has an increasing rate of diabetes, infectious disease and cardiovascular diseases and cancer, due to smoking and other lifestyle factors. Other health challenges are child abuse, abortion, violence, sexually transmitted diseases, substance abuse, low oral health, stressors of mental health and the effects of contamination of the traditional diet.[153]

> "Greenland experienced a major health transition during the twentieth century and especially during the latter half of the century. In 1950, mortality was high and the main causes of death were tuberculosis and acute infectious diseases, During the 1950s, the importance of these diseases as causes of death diminished sharply and total mortality decreased. However, as mortality from infections, heart diseases and accidents continued to decrease, new causes of death gained importance, particularly cancer and suicide".

Health care organization, expenditures and financing—a comparison between Norway, Sweden, Finland, Greenland and Russia

Norway, Sweden, Greenland and Finland generally have very similar health care systems. The Nordic model is characterized by significant decentralization, down to the municipality level, with a high degree of both political and fiscal autonomy, and largely free health care has been in place for decades.

Norway, Sweden, Greenland and Finland are similar in their sources of health care financing, which entails taxation from different levels of government, grants from the central government, health insurance funded by employer and employee contributions, and user charges for specific services. A private sector exists, accounting for about 15 per cent in Norway and Sweden and 25 per cent in Finland.[154]

In Norway, the delivery of primary health care and public health services is the responsibility of municipalities, whereas "specialized health services" (including general and psychiatric hospitals, ambulances, substance abuse treatment and patient transportation) are provide by regional health authorities. The Swedish system differs slightly from this model in that municipalities are responsible for long-term care and home care only, whereas public health, hospitals and primary care are the responsibility of 18 county councils.

Northern-Finnish patients have limited access to health care services in circumpolar areas across the Nordic countries for two reasons. First, health professionals in Norway and Sweden do not speak Finnish, which presents a language barrier. Second, the Social Insurance Institution of Finland does not cover the expenditures of travel or the costs of medicine. In addition, it seems that in circumpolar areas, the density of Finnish service providers is greater than Swedish ones, causing many Swedish citizens to transfer to Finnish health care providers every year.[155] However,

---

[153] P. M. D. Bjerregaard and Young, 2008, p. 33.

[154] T. K. Young, et al., 2012, pp. 158-161.

[155] Vuori, et al., 2010, pp. 512-514.

studies have found that long distances to medical care or Sami ethnicity have no influence on the cancer patient survival in Northern Finland.[156]

The Greenland government has a separate and independent health care system from that of Denmark, although much of the bureaucracy is staffed by Danish people. The Ministry of Health (Departementet for Sundhed/Peqqissutsimut Naalakkersuisoqarfik) has overall responsibility for all health services, from the operation of the tertiary care Queen Ingrid Hospital in Nuuk to health centres and rural hospitals in towns and villages. Greenland is organized into 16 health districts. Danish is the dominant language spoken because a large proportion of the medical staff is recruited from Denmark.

Since the 1990s, health reforms in Russia have focused on financing and decentralization. The regions are key players in health care provision and the impact of reform varies widely across the country. The remoteness and small size of indigenous settlements affects access to, and the expense of medical care. All indigenous peoples of Russia are entitled to free medical care coverage, which includes a compulsory annual check-up at state and municipal health care facilities. Yet federal and regional health care programs do not always provide medical brigades to visit remote areas. Medical personnel often lack modern, mobile equipment that allows them to go out and examine indigenous peoples in remote settlements, such as reindeer herding camps. Nomadic reindeer herding is the traditional livelihood of many indigenous peoples in the Russian north. Working with indigenous peoples out in the tundra is complicated due to the practical difficulties of carrying out examinations in the constantly moving reindeer herding camps, as well as difficulties with controlling the prescribed treatment. Poorly equipped health care facilities and lack of investment means that it is extremely difficult to retain medical staff and attract specialists to come and work in rural hospitals.[157]

A major challenge in international comparison of health care systems is that different countries have different health care systems with different financial management practices. However, a basic measure in the international comparison of health care systems is health care expenditures. It provides a glimpse of the health care resources available to, and used by the various health care agencies. Conversely, there is international agreement on the inclusion criteria and classification of types of expenditures in the form of the System of Health Accounts (SHA) developed by the organization for Economic Cooperation and Development (OECD).[158,159] The Nordic countries, all have similar levels of per capita health expenditures, with health care accounting for 8-10 per cent of GDP.[160] In Russia, health care expenditure accounts for 5 per cent of GDP, while in the Komi Republic, the per capita expenditures are 15 per cent higher than the national average. In northern Norway, the per capita expenditures are 25-30 per cent higher than the national average, whereas in northern Sweden and Finland the difference is less than 10 per cent. Greenland reports a lower level of per capita health expenditure than Denmark, the only instance where expenditures in the north are lower than in the south.

---

[156] Soininen and Pukkola, 2008, p. 33.

[157] MRG), 2013, pp. 186-188.

[158] Further details are available from the SHA manual. Available from: http://www.oecd.org/health/healthdata.

[159] T. Kue Young (2008) Circumpolar Health Indicators: Sources, Data and Maps. Supplements 3. International Journal of Circumpolar Health. pp. 115-126.

[160] OECD health Data from 2 periodes; 2000-2004 and 2005-2007 and Russian data from WHO.

Hospital and primary care

Hospital services are core to any health care system. A variety of hospitals are located in the circumpolar regions, from highly specialized ones such as the university hospitals in Tromsø, Umeå and Oulu, to small ones in the remote towns of Greenland. The rate of hospital beds per 100,000 is the most commonly available indicator, which is more or less comparable across different jurisdiction.[161] In northern Norway there were 337 hospital beds per 100,000. The same numbers for Northern Sweden were 308, Finland 226, Greenland 185 (Nuuk), and Komi Republic 977.40 The Russian region have the highest bed availability, with around 1,000 hospital beds per 100,000.[162]

Use of health care in the main Sami areas of Norway

In 2011 a study investigating the current health expenditures in somatic hospital and specialist service in the Sami municipalities found that "the overall public hospital expenditure rate in Sami municipalities is above the national average and equivalent to corresponding municipalities in the same geographical area. However, there was a considerable variation among the Sami municipalities. The age groups 35-49 and 50-64 in all Sami municipalities have higher expenditure rates than the national average regarding outpatient contacts and hospitalizations, while the expenditure rate on the elderly (80 years or older) is below the national average in most Sami municipalities".[163] However, this study did not indicate how the Sami patients experience the quality of care in the patient-physician relationship.

Health care delivery for the Sami peoples

The Norwegian government was the very first State to ratify the United Nations International Labour Organization (ILO) Convention No. 169 on the rights of indigenous peoples in 1990 (Sweden and Finland have not ratified this Convention), which further strengthened the rights of the Norwegian Sami. Today the Sami have their own jurisdiction area where Sami and Norwegian languages are granted equal status as official languages. The Sami peoples of Norway have the legal right to all public services in their own language, including health services.

Sweden recognized the Sami as indigenous peoples in 1977.[164] As such, the Sami enjoy special protection and are granted innate rights pertaining to cultural and linguistic rights, protected under Swedish law, as well as through international conventions and declarations. However, has thus far refrained from ratifying ILO Convention No. 169 on the rights of indigenous peoples.[165]

Better health care service for Sami people has been raised on the political and health professional agenda for many years and from numerous sides. Health care, with differences in health gradients between the northernmost county of Norway (Finnmark), where many Sami live, and the counties farther south in Norway, government actions has been implemented since the 1960s to

[161] T. K. Young, et al., 2012, pp. 161-163.

[162] K. Young, 2008, p. 123.

[163] M. Gaski, Melhus, Deraas and Forde, 2011, pp. 8-9.

[164] Swedish Government, 1999, p. 16.

[165] Swedish Government, 1999.

strengthen the Sami peoples.[166] Since 1980, problems of underutilization of health services and communication between health workers and Sami patients were brought into focus, and the result was that the first outpatient psychiatric clinic was funded in the Sami core area of Karasjok with Sami-speaking therapists. Several years later, an outpatient clinic with Sami clinicians provided services in internal medicine, rheumatology, and other specialties.

In 2002, the Sami Centre for Mental Health (SANKS) was established. It is a multi-professional training centre for Sami mental health workers, and many of the therapists are Sami speaking. SANKS offers psychiatric treatment and assessment to patients in addition to counselling, teaching and research.[167] Treatment modalities include various outpatient treatments as well as treatment at psychiatric wards for adult, youth and families. Due to long distance between Sami municipalities, small branches have been established in some other regions, where the Sami people reside and telecommunications is frequently used.[168]

"Norway is the only country that has a specific Sami focus on public health for the Sami population, acknowledging the need for culturally and linguistically adapted health services. Although health and social services for the Sami had been established in the 1980s, the first national plan for health and social services for the Sami population was made in 1995 (NOU 1995: 6 Plan for helse- og sosialtjenester til den samiske befolkning i Norge). Where the Swedish and Finnish health care system and public health policies are concerned, the Sami seem to be nothing less than fully assimilated. A main reason that Norway is a leading country can be explain by the considerable number of Sami health and social services workers compared with the other Nordic countries who advocated for an ethnic-specific health service."

However, many Sami peoples claim that the Norwegian health services do not ensure the needs of Sami patients.[170] Also, it is likely that the issue of health services is similar and even worse in the other Nordic countries. While some studies have been conducted,[171] the existence of health services research particularly investigating health care utilization among Sami in Norway, Sweden, Finland and Russia need more attention.[172]

Patient satisfaction

Health care systems are designed to serve consumers (users, clients, patients). Part of the assessment of the quality of services provided is the level of satisfaction by those who have used the services. There are some studies of Sami patients and their providers. In a study by Turi et al. (2009)[173] there is an attempt to measure the frequency in the use of health services. In the study

---

[166] Margrete Gaski, 2011.

[167] www.sanks.no.

[168] Baarnhielm, Javo and Mosko, 2013, pp. 40-55.

[169] Hassler, Kvernmo and Kozlov in P. M. D. Bjerregaard and Young, 2008, pp. 166-167.

[170] Norge Sosial- og helsedepartementet, 1999.

[171] Margrete Gaski, 2011; Lund et al., 2007; Turi, 2011.

[172] P.M.D. Bjerregaard and Young, 2008, pp. 166-167.

[173] Turi, 2011, pp. 1-10.

of Sami adolescents (15-16 years old) and their non-indigenous peers it was found that Sami and non-Sami youth use health services with equal frequency. In another study of mental health care,[174] Sami patients showed less satisfaction with all investigated treatment parameters than their Norwegian peers, including contact with staff and treatment alliance. In another study by Nystad et al. (2008),[175] Sami-speaking patients expressed that they are less satisfied with the municipality general practitioner service than the Norwegian speakers and that misunderstandings between physician and patient due to language barriers were more frequent.

Sami children and adolescents

In the Nordic countries today, Sami youth come of age in a society in which their personal values, culture and language have a completely different status compared to the conditions under which their parents were raised. Young people who are proficient in the Sami language and culture enjoy a more liberated and less politicized definition of "Saminess" than did the preceding generation. Many adolescent Sami express a complex identity including Norwegian, Swedish or Finnish and Sami culture and language; some identify themselves with another ethnicity as well. Many of the younger Sami are from families where their parents' and grandparents' generations were the targets of force assimilation policies. This experience has encouraged discussion between the Sami generations, particular when individuals of similar backgrounds choose different solutions in order to form their identity. A recent report published by the Nordic Ombudsmen for Children[176] indicated that Sami children are still bullied due to their ethnicity. However, most of them are proud of their Sami identity. At the same time, it is often difficult for some Sami children and adolescents to be honest about their Sami background. There is a need to place more focus on discrimination, health and well-being of Sami children and adolescents, to understand how colonization and Sami identity interact to influence health care access and utilization by Sami peoples.

Elderly Sami health and well-being

Today many elderly Sami, especially outside the defined Sami core areas, have lived their lives in a world of tension trying to strike a balance between assimilation, revitalization, and ambiguity, when it comes to their Sami identity and culture. Considering the history of assimilation, stigmatization, and discrimination, it seems reasonable to assume that a Sami heritage contested throughout a lifespan might have a significance impact on health and well-being in old age.[177] Postcolonial theory provides a framework for understanding how indigenous peoples' health is closely related to historical, social, political, and economic factors and forces. There seems to be a wide consensus regarding the significance of cultural competence in interactions between health care providers and indigenous patients. Theories on cultural competence ask for "culturally based care knowledge, acts, and decisions used in sensitive and knowledgeable ways to appropriately and meaningfully fit the cultural values, beliefs, and lifeways of clients".[178] Efforts are made to find cultural-specific features of the Sami experience of well-being to develop appropriate and

---

[174] Sorlie and Nergard, 2005, pp. 304-310.

[175] Nystad, Melhus and Lund, 2008.

[176] In Norwegian, *Barneombudene i Norden*, 2008.

[177] Blix, Hamran and Normann, 2013, pp. 264-265.

[178] Leininger and McFarland, 2006, p. 15.

culturally safe social and health care services.[179] Traditional Sami cultural aspects, such as Sami language, traditional Sami foods, spirituality and way of life, are important aspects that are being emphasized in the care of elderly Sami, especially those suffering from dementia.

There has been very little attention paid to the needs of elderly Sami peoples in the health care system and this area requires strengthening in the future, especially when it comes to cultural-specific features in health care services. The development of cultural competent standards of care for health providers is a necessary pre-condition to achieve this goal.

Use of traditional medicine

Integrating traditional healing within health services for indigenous peoples has currently taken on a much stronger focus. Traditional healing is a part of traditional knowledge among indigenous peoples. Knowledge traditions and world views constitute the context for the health care system of a society. In recent studies in the Arctic region it was found that the therapist showed little awareness of their client's use of traditional healers. While over a third of the Sami clients had used traditional healers in relation to their current health problems, less than half reported that this was given any consideration during the hospital stays.[180]

Other studies found that some Sami users were giving greater importance to religion and spirituality and were less satisfied with the public psychiatric services than those Sami patients who had not used traditional or complementary treatments. Studies suggest that different aspects of traditional healing within the health services to the Sami community should be given greater consideration.[181]

It is likely that the issues regarding the use of traditional medicine is similar and relevant to circumstances among the indigenous peoples in the other Nordic countries and among the Inuit in Greenland, but this is an area that needs to be a higher priority area for health services research.

Health status and health care delivery in Greenland

Greenland is a Danish colony, and in the last few decades, the home rule government has been given extensive powers to govern. The future goal is to attain full independence. The conditions for health care in Greenland differ in a number of ways from the Sami in the Nordic countries, because of geographic and climatic conditions. The health care system is obligated to deliver equal care to all citizens regardless of their place of residence. This requires a large number of small, cost-effective health centres capable of providing acute care because the expenses for transport of patients and staff are very high.[182] Due to their small size and isolation, towns and villages in Greenland often need to be self-sufficient and are very vulnerable to external factors.[183] No private providers of health care services exist in Greenland, but private dental care, physiotherapy, psychotherapy and treatment for alcohol and drug abuse are available in Nuuk.

---

[179] Tervo, Muller-Wille and Nikkonen, 2003, p. 120.

[180] Sorlie and Nergard, 2005.

[181] Sexton and Sorlie, 2008, pp. 135-146.

[182] Bjerregaard and Stensgaard 2008 Greenland in P. M. D. Bjerregaard and Young, 2008, pp. 34-37.

[183] Niclasen and Mulvad, 2010, p. 438.

In the last 50 years, Greenland as well as other indigenous societies in the circumpolar regions has undergone rapid social, environmental and economic changes, which have influenced all aspects of their life, impacting on living conditions and health care. In the past, perinatal complications, acute and chronic infectious diseases and injuries dominated as the leading causes of morbidity.[184] Recently, chronic and lifestyle diseases and disabilities dominate morbidity concerns despite the fact that the "old" diseases have not decreased to the same low levels found in Western countries. Furthermore, the burden of poor health related to social conditions does not appear to be decreasing.[185]

Specific health care access study shows that 83 per cent of the population in Greenland had been in contact with a primary health care centre within the last year (2011). Females were more frequent users than males. Personal contact was the most frequent type of consultation (75.8 per cent), followed by telephone (14.8 per cent) and e-mail (9.8 per cent) consultations. Musculoskeletal symptoms accounted for the most frequent basis for diagnoses.[186]

Self-rated health (SRH) is a relevant variable in primary health care and in general public health assessments and monitoring. In a recent study with Inuit and Sami youth from Norway, poor SRH was reported to be three times higher among Inuit than Sami. A cause of great concern is that Inuit female youth were reported with the poorest SRH. Suicidal thoughts and risk were associated with poor SRH.[187] Another study shows that aggregate acculturation[188] is a strong risk factor for substandard SRH among the Inuit of Greenland.[189]

Mental problems are thus increased in parallel with the societal change and development. The suicide rate in Greenland, especially among men, is among the highest in the world. The highest incidence is found among males aged 15-24 years. The highest suicide rate is in the capital, Nuuk, and in Eastern Greenland. However, the incidence of attempted suicide using medicine was high in the Nuuk, especially among females. The highest incidence of suicide attempts using medication was observed among females in the age group 15-19 years, who, as mentioned earlier, had the lowest self-rated health. Together this reflects considerable risk and psychosocial vulnerability among young people in Greenland.[190]

Today, a major threat to the Greenlandic health care system is the lack of staff on all professional levels and their rapid turnover, especially for the small towns and remote villages.[191] This reduces health care in several ways, "especially to continuity in care, the surveillance of health and services and preventive or health promotion efforts". In 2007 the first public health program in Greenland, Inuuneritta ("let us have a good life) was proposed. The goal of the program is to meet

---

[184] P. M. D. Bjerregaard and Young, 2008, pp. 15-16.

[185] Niclasen and Mulvad, 2010, pp. 439-440.

[186] M. L. Pedersen, Rolskov, Jacobsen and Lynge, 2012, p. 1.

[187] Spein et al., 2013, p. 1.

[188] Acculturation for indigenous peoples is related to the process of colonization over centuries as well as the ongoing social transition experienced in the Arctic today. Changing living conditions and lifestyle affect health in numerous ways in Arctic indigenous peoples.

[189] Eliassen, Braaten, Melhus, Hansen and Broderstad, 2012, pp. 4-6.

[190] Bloch, Drachmann and Pedersen, 2013, pp. 2-3.

[191] Niclasen and Mulvad, 2010, p. 442.

the health challenges among the Inuit in Greenland. Inuuneritta focuses on diet, physical activity, alcohol and drug abuse, smoking, violence and sexual health. It also includes programs on suicide prevention, early interventions for the health and development of children and dental health.[192]

In 2008, a new plan for reorganization of the health care system was proposed. Researchers Niclasen and Mulvvad (2010) describe the important issues of the plan as follows:

> "A fundamental component of the structural reorganization is tying all parts of the health care system together through telemedicine and in the future with a joint electronic patient file. The rapid epidemiological changes make surveillance and monitoring of health particularly important, and data on core indicators of health and health care are urgently needed. Furthermore, better steering instruments on resource allocation and quality, and securing best clinical practice are areas where focus in the future is needed".

In order to attract students, the nursing education has been extended to include a university-based bachelor's degree, and to meet the needs for high-quality health care in the small villages, a specialized training program to qualify nurses to work without direct supervision by a medical doctor is planned. Also medical doctors are offered a one-year specialization in Arctic health, for working in the rural areas in Greenland.

Giving birth in Greenland

In 2001-2003, new policies and guidelines for pregnancy and childbearing were introduced, which led to an increase in the proportion of deliveries at the Queen Ingrid´s Hospital in Nuuk. However, these changes were met with some public criticism.[193] The guidelines for transfer and visitation were set into motion in 2002, and females are referred for birth either in their own community or, in the case of at-risk pregnancy, sent to the national referral hospital during the last trimester. However, the new national health policy (2009) not only transfers females in the case of at risk pregnancy, but also consolidates low-risk pregnancies in clusters at regional hospitals. It is estimated that 40-50 per cent of the pregnant females will be transferred out of their local communities during the last two to four weeks of pregnancy and then come back one to two weeks after birth.[194]

> Inuit childbirth is the women's own personal act, and the unborn child is a living part of the community. ...in other indigenous cultures where birth is not only considered a personal event, but is also one of the ways that the child and family are linked to the community.[195]

The new policies and guidelines for pregnancy have changed the focus on birth as a personal and community act to birth within the private and political arena. Between 1953 and 1992 women in Greenland gave birth in their local communities and as late as 2000, it was still uncommon for women to leave their communities to give birth. Females often feel isolated when they have to go to the larger cities, where hospital nurses and doctors do not speak Greenlandic. Greenlandic perinatal policy did not include economic support for women desiring to have family with them

---

192 Niclasen and Mulvad, 2010, p. 443.

193 P. Bjerregaard and Olesen, 2010, pp. 480-485.

194 R. Montgomery-Andersen, Douglas and Borup, 2013, p. 80.

195 R. Montgomery-Andersen, et al., 2013, p. 80.

when they were transferred for birth; this was up to the individual families.[196] In a country with its own unique culture and cultural norms, it is important that when changing policy that women and their families are a part of the dialogue around change. This has not happened in Greenland, because decisions regarding birth setting have been made by policymakers, health and government officials and were fashioned after the Danish system, where the Inuit females and families themselves were often not a part of the dialogue.

Gender-based violence among Inuit in Greenland

In the international literature, Gender Based Violence (GBV) is applied to a broad range of related life events. The World Health Organization (WHO) defines violence as a health problem. "The intentional use of physical force or power, threatened or actual, against oneself, another person, or against a group or community that either result in or has a high likelihood of resulting in injury, death, psychological harm, mal development, or deprivation".[197] Violence as a public health problem has traditionally focused on violence that occurs in public space and assessed as a cause of injuries. The more recent definition stated above, broadens the potential harmful effect to include not only physical injuries. The United Nations definition is often applied when addressing the specific form of violence which women are subjected to: "Any act of gender-based violence that result in, or is likely to result in, physical, sexual or psychological harm or suffering to women, including threats of such acts, coercion or arbitrary deprivation of liberty, whether occurring in public or private life".[198]

Few studies have been written by indigenous peoples in the Arctic region. One study has compared reported violence in Greenland and Denmark, where a health survey addressed the same questions to both women and men. The overall prevalence of reported violence was higher in Greenland than Denmark and the gender focuses of violence differed. In Greenland, women reported the same high level of severe violence as men, whereas in Denmark the men reported violence, rather than women. However, the types of violence reported by women in Greenland differed from the types reported by men, as women were more often sexually abused and abused as children. To date, no studies have been undertaken that have addressed gender-based violence among Sami peoples. However, a recent study began in Norway on Gender-Based Violence, Ethnicity and Mental Health. There is also a subproject in the Population-based Study on Health and Living Conditions in Areas with Mixed Sami and Norwegian Settlements, titled the SAMINOR Questionnaire Study.[199] It is known that the elderly in northern Norway (where most Sami reside) are more likely to be exposed to family violence than seniors in general, living in South Norway.[200]

Linguistic barriers in health care setting

Effective communication between a patient and the provider is paramount in a health care setting. Therefore, language barriers present a formidable obstacle to accessing adequate health care. Language differences have been shown to be a serious barrier among various cultural and

---

[196] R. A. Montgomery-Andersen, et al., 2010, p. 301.

[197] Krug, 2002.

[198] United Nations General Assembly Declaration on the Elimination of Violence Against Women, 1993.

[199] http://uit.no/prosjekter/prosjekt?p_document_id=261008.

[200] Sited from: http://www.nordlys.no/nyheter/article6915937.ece.

ethnic groups.[201] A study carried out in 1980 concluded that linguistic and cultural barriers prevented Sami patients from going to the doctor, leading to an inferior health service for Sami people.[202] In Norway (as well in Sweden and Finland) all municipalities and counties with Sami peoples are responsible for solving language barriers associated with services, so that the basic user rights can be met. Research indicates that Sami patients experience linguistic and cultural barriers in the meeting with the health services.[203] For many Sami, it is important to be able to use their mother tongue in conversations with their doctor, nurse, social worker and other health care personnel. Language barriers can lead to inadequate health care and treatment for Sami patient. Sami patients often do not receive health services in their own language, because only a few health workers can speak Sami. Further, interpreter services are poorly developed in the rural Sami areas. Many Samis are also reluctant to admit that they do not understand the majority language or are in need of interpretation. Some Sami therefore fail to seek health care services, even when they have significant care needs.[204] Surveys have indicated that there is severely limited use of interpreters in health and child welfare services.

Today, children under school age and elderly Sami are completely monolingual in the Sami language. At the same time, bilingual Sami have difficulty communicating in Norwegian, especially when they are seeking health care.

In the report titled "Discrimination of the Sami—the rights of the Sami from a discrimination perspective" (2008), by the Ombudsman against Ethnic Discrimination (DO) in Sweden, reported that many Sami are met with discrimination and prejudice when they seek medical care for their Sami-speaking children:

> "In their contact with the DO, parents of Sami-speaking children describe that when they seek medical care, they feel insulted by medical staff. Several parents have experienced situations where doctors, nurses and speech therapists have commented on the fact that the child and his/her parent speak Sami with each other. Examples of such comments include "Speak Swedish. We live in Sweden". "Can the child only speak Sami?" and "When is this child going to learn Swedish?" The perceived insinuation is that the child is not fully functional because he or she speaks his/her mother's tongue better than Swedish".[205]

Cultural barriers in health care settings

Indigenous peoples often hold different priorities and perception of health than their mainstream majority peers. This can stem from traditional cultural or religious beliefs about health and well-being, different customary practices around health care, or living in distinct locations with unique health challenges. In order to achieve better equity in health outcomes, these different viewpoints must be taken into consideration in policy development and service delivery.[206]

---

[201] Marrone, 2007, pp. 192-193.

[202] Fugelli, 1991.

[203] Nystad, et al., 2008, pp. 119-120.

[204] NorwegianHealthAuthorities, 2009.

[205] Pikkarainen and Brodin, 2008, p. 30.

[206] MRG, 2013, p. 18.

"In the discourse about health services for Sami patients in Norway the last few years, attention is given to cases where the health services is accused of not taking care of the needs of Sami patients. The system do not allow for neither language nor cross-cultural communication or the patients view of health".[207]

The lack of language and cultural understanding can lead to symptoms of disease being misinterpreted and treatment not provided all of which can have serious consequences. There are indications that there is an underreporting of disease in the Sami community, particularly in relation to somatic and mental health, medical care at birth and chronic diseases.[208]

Dental health care and dental treatment

Dental health is an important aspect of general health and well-being for both children and adults. In Norway, reports from the National Bureau of Statistics have consistently reported a lower oral health status in the three northernmost counties, the worst being the northernmost county (Finnmark), especially in some of the communities with a large proportion of indigenous Sami population.[209] By offering free dental examinations, the scientists at the Arctic University of Norway will be able find out why people in the Sami municipalities (in Finnmark) have lower oral health than the national average.[210]

In Greenland, dental carries burden is high in children compared to the other Nordic countries, and the strengthening of oral health promotion and disease prevention is urgently needed.[211] In a study by Koposova et al. (2013), dental prevalence was higher among the Russian children than the Norwegian children.[212]

Environmental factors affecting health for indigenous people

There have been concerns about pollutants in marine foods and reindeer meat; however, recent research does not give any reason to believe that the consumption of marine foods and reindeer meat presents a high health risk for the Sami and Inuit peoples.[213] Radioactive contamination resulting from the Chernobyl accident in Russia has affected south-Sami peoples in central Norway and Sweden. Radioactive exposure was largely food borne in reindeer because radioactive pollutions from Chernobyl were carried by wind and spring rain patterns in high concentrations to central Sweden and Norway. Most detrimental was the contamination of lichen, the main winter staple of Scandinavia's reindeer. Many reindeer had to be destroyed, because of high level of radioactive pollutions.[214] The Chernobyl accident has had a major impact on the psychosocial health of the South Sami reindeer herds in Norway and Sweden. The Samis are still concerned about the

---

[207] Margrete Gaski, 2011, p. 9.

[208] NorwegianHealthAuthorities, 2009.

[209] Adekoya, 2012, pp. 31-38.

[210] http://uit.no/nyheter/artikkel?p_document_id=353106&p_dim=88108.

[211] Petersen and Christensen, 2006, pp. 35-44.

[212] Koposova et al., 2013, pp. 3-11.

[213] Symon and Wilson, 2009.

[214] Bloch, et al., 2013.

impact from the nuclear accident that may affect their health and future prospects for reindeer husbandry.[215]

The Sami and Inuit peoples in the Arctic are primarily exposed to pollutants through traditional food and water, but also through the air. Pollutants are particularly a problem for indigenous peoples, who mainly live on traditional diets. Although the largest emissions of pollutants do not happen in the Nordic countries and in Greenland, the air currents which transport airborne contaminants to the Arctic are particularly worrisome. Therefore, this is an issue for the Sami and Inuit peoples. Long-range pollution seems to have shown a downward trend in recent years, but local pollution from industries could be a problem for indigenous health and the environment.[216] Recently, in northern Sweden there has been a mining dispute where hundreds of Sami and other activist have protested against iron mining plans in the Sami traditional reindeer herding lands in Kallak. According to Swedish law, the Sami peoples cannot claim ownership of the land where they have lived for nearly 9,000 years, but have the right to use it for herding. The mining dispute has led to renewed calls for the government to adopt changes that recognize Sami ownership rights over the land. "Legally, Sweden has a long way to go to take full responsibility for the Sami people", said Christina Allard, an associate professor at Lulea University. Sweden, unlike Norway and many other countries has yet to sign legally binding international conventions that protect the rights of indigenous peoples.[217] In the future, local pollution from new industries in the Arctic area will have a major impact on the living conditions and psychosocial health of the indigenous peoples living in the circumpolar areas.

Conclusion

The delivery of high-quality health care to indigenous peoples in the circumpolar areas poses significant challenges. These include the need to develop culturally sensitive health services for the indigenous Sami and the Inuit peoples taking into account language barriers, cross-cultural misunderstandings and racial discrimination. The goal is for health and social services to be of the same quality that is provided for the rest of the population. Entering into the health care system (access to care) and receiving appropriate health care and for the services to be effective (quality of care) are key factors in ensuring good health outcomes. Often the health and social services practitioners are perceived as representatives of majority cultural values and norms that have, throughout history oppressed indigenous peoples, resulting in a deeply felt mistrust of health care institutions. Current health policies and practices favour western standardized health care systems, where the voices of indigenous peoples are often absent. Circumpolar health care systems must take into account the influence of indigenous peoples' view of health and well-being and to develop specific interventions to increase access and utilization among indigenous peoples. This requires health providers to critically reflect on whether policies and practices promote or compromise indigenous health and well-being. Indigenous peoples should not be a passive consumer of health care, but rather an active partner in the development of high quality of care, that ensure good health outcomes for indigenous peoples in the circumpolar areas.

---

[215] Sjolander, 2011.

[216] Symon and Wilson, 2009.

[217] AP News — Sweden's Indigenous Sami in fight against miners by Malin Rising. Aug. 29. 2013.

References

(MRG), M. R. G. I. (2013). State of the World's Minorities and Indigenous Pepole 2013. London.

Adekoya, S. M. (2012). Oral health of adults in Northern Norway: a pilot study. Tromsø: University of Tromsø.

Baarnhielm, S., Javo, C., and Mosko, M. O. (2013). Opening up mental health service delivery to cultural diversity: current situation, development and examples from three northern European countries. Adv Psychosom Med, 33, 40-55. doi: 10.1159/000348730

Bjerregaard, P., and Olesen, I. (2010). Giving birth in Greenland: secular change in acceptance of hospital deliveries. Int J Circumpolar Health, 69(5), 480-485.

Bjerregaard, P. M. D., and Young, T. K. (2008). Health transitions in arctic populations. Toronto [Ont.]: University of Toronto Press.

Blix, B. H., Hamran, T., and Normann, H. K. (2013). Struggles of being and becoming: a dialogical narrative analysis of the life stories of Sami elderly. [Research Support, Non-U.S. Gov't]. J Aging Stud, 27(3), 264-275. doi: 10.1016/j.jaging.2013.05.002.

Bloch, L. H., Drachmann, G. H., and Pedersen, M. L. (2013). High prevalence of medicine-induced attempted suicides among females in Nuuk, Greenland, 2008-2009. Int J Circumpolar Health, 72. doi: 10.3402/ijch.v72i0.21687.

Brustad, M., Pettersen, T., Melhus, M., and Lund, E. (2009). Mortality patterns in geographical areas with a high vs. low Sami population density in Arctic Norway. [Comparative Study]. Scand J Public Health, 37(5), 475-480. doi: 10.1177/1403494809106502.

Eliassen, B. M., Braaten, T., Melhus, M., Hansen, K. L., and Broderstad, A. R. (2012). Acculturation and self-rated health among Arctic indigenous peoples: a population-based cross-sectional study. BMC Public Health, 12, 948. doi: 10.1186/1471-2458-12-948.

Fugelli, P. (1991). Den norske lege i Sameland (pp. S. 86-100). Rovaniemi: Laplands universitet.

Gaski, M. (2011). Aspects of health services in Sami areas (Vol. nr. 124). Tromsø: Universitetet i Tromsø, Institutt for samfunnsmedisin.

Gaski, M., Melhus, M., Deraas, T., and Forde, O. H. (2011). Use of health care in the main area of Sami habitation in Norway - catching up with national expenditure rates. Rural Remote Health, 11(2), 1655.

Hansen, K. L. (2011). Ethnic discrimination and bullying in relation to self-reported physical and mental health in Sami settlement areas in Norway: the Saminor study (Vol. nr. 115). Tromsø: Universitetet i Tromsø, Institutt for samfunnsmedisin.

Hansen, K. L., Melhus, M., Hogmo, A. and Lund, E. (2008). Ethnic discrimination and bullying in the Sami and non-Sami populations in Norway: the SAMINOR study. Int J Circumpolar Health, 67(1), 97-113.

Hansen, K. L., Melhus, M. and Lund, E. (2010). Ethnicity, self-reported health, discrimination and socioeconomic status: a study of Sami and non-Sami Norwegian populations. Int J Circumpolar Health, 69(2), 111-128.

Hansen, K. L. and Sorlie, T. (2012). Ethnic discrimination and psychological distress: a study of Sami and non-Sami populations in Norway. Transcult Psychiatry, 49(1), 26-50. doi: 10.1177/1363461511433944

Hassler, S., Johansson, R., Sjolander, P., Gronberg, H. and Damber, L. (2005). Causes of death in the Sami population of Sweden, 1961-2000. [Research Support, Non-U.S. Gov't]. Int J Epidemiol, 34(3), 623-629. doi: 10.1093/ije/dyi027.

Hassler, S., Sjölander, P. and Ericsson, A. (2004). Construction of a database on health and living conditions of the swedish saami population (pp. S. 107-124 : ill.). Umeå: Umeå universitet.

Ikaheimo, T. (2010). Unique information about the health systems of the North. [Editorial]. Int J Circumpolar Health, 69(5), 414.

Kaiser, N., Sjolander, P., Liljegren, A. E., Jacobsson, L. and Renberg, E. S. (2010). Depression and anxiety in the reindeer-herding Sami population of Sweden. [Research Support, Non-U.S. Gov't]. Int J Circumpolar Health, 69(4), 383-393.

Koposova, N., Eriksen, H. M., Widstrom, E., Handegard, B. H., Pastbin, M. and Koposov, R. (2013). Caries prevalence and determinants among 12-year-olds in North-West Russia and Northern Norway. [Research Support, Non-U.S. Gov't]. Stomatologija, 15(1), 3-11.

Krug, E. G. (2002). World report on violence and health. Geneva: World Health Organization.

Kulonen, U.-M., Pulkkinen, R. and Seurujärvi-Kari, I. (2005). The Saami: a cultural encyclopaedia (Vol. 925). Helsinki: Seura.

Leininger, M. M. and McFarland, M. R. (2006). Culture care diversity and universality: a worldwide nursing theory. Sudbury, Mass.: Jones and Bartlett.

Lund, E., Melhus, M., Hansen, K. L., Nystad, T., Broderstad, A. R., Selmer, R. and Lund-Larsen, P. G. (2007). Population based study of health and living conditions in areas with both Sami and Norwegian populations--the SAMINOR study. [Comparative Study].

Research Support, Non-U.S. Gov't]. Int J Circumpolar Health, 66(2), 113-128.

Marrone, S. (2007). Understanding barriers to health care: a review of disparities in health care services among indigenous populations. [Review]. Int J Circumpolar Health, 66(3), 188-198.

Minde, H. (2005). Assimilation of the Sami: implementation and consequences (Vol. nr 3/2005). [Kautokeino]: Resource Centre for the Rights of Indigenous Peoples.

Montgomery-Andersen, R., Douglas, V. and Borup, I. (2013). Literature review: The "logics" of birth settings in Arctic Greenland. Midwifery, 29(11), e79-88. doi: 10.1016/j.midw.2013.06.014

Montgomery-Andersen, R. A., Willen, H. and Borup, I. (2010). "There was no other way things could have been." Greenlandic women's experiences of referral and transfer during pregnancy. Anthropol Med, 17(3), 301-313. doi: 10.1080/13648470.2010.526696

Niclasen, B. and Mulvad, G. (2010). Health care and health care delivery in Greenland. [Review]. Int J Circumpolar Health, 69(5), 437-447.

Norge Sosial- og helsedepartementet. (1999). Mangfold og likeverd: regjeringens handlingsplan for helse- og sosialtjenester til den samiske befolkningen i Norge : høringsutkast. Oslo: Statens forvaltningstjeneste, Informasjonsforvaltning.

NorwegianHealthAuthorities. (2009). Samhandlingsreformen: rett behandling - på rett sted - til rett tid. [Oslo]: [Regjeringen].

Nystad, T., Melhus, M. and Lund, E. (2008). Sami speakers are less satisfied with general practitioners' services. Int J Circumpolar Health, 67(1), 114-121.

Omma, L. (2013). Ung same i Sverige: livsvillkor, självvärdering och helsa (Vol. 1543). Umeå: The University, Faculty of Medicine.

Pedersen, M. L., Rolskov, A., Jacobsen, J. L. and Lynge, A. R. (2012). Frequent use of primary health care service in Greenland: an opportunity for undiagnosed disease case-finding. Int J Circumpolar Health, 71, 18431. doi: 10.3402/ijch.v71i0.18431

Pedersen, P., Høgmo, A. and Solbakk, J. T. (2012). Sápmi slår tilbake: samiske revitaliserings- og moderniseringsprosser i siste generasjon. Kárášjohka: ČálliidLágádus.

Petersen, P. E. and Christensen, L. B. (2006). Dental health status and development trends among children and adolescents in Greenland. Int J Circumpolar Health, 65(1), 35-44.

Pikkarainen, H. and Brodin, B. (2008). Discrimination of the Sami: the rights of the Sami from a discrimination perspektiv. Stockholm: Ombudsmannen mot etnisk diskriminering (DO).

Sexton, R. and Sorlie, T. (2008). Use of traditional healing among Sami psychiatric patients in the north of Norway. Int J Circumpolar Health, 67(1), 135-146.

Silviken, A., Haldorsen, T. and Kvernmo, S. (2006). Suicide among Indigenous Sami in Arctic Norway, 1970-1998. [Research Support, Non-U.S. Gov't]. Eur J Epidemiol, 21(9), 707-713. doi: 10.1007/s10654-006-9052-7.

Sjolander, P. (2011). What is known about the health and living conditions of the indigenous people of northern Scandinavia, the Sami? [Research Support, Non-U.S. Gov't].

Review]. Glob Health Action, 4. doi: 10.3402/gha.v4i0.8457.

Slaastad, T. I. (2012). Samisk statistikk 2012 (Vol. 2012/3). Oslo: SSB.

Soininen, L. and Pukkola, E. (2008). Mortality of the Sami in northern Finland 1979-2005. [Comparative Study]. Int J Circumpolar Health, 67(1), 43-55.

Sorlie, T. and Nergard, J. I. (2005). Treatment satisfaction and recovery in Saami and Norwegian patients following psychiatric hospital treatment: a comparative study. [Comparative Study

Research Support, Non-U.S. Gov't]. Transcult Psychiatry, 42(2), 295-316.

Spein, A. R., Pedersen, C. P., Silviken, A. C., Melhus, M., Kvernmo, S. E. and Bjerregaard, P. (2013). Self-rated health among Greenlandic Inuit and Norwegian Sami adolescents: associated risk and protective correlates. [Research Support, Non-U.S. Gov't]. Int J Circumpolar Health, 72. doi: 10.3402/ijch.v72i0.19793.

Swedish Government, I. (1999). The Sámi - an indigenous people in Sweden. It is about the possibilities to ratify the ILO Convention 169. 25.

Symon, C. and Wilson, S. J. (2009). AMAP assessment 2009: Human health in the Arctic. Oslo: Arctic Monitoring and Assessment Programme.

Tervo, H., Muller-Wille, L. and Nikkonen, M. (2003). Health culture within the context of the northern environment. Int J Circumpolar Health, 62(2), 167-181.

Turi, A. L. (2011). Internalizing symptoms and health service use in indigenous Sami and non-indigenous adolescents in Arctic Norway. [Tromsø]: Department of Psychology, Faculty of Health Sciences, University of Tromsø.

Vuori, J., Kylanen, M. and Tritter, J. (2010). Transfer of patients from health care centres to special care services: analysis of travel distances in Nordic countries. Int J Circumpolar Health, 69(5), 512-518.

Williams, D. R. and Mohammed, S. A. (2009). Discrimination and racial disparities in health: evidence and needed research. [Research Support, N.I.H., Extramural].

Research Support, Non-U.S. Gov't Review]. J Behav Med, 32(1), 20-47. doi: 10.1007/s10865-008-9185-0.

Young, K. (2008). Circumpolar Health Indicators: Sources, Data and Maps. Int J Circumpolar Health, Supplement 3.

Young, T. K., Rawat, R. and Dallmann, W. K. (2012). Circumpolar health atlas. Toronto: University of Toronto Press.

CHAPTER FOUR

ACCESS TO HEALTH SERVICES BY INDIGENOUS PEOPLES IN CENTRAL, SOUTH AMERICA AND THE CARIBBEAN REGION

DR. MYRIAM DE ROCIO CONEJO MALDONADO

CHAPTER FOUR

ACCESS TO HEALTH SERVICES BY INDIGENOUS PEOPLES IN CENTRAL, SOUTH AMERICA AND THE CARIBBEAN REGION

DR. MYRIAM DE ROCIO CONEJO MALDONADO

Introduction

Central, South America and the Caribbean region have vibrant and politically active indigenous populations that comprises between 45 and 50 million peoples who belong to almost 600 indigenous groups.[218] The highest numbers of indigenous peoples are found in Mexico, Peru, Guatemala, Bolivia and Ecuador. According to World Bank figures, 12.76 per cent of the entire population and approximately 40 per cent of the rural population is indigenous.[219] Indigenous peoples represent a disproportionate number of the poorest, in a region that has the world's greatest income disparity. Indigenous peoples live in a range of diverse settings, from tropical forest villages to mountain towns and in the largest cities. Many have strong attachments to their traditional territories which are located in the rural areas however, more and more indigenous peoples are either migrating or being displaced to regions or countries that are long distances from their communities. The number of indigenous peoples living in urban areas has also increased where there is dependency on urban clusters for their livelihood.[220]

Over the past two centuries, colonialism has influenced indigenous communities, resulting in highly mixed populations in the Caribbean, linked to the importation of slaves from Africa to the almost destruction of indigenous groups such as the Taino in Cuba, Puerto Rico, the Dominican Republic and Jamaica. While some indigenous groups were able to remain in isolation, others were forced into cities and towns or settled in less hospitable lands or pushed off their lands altogether. In many cases, indigenous peoples were to be incorporated, voluntarily or involuntarily, into the mainstream population where they might or might not self-identify as indigenous peoples. While they could live and work in the same way as their non-indigenous neighbours, many were forced into the worst socioeconomic roles. For example, many indigenous peoples of mixed descent in Mexico left their homes, crossing state and national borders to take up marginalized labour roles, especially in the United States as agricultural labourers, construction workers and domestic workers.[221]

---

[218] http://www.iwgia.org/regions/latin-america/indigenous-peoples-in-latin-america.

[219] It should be noted there is a lack of specific information on indigenous peoples' health the Caribbean region.

[220] http://www.iwgia.org/regions/latin-america/indigenous-peoples-in-latin-america.

[221] Raul Montenegro and Carolyn Stephens "Indigenous health in Latin America and the Caribbean" www.thelancet.com, Vol 367, June 3, 2006.

Despite State subjugation policies aimed at their destruction, indigenous peoples are still managing to uphold and rebuild their identity, language and culture, as well as their traditional social, legal and political systems, or a large part thereof. Central America, South America and the Caribbean's history and very essence are rooted in the cultural and social foundations of indigenous peoples. Throughout history, indigenous peoples have developed different forms of resistance and currently, having gained strength, indigenous movements are reclaiming their land rights, respect for their cultural values, languages, customs and institutions and the right to decide their development priorities. Indigenous movements in Central America, South America and the Caribbean have grown markedly in recent decades and have increased their organizational capacity as political actors, demanding increasingly higher levels of participation.[222]

International legal framework for intercultural health

There are a number of the legally binding instruments on the right to health that have relevance to indigenous peoples. These include the Universal Declaration of Human Rights;[223] International Covenant on Economic, Social and Cultural Rights;[224] Convention on the Rights of the Child;[225] Convention on the Elimination of all Forms of Discrimination against Women;[226] and the Millennium Summit Declaration.[227]

Other instruments include:

The *International Convention on the Elimination of All Forms of Racial Discrimination* (CERD, 1965) is a legal mechanism that obliges all Member States of the United Nations to eliminate racial discrimination, as well as to act against racism. U.N. Committee on the Elimination of Racial Discrimination CERD) has emphasized that:

> [I]n many regions of the world indigenous peoples have been, and are still being, discriminated against and deprived of their human rights and fundamental freedoms and in particular that they have lost their land and resources to colonists, commercial companies and State enterprises. Consequently, the preservation of their culture and their historical identity has been and still is jeopardized.[228]

The *International Labor Organization Convention No. 169* (ILO, 1989) on indigenous and tribal peoples, which has been ratified in Latin America by Mexico, Guatemala, Honduras, Nicaragua, Costa Rica, Colombia, Ecuador, Peru, Bolivia, Paraguay, Chile, Brazil, Uruguay and Argentina, defines, inter alia, the rights of indigenous peoples to ownership and possession of land, recognition of their values and practices, making decisions about their own priorities, customary law, social security and health, equality regarding contracts and conditions of employment, and education at all levels.

---

[222] http://www.ilo.org/indigenous/Activitiesbyregion/LatinAmerica/lang--en/index.htm.

[223] The Universal Declaration of Human Rights http://www.un.org/en/documents/udhr/.

[224] International Covenant on Economic, Social and Cultural Rights
http://www.ohchr.org/EN/ProfessionalInterest/Pages/CESCR.aspx.

[225] Convention on the Rights of the Child http://www.ohchr.org/en/professionalinterest/pages/crc.aspx.

[226] Convention on the Elimination of all Forms of Discrimination against Women
http://www.ohchr.org/Documents/ProfessionalInterest/cedaw.pdf.

[227] Millennium Summit Declaration http://www.un.org/millennium/declaration/ares552e.htm.

[228] U.N. Committee on the Elimination of Racial Discrimination (CERD), General Recommendation XXIII: Indigenous Peoples, U.N. Doc. CERD/C/51/misc 13/Rev 4, at 3 (1997) [hereinafter CERD General Recommendation on Indigenous Peoples].

In Article 5, of ILO Convention 169 states that in applying the provisions of this Convention:

a. the social, cultural, religious and spiritual values and practices of these peoples shall be recognized and protected, and due account shall be taken of the nature of the problems which face them both as groups and as individuals;

b. the integrity of the values, practices and institutions of these peoples shall be respected;

c. policies aimed at mitigating the difficulties experienced by these peoples in facing new conditions of life and work shall be adopted, with the participation and co-operation of the peoples affected.

Article 25 of ILO Convention 169 states:

1. Governments shall ensure that adequate health services are made available to the peoples concerned, or shall provide them with resources to allow them to design and deliver such services under their own responsibility and control, so that they may enjoy the highest attainable standard of physical and mental health.

2. Health services shall, to the extent possible, be community-based. These services shall be planned and administered in co-operation with the peoples concerned and take into account their economic, geographic, social and cultural conditions as well as their traditional preventive care, healing practices and medicines.

3. The health care system shall give preference to the training and employment of local community health workers, and focus on primary health care while maintaining strong links with other levels of health care services.

4. The provision of such health services shall be coordinated with other social, economic and cultural measures in the country.

The *Declaration and Program of Action of Vienna (1993)* recognizes the significance of both the participation and the contribution of indigenous populations in social and economic development, and calls upon states to guarantee the fulfilment of the rights and fundamental freedoms of indigenous populations, as well as to recognize and respect cultural diversity and their systems for social organization.

The *Declaration and Program of Action of Durban* (2001) reaffirms the need to fulfil human rights and fundamental freedoms of indigenous peoples and the need to combat racism, racial discrimination, xenophobia, and related intolerance that affects them.

The *United Nations Declaration on the Rights of Indigenous Peoples* (2007) commits, as does ILO Convention 169, all subscribing States to respect the cultural expressions of indigenous groups in all fields, including health. The UN Declaration states in Article 24:

1. Indigenous peoples have the right to their traditional medicines and to maintain their health practices, including the conservation of their vital medicinal plants, animals and minerals. Indigenous individuals also have the right to access, without any discrimination, to all social and health services.

2. Indigenous individuals have an equal right to the enjoyment of the highest attainable standard of physical and mental health. States shall take the necessary steps with a view to achieving progressively the full realization of this right.

The Inter-American instruments ensuring the right to health and other human rights of indigenous peoples include:

- American Declaration on the Rights and Duties of Man
- American Convention on Human Rights
- Additional Protocol to the American Convention on Human Rights
- Inter-American Convention on Prevention of Violence Against Women ("Belem Do Para")
- Inter-American Convention to Prevent Torture
- Inter-American Convention on the Elimination of All Forms of Discrimination Against Persons with Disabilities

These are, inter alia, some international mechanisms that have the mandate to address the health rights of indigenous peoples in the Central, South America and the Caribbean region such as:

- The United Nations Permanent Forum on Indigenous Issues was created in 2000 and has made recommendations urging all Member States to include the intercultural perspective within their health policies, programs and services, with special reference to reproductive health, as well as to reassess the role played by healers and midwives as agents for the exchange between ancestral medicine and western medicine.

- Resolutions CD37.R5 (1993), CD40.R6 (1997), and CD.47.R13 (2006) of the Pan American Health Organization (PAHO) establishes guidelines to address health with an integrated and intercultural approach, and the incorporation of indigenous wisdom, knowledge about medicines and therapies for health care, in relation to the geopolitical and social context of indigenous peoples, the promotion of health and the renewed primary health care strategy (PHC-R).

- Resolutions of the Meetings of Health Ministers of the Andean Subregion (REMSA) address different questions. REMSA XVII/296 (1993) made health care a priority for the indigenous populations in the subregion, and REMSA XXVII/417 (2006) and REMSA XXVIII/438 (2007) allowed the creation of the Andean Commission for Intercultural Health, as well as the elaboration of the Andean Intercultural Health Plan as a response to those initiatives oriented to provide health services with an intercultural approach for the countries in the Andean subregion.

The legal norms and international mechanisms mentioned above relate to the need to respect the health rights of indigenous peoples; establish laws, policies and programs to diminish or combat inequality in the area of access to health care; and guaranteeing health with the provision of culturally appropriate health services. Further, there must be interaction between traditional/ancestral medicine and conventional medicine in order for them to complement each other. Indigenous peoples must be able to participate in the development and planning of health services on equal terms in order to improve their own health situation.

Health issues in Central America, South America and the Caribbean

Many indigenous peoples in Central America, South America and the Caribbean still live in isolated environments where conditions are harsh. People living within natural ecosystems are exposed to many health hazards produced mostly by the exacting environment. In the past, health risks were linked to basic access to foods, water and shelter and, in many contexts, risks from predators.[229] Health and well-being prior to colonization was closely related to sophisticated knowledge and use of the local ecosystems. The early period of colonialism brought new diseases that were especially lethal for communities in the coastal areas.[230] Current-day problems still have a major impact on indigenous peoples' lives in the region. The security of indigenous peoples' lands, territories and resources has become a competition between the governments of the region in the areas of agricultural, mining and energy generation initiatives particularly in Argentina, Bolivia, Brazil, Chile, Guatemala, Honduras, Mexico, Panama and Peru. This has had negative impacts on indigenous peoples, particularly for indigenous peoples living in remote areas and forest zones, including those living in voluntary isolation in the Amazon rain forest.

Indigenous peoples and their communities in most Central and some South American States continue to face limited economic opportunities, poor access to social services, high levels of public insecurity and the strong influence of organized criminal enterprises. All of these challenges are exaggerated by the generally weak state presence in remote geographical zones, as well as by fragile institutions, uneven justice administration, politicized judicial systems, and continuing high levels of corruption and impunity particularly in Central and South America.[231] This situation has resulted in major inequalities between indigenous peoples and their non-indigenous counterparts. Indigenous peoples experience the worst social conditions and thus health profiles include the highest rates of morbidity and mortality and the least access to health services compared to the rest of the population. According to unpublished data, in 2003 the average rate for infant mortality in Colombia was 19 per 1,000 infants, but for the Wayuu indigenous group the infant mortality rate was 111 per 1,000.[232] In terms of morbidity rates in Bolivia, the Guaraní, with a population of 153,483 have a prevalence of tuberculosis five to eight times that of the national average.[233] Indigenous peoples are more likely to suffer from substance abuse, depression and other mental disorders that are obstacles to the enjoyment of the right to the highest attainable standard of physical and mental health. HIV/AIDS and other sexually transmitted diseases are also spreading in indigenous communities. At the same time, indigenous communities are faced with economic exploitation of indigenous women and lack of information about physical and mental health.[234]

The right to life for indigenous peoples in the region is frequently at risk due to higher mortality and morbidity rates compared to the general population. The health and personal integrity of indigenous peoples is at risk throughout their lives—from infancy where there are high mortality rates, and throughout life where there is a great prevalence of disease and death at early age. Among the Maya in Guatemala, life expectancy for indigenous peoples is 17 years shorter than for

[229] Raul Montenegro and Carolyn Stephens, "Indigenous health in Latin America and the Caribbean" www.thelancet.com, Vol 367, June 3, 2006.

[230] Raul Montenegro and Carolyn Stephens, "Indigenous health in Latin America and the Caribbean" www.thelancet.com, Vol 367, June 3, 2006.

[231] Minorities Rights Group International State of the World's Minorities and Indigenous Peoples 2012, p. 90.

[232] Raul Montenegro and Carolyn Stephens, "Indigenous health in Latin America and the Caribbean" www.thelancet.com, Vol 367, June 3, 2006.

[233] Raul Montenegro and Carolyn Stephens, "Indigenous health in Latin America and the Caribbean" www.thelancet.com, Vol 367, June 3, 2006.

[234] Pan American Health Organization (PAHO), "Human Rights and Health: Indigenous Peoples" 2008, p. 2.

the non-indigenous population.[235] In Bolivia, 9 per cent of Guaraní peoples have access to safe drinking water which impacts on the enjoyment of the right to health. Lack of infrastructure and medical services also impact on indigenous peoples' right to health, particularly in physically isolated communities.[236]

The other major concerns include the general lack of disaggregated data by ethnicity and gender in most of the countries in the regions. This makes it difficult to obtain a precise picture of the overall health situation of indigenous peoples. On the other hand, there are data available on the current health of indigenous peoples but it is scattered, depending on individual groups of scientists and their studies, but it is not available on government databases. Some countries such as Brazil have made efforts to gather data, and even have a specific indigenous office within the government that is tasked with obtaining information on groups in isolation.[237]

Indigenous peoples make up to 40 per cent of the rural population in the region, where there is often little or no access to conventional health services. As a result, at least 80 per cent of indigenous peoples depend mainly on traditional therapists for medical assistance".[238] The infant mortality rate is 54 per 1,000 live births[239] expressed as profound and disturbing disparity; "infant mortality rates among indigenous children are 60 per cent higher than among non-indigenous children".[240]

The indigenous population in Mexico is estimated to be 12.6 per cent of the wider population and 80.6 per cent of the indigenous population are considered to be extremely poor. Maternal mortality rates in the states of Guerrero, Chiapas and Oaxaca are 103.2, 82.7 and 80.6 per 100,000,[241] respectively. In the rural areas of these three states the probability of death due to preventable diseases is 181 per cent higher than the probability in the urban centres of the same states.[242] In the case of Guatemala indigenous peoples are 42.8 per cent of the total population and 86.6 per cent[243] of this indigenous population live in poverty. The maternal mortality rate has reached 211 per 100,000.[244] The infant mortality rate has reached 51.1 per 1,000 live births.

---

[235] Pan American Health Organization (PAHO), "Human Rights and Health: Indigenous Peoples" 2008, p. 2.

[236] "State Policy: From Custody to the Policy of Rights—a Solved Issue?" in: Indigenous Peoples in Voluntary isolation and initial contact, Antenor Vaz, IWGIA, Copenhagen, 2013, p. 12.

[237] Raul Montenegro and Carolyn Stephens, "Indigenous health in Latin America and the Caribbean" www.thelancet.com, Vol 367, June 3, 2006.

[238] Cevallos, Rodrigo, "Prestación de servicios de salud en zonas con pueblos indígenas", http://www2.paho.org/hq/dmdocuments/2009/servicios%20salud%20zonas%20indigenas.pdf, p. 19.

[239] "Mortalidad infantil y en la niñez de pueblos indígenas y afrodescendientes de América Latina: inequidades estructurales, patrones diversos y evidencia de derechos no cumplidos", CEPAL y CELADE, Naciones Unidas, Santiago de Chile 2010http://www.eclac.cl/Celade/publica/bol62/BD6206.html.

[240] "Mortalidad infantil y en la niñez de pueblos indígenas y afrodescendientes de América Latina: inequidades estructurales, patrones diversos y evidencia de derechos no cumplidos", CELADE-CEPAL http://www.eclac.cl/publicaciones/xml/1/41581/LCW.348Oct_2010.pdf.

[241] http://www.ipsnoticias.net/2011/10/mexico-muerte-materna-destino-fatal-de-campesinas-e-indigenas/.

[242] La salud de la población indígena en México, José Luis Torres, Renata Villoro, Teresita Ramírez, Beatriz Zurita, Patricia Hernández, Rafael Lozano, Francisco Franco, Revista Calidoscopio de la Salud.

[243] "Los pueblos indígenas y la pobreza en América Latina: un análisis empírico", Estudios socio demográficos en pueblos indígenas, Serie E, No. 40 (LC/DEM/G.146), Santiago de Chile, División de Población, Centro Latinoamericano y Caribeño de Demografía (CELADE).

[244] http://www.s21.com.gt/nacionales/2012/02/13/mortalidad-materna-se-triplica-indigenas.

In Chile the indigenous population is estimated to be 10.3 per cent[245] of the total population, and 16 per cent of the indigenous population lives in poverty. The infant mortality rate in general is 11 per 1,000 live births, while the rate for the indigenous peoples is 12.8 per 1,000 live births.[246] In Bolivia the indigenous population is 52 per cent[247] of the total population. Poverty among indigenous peoples has reached 64.3 per cent.[248] The maternal mortality rate in Potosí, the province with the largest indigenous population, is 496 per 100,000.[249]

In Peru the indigenous population is 40.25 per cent of the total population and 79 per cent of the indigenous population is poor. The Peruvian Institute for Statistics has no consolidated number for the infant mortality rate for indigenous children but has indicated that in indigenous communities the infant mortality rate goes from 99 to 153 per 1,000 live births. In Puno, one of the provinces with a large indigenous population, the maternal mortality rate reaches 36 per 100,000.[250]

In Ecuador, according to the 2011 census, the indigenous population is 7.1 per cent of the total population, and 49.9 per cent[251] of the indigenous population is poor. The infant mortality rate among indigenous children is 67.6 per 1,000 live births, while the rate for the population in general is 29.9[252] per 1,000 live births. The maternal mortality rate is 210 per 100,000.[253]

The above figures provide a visible overview of the health gaps that still exist between the indigenous peoples and the rest of the population. Indigenous peoples' health disparities are linked to social, cultural, economic and political factors. There are national and international norms that go towards enhancing and supporting indigenous peoples, particularly in the area of health, as well as national efforts to improve the situation of indigenous persons. However, these actions are clearly not enough for achieving health equity for indigenous peoples. There is a need for recognizing a human-rights-based approach which calls for the inclusion of interculturality and recognition of collective rights.

A gap persists between advances in intercultural health and concrete possibilities of contributing to improving health conditions for indigenous peoples, in spite of the fact that there exists an important basis of information on the fundamental concepts and data on beliefs, expressions and cultural practices of indigenous peoples in various countries.

[245] "La identificación de poblaciones indígenas en los censos de América Latina", in: América Latina: aspectos conceptuales de los censos del 2000, CEPAL/CELADE, Santiago de Chile, p. 361.

[246] http://celade.cepal.org/redatam/PRYESP/SISPPI.

[247] "La identificación de poblaciones indígenas en los censos de América Latina", in: América Latina: aspectos conceptuales de los censos del 2000, CEPAL/CELADE, Santiago de Chile, p. 361.

[248] "Los pueblos indígenas y la pobreza en América Latina: un análisis empírico", Estudios socio demográficos en pueblos indígenas, Serie E, No. 40 (LC/DEM/G.146), Santiago de Chile, División de Población, Centro Latinoamericano y Caribeño de Demografía (CELADE).

[249] http://www.un.org/spanish/News/story.asp?newsID=2649#.Ukj8YtjIwis.

[250] "SITUACIÓN DE LAS MUJERES EN LOS PUEBLOS INDÍGENAS DE AMÉRICA LATINA. OBSTÁCULOS Y RETOS", Judith Bocos Ruiz.

[251] http://websie.eclac.cl/sisgen/ConsultaIntegrada.asp?idAplicacion=14.

[252] http://celade.cepal.org/redatam/PRYESP/SISPPI/.

[253] http://www.opsecu.org/jspui/bitstream/123456789/130/1/130.pdf.

Interculturality and health

It must be recognized that advancements in establishing norms for compliance with health rights of indigenous peoples are the result of the hard struggles by indigenous peoples themselves. They have promoted actions to the States demanding recognition of their rights, the elaboration of public policy and plans to revert situations of inequality in which they live, their social and economic marginalization, and their exclusion through racial discrimination, as well as addressing their deplorable health situation in comparison to other social and cultural groups.

The elaboration of policies, plans and projects and other initiatives for indigenous peoples have taken place in the Central, South America and the Caribbean region since the beginning of the 1990s. Several countries in the region have included an intercultural approach for health in their development plans. At the same time, sociocultural and linguistic barriers continue to exist, as well as barriers in terms of geographic access to health services and the lack of recognition of indigenous peoples' own knowledge and practices regarding the holistic connection between health, disease and healing. These barriers generate resistance and lack of trust among indigenous peoples in terms of using conventional medicine health services.

Such barriers may be overcome through the incorporation of an intercultural approach in the provision of health services, in order to guarantee intercultural management models and health care; culturally relevant health services and medical staff with intercultural competencies. There is also a need to articulate traditional/ancestral medicine with conventional medicine through intercultural-related health mechanisms. In this sense, it is important to reorient health services, include intercultural education and training for health professionals and to have health information systems that improve the provision of health services based on an intercultural approach.

Reorientation of health services

The reorientation of health services towards an intercultural approach implies respect for and compliance with the individual and collective rights of indigenous peoples; the recognition of diverse knowledge and wisdom regarding the process of health-disease-treatment-healing; interaction of knowledge and practices between conventional medicine and the knowledge that indigenous peoples possess, as well as their complementary role; and the achievement of equity in health for both indigenous individuals and collectives.

One must have in mind that intercultural health, if it is to be presented as a reference for transversal interest with application to any society, cannot be imposed within the state only by decree. If it is not valued and given the consensus of all sectors involved, unfortunate situations may arise that would result in serious difficulties for health care and hide the reasons for the lack of equity for indigenous peoples. Interculturality promotes a horizontal dialogue between cultures, a respectful relationship with no hierarchies. This means the inhibition of one's criteria and criticisms and one's prejudices, as well as concentrating on cultural practices that are often quite different from the rest of society. It is a matter of limiting ethnocentrism, which is the trend for interpreting other cultures based on the principles of one's own culture. Therefore, key words regarding the concept of interculturality are: respect for diversity, interaction, dialogue and horizontality.[254]

---

[254] Cited in "Diagnostico y Fortalecimiento de la Inclusión de Interculturalidad en la Formación del personal de Salud" (informe de avance), Martha Escobar, MSP Ecuador 2013.

Interculturality must be considered as an initiative for changing the health conditions, as long as change serves to improve epidemiology indicators, that is, to get people to live longer and better. If, on the other hand, change is understood as only having the objective of giving new value to traditional medicine, it will be difficult for health services to improve, and therefore to produce improvements in the health of the population.[255]

In this sense, countries in Latin America with indigenous peoples have incorporated the intercultural approach in their laws, policies, management and health care models, and technical norms, in order to contribute to health equity according to the sociocultural contexts of indigenous peoples. The big challenge is to make those instruments function.

In Guatemala, the Inclusive Health Model (MIS, Modelo Incluyente de Salud) has been implemented since 2003 by the Consorcio Médicos del Mundo Navarra-CORDAID in coordination with the Ministry of Public Health and Social Assistance (MSPAS, Ministerio de Salud Pública y Asistencia Social) and with the financial support of the European Commission and the Government of Navarra. It is a model for individual, family and community care at the primary level, based on three pillars: the right to health, interculturality, and gender perspective.[256] The intercultural approach of MIS recognizes the existence of health concepts and practices that originate from cultural diversity and promotes interactive processes (it includes referral and cross-referral) between different knowledge and practices of care and treatment.[257]

In Mexico, the National Program for Action "Salud y Nutrición para los pueblos indígenas"[258] (Health and Nutrition for indigenous peoples) has the responsibility for promoting the strategy for good quality health services with cultural sensitivity and has been able to implement "Unidades de Salud Competentes"[259] (competent health units), which make health services culturally adequate (cultural infrastructure and equipment), incorporating medical staff with intercultural capacities, intercultural care of births and intercultural services including indigenous traditional medicine. The implementation of the National Health Program 2007-2012 has made it possible to promote integrated intercultural policies, increase the knowledge and use of traditional/ancestral medicines according to requirements of the population, as well as the application of mixed models for care that combine traditional/ancestral medicine with conventional medicine.

In Bolivia, successful experiences have been identified. These have been supported by the Ministry of Health and Sports (Ministerio de Salud y Deportes) and carried out by agencies for international cooperation together with public health institutions.[260] One case is from the Department of Potosí,[261] and its main components are the articulation of diverse health systems. Integrating

[255] Salud Intercultural: Crítica y problematización a partir del contexto boliviano, Susana Ramírez Hita, La Paz, ISEAT, 2011, pp. 31-38.

[256] Del Dicho al Hecho: Los avances un primer nivel de atención en salud incluyente, Medicus Mundi Navarra—Guatemala, Sacatepéquez, Guatemala, 2008, p.7: http://www.saludintegralincluyente.com/ftp/saludintegralincluyente/DOCU-MENTOS/PDF/antecedentes/guatemala/DEL%20DICHO%20AL%20HECHO.pdf.

[257] Ibid. p. 47.

[258] http://ssj.jalisco.gob.mx/sites/ssj.jalisco.gob.mx/files/programapueblosindigenasfinal_1.pdf.

[259] http://guerrero.gob.mx/programas/programa-de-salud-y-nutricion-para-los-pueblos-indigenas-prosani/.

[260] Vice-Ministry of Traditional Medicine and Inter-culturality: http://www.sns.gob.bo/index.php?ID=ViceMedicinaTradicional.

[261] Program designed and implemented by the Italian Development Cooperation and the Department of Posotí: "Programa de Apoyo al Desarrollo del Sistema Socio-Sanitario del Departamento de Potosí": http://www.utlamericas.org/2013/?page_id=645&lang=es.

diversity in hospitals includes having adequate spaces for both conventional medicine and traditional medicine, training human resources about interculturality incorporating graduate studies on intercultural health, and making the premises culturally adequate with construction and equipment that facilitates an intercultural approach, combined with community participation in health units and adequate housing for family.

In Peru, the Ministry of Health (MINSA), following the guidelines for sector policies for the period 2002-2012, incorporates the intercultural approach in management by respecting cultural diversity, strengthening traditional medicine, and complementing it with conventional medicine.[262] An example of this is caring for births in culturally adequate health units that provide maternal and neonatal care in the Department of Ayacucho. The most important results have been an increase in the number of people from indigenous peoples seeking birth care and a decrease in maternal deaths, mainly of indigenous women. This model counts on community participation, as well as the participation of regional governments, the support of civil society organizations, NGOs and agencies for international cooperation.[263]

In Chile, the Ministry of Health incorporates the intercultural approach by organizing and providing health services that are culturally appropriate (protocols, construction, equipment, pertinent health staff and information systems), strengthening the health system of indigenous peoples, and complementing conventional medicine with traditional medicine. An example of the way traditional medicine is strengthened is the program for intercultural health for the Mapuche (Hospital Makewe, Health Center Boroa Filulawen and Intercultural Hospital Nueva Imperial), which involves the indigenous world view, or *cosmovisión*, and knowledge of ancestral medicine in the processes for self care and promotion of individual, family and community health.[264]

In Ecuador, the Modelo de Atención Integral de Salud Familiar, Comunitario e Intercultural (MAIS-FCI, Integral Care Model for Family, Community and Intercultural Health) recognizes the management and care of intercultural health by implementing mechanisms to allow health promotion from the various world views and knowledge approaches, culturally appropriate health services, staff with intercultural competencies for improving sociocultural access, enhancing the wisdom of different peoples, and coordination between conventional health systems and the traditional and ancestral wisdom.[265]

In this sense, it is possible to highlight important experiences the Pan American Health Organization (PAHO) has recognized. One of them is "Improving the life conditions and the defence of the identity of the Andean population of Cotacachi-Ecuador",[266] which has the objective of reducing maternal mortality among indigenous women by strengthening the competencies of health staff

---

[262] UNFPA, Atención en Salud con Pertinencia Intercultural, Módulo Técnico - Teórico, Lima, 2011, p. 17: http://www.unfpa.org.pe/publicaciones/publicacionesperu/SSL-Atencion-en-Salud-Modulo-Tecnico.pdf.

[263] Ibid. p. 75.

[264] CCTCEM, Salud intercultural y la patrimonialización de la Salud Mapuche en Chile, 22, Junio de 2013: http://www.enelvolcan.com/jun2013/261-salud-intercultural-y-la-patrimonializacion-de-la-salud-mapuche-en-chile.

[265] Manueal del Modelo de Atención Integral del Sistema Nacional de Salud Familiar, Comunitario e Intercultural (MAIS-FCI), p. 40.

[266] PAHO/WHO honours efforts to improve gender equity in health in Latin America, 7 June 2013: http://www.paho.org/hq./index.php?option=com_content&view=article&id=8769%3Apahowho-honors-efforts-to-improve-gender-equity-in-health-in-latin-america&catid=740%3Anews-press-releases&Itemid=1926&lang=en.

in the area of intercultural and ancestral health assistance. With this purpose, a system of referral and cross-referral was established and a certificate was issued to midwives in order to link them to the maternal health services. This initiative has increased the number of institutional births by 45 per cent, and it has helped to bring down to zero the number of maternal deaths in the last four years. It has been carried on by Ecuador's Red Cross in cooperation with the Ministry of Public Health, the municipal government in Cotacachi and indigenous community organizations, and it has counted on the support of the Agencia Catalana de Cooperación al Desarrollo (España) and the United Nations Population Fund (UNFPA).

For most of the countries (Bolivia, Peru, Ecuador and Guatemala) the main effort is directed towards allowing culturally adequate births for women. This includes providing spaces in hospitals and health centres, allowing relatives and a midwife to assist women, and returning the placenta to the women, providing traditional herbal teas and foods pre- and post-delivery, and using infusions. While this has been an important achievement as a women's rights concern, there has been no formal evaluation process of this service. Currently, there is no evidence on whether the program improves the quality of service for indigenous women.

In this sense, the recommendations regarding management and care of health services are:

≡ to promote the implementation of the legal and programmatic norms at the level of organizational structure of the Ministries of Health and of the communities;

≡ to promote the complementary actions with equity between conventional medicine (biomedicine), traditional medicine (ancestral and popular medicine), and culturally pertinent alternative medicine;

≡ to strengthen the experiences regarding health services with intercultural pertinence and to seek their replication as validated and sustainable practices;

≡ to reinforce the formation of management, technical and sociopolitical capacities of human resources with an intercultural approach; and

≡ to promote from the territory the articulation and strengthening of ancestral medicine.

In addition, in relation to the management of the knowledge, it is necessary to promote plans for institutional and community education and communication with an intercultural approach and identity; to carry out research on the world view and ancestral knowledge and practices in the process addressing health, disease, care issues; and to systematize, publish and share experiences of intercultural health already validated, sustainable and replicable.

Human Resource Training in Health

The Pan American Health Organization (PAHO)[267] promotes "the integral training of human resources in health to respond to the epidemiologic profile and sociocultural context of the community by formal and non-formal education, applying the "learning by doing" paradigm through the exchange of experiences, and taking advantage of theoretical and technical capacities for the intercultural approach in health".

---

[267] Organización Panamericana de la Salud-Organización Mundial de la Salud (OPS-OMS) (1998). "Incorporación del Enfoque Intercultural de la Salud en la Formación y Desarrollo de Recursos Humanos". OPS-OMS, Washington (E.U.A.).

To promote health care with equity that is responsive to the needs of various ethnic groups, including prevention services, the training of human resources in health aims to improve the technical and human skills of the institution's staff. This training is envisaged to have positive effects including improved respect for patients, acknowledgement of their treatment experiences and recognition of the world views.

Among advances in this area a study within the framework of the Andean Plan for Intercultural Health of ORAS-CONHU shows advances in the "Intercultural approach in university training of human resources for health in the Andean region", which allows one to observe how, since the last decade, countries have had a significant increase in applying the inclusion of the intercultural approach in the training of health professionals. This document contributes to: 1) the analysis of curricula about interculturality in health of the current education opportunities offered by educational institutions in the subregion at the undergraduate and graduate levels; 2) the update of the existing inventory on offerings in education and training in interculturality in health; and 3) the elaboration of a proposal of academic contents regarding interculturality in health that should be incorporated in the education curricula for health professionals at the undergraduate and graduate levels.

In 2005, the important contribution made by the Indigenous Fund started the Program of Education and Training through the Universidad Indígena Intercultural (Intercultural Indigenous University). This program has promoted education with an intercultural perspective for indigenous and non-indigenous professionals in positions of leadership to take charge of the tasks of articulation, participation and decision-making affecting politics, economics and social organization of their respective societies. This program has a master's degree in Intercultural Health within the Universidad de la Región Autónoma de la Costa Caribe Nicaragüense, with the following academic objectives: "to contribute to the improvement of life conditions and the health status of indigenous peoples and Afro-descendant and ethnic communities, as well as to the generation of new paradigms based on an intercultural vision of health within the framework of compliance of the Millennium Development Goals and the objectives of the Second International Decade of the World's Indigenous Peoples" and "to promote space for dialogue and negotiations on current topics related to health in Latin American countries, such as: structural reforms, problems of social exclusion, inequity, institutional racism and geographical marginalization; as well as other integral problems a multi-ethnic and multicultural society faces".[268] In this scenario health and education face joint challenges in terms of contributing to the development of public policies for a multicultural country; undoubtedly universities are called upon to contribute in these transformation processes.

Inclusion of the ethnic variable in health registers

A clear process is required for the production of systematic, relevant and pertinent information for the design and monitoring of public health policies that ensure compliance with the individual and collective rights of indigenous peoples and other ethnic groups. Such a process is necessary for knowing the epidemiologic profiles of the various indigenous peoples in a constant and rigorous way, with the following objectives: a) to identify health inequalities and inequities between countries, between peoples, and among countries and peoples; b) to collect, process, analyse and

[268] Antecedentes, situación actual y perspectivas de la salud intercultural en América Latina, Víctor Manuel del Cid Lucero, URACCAN, Noviembre 2008, p. 8.
http://www.fondoindigena.org/apc-aa-files/74656d706c6174653132333435363738/FI___m30asi_1.pdf.

spread all the pertinent information for the development of peoples, as well as to elaborate a legal and normative framework, as well as public policies on health information, for making indigenous peoples visible in the statistical systems of health.[269]

Currently, most of the systems of information regarding health in the Latin American countries do not produce disaggregated data based on ethnic groups, peoples or communities. Because of that, it is not possible to formulate differentiated epidemiologic diagnosis or to determine their morbidity and mortality profiles.

Within a framework of rights, the invisibility of indigenous peoples and Afro-descendants in the information systems of health, and consequently, the lack of information about their health conditions, is by itself an expression of ethnic discrimination, which must be overcome in light of the recommendations provided by international bodies and the current demands from such groups.[270]

It is necessary to overcome the sort of planning that has the purpose of reaching homogeneous perceptions, which is sustained on the notion that there are no differences among the epidemiologic profiles of the various peoples. That planning considers that no specific policies focused on those various peoples will be required. Thus, as long as no epidemiological evidence is produced and health inequalities and inequities are not consistently and rigorously identified for countries, ethnic groups and regions in Latin America, concrete health policies and plans for these groups will be restricted to initiatives of a cultural character, limiting the transversal nature of the approach and mainly, impeding the elaboration of health objectives that are both demandable and apt for evaluation.[271]

As indicated by international bodies, the challenge of overcoming health inequities implies focusing actions specifically targeted to those peoples and communities whose rights have been violated most, to concentrate on the groups with the highest risks of preventable morbidity and premature mortality. Thus four specific steps are critical. First, to assess the damage; second, to identify their social determinants, both structural and immediate; third, to design interventions that are focused, efficient and pertinent; and fourth, to monitor advances in terms of equity and fulfillment of rights.[272]

A balance of the process of inclusion of the ethnic approach in the sources of data (see Table 1) allows us to verify that the main advancement has been the incorporation of variables for ethnic identification in the sources of social and demographic data, mainly in the population census. Such incorporation has fallen behind, on the other hand, in surveys and vital statistics, for which achievements are rather heterogeneous.

---

[269] "Elementos para la incorporación del enfoque étnico en los sistemas de información en salud (SIS). Guía básica", Ana María Oyarce, Malva-marina Pedrero, Octubre 2012.

[270] Permanent Forum on Indigenous Issues, Follow-up to the recommendations of the Permanent Forum: (a) Economic and Social Development Report of the international technical expert meeting on "Keeping track—indicators, mechanisms and data for assessing the implementation of indigenous peoples' rights", E/C.19/2011/11; Permanent Forum on Indigenous Issues, Implementation of recommendations on the six mandated areas of the Forum and on the Millennium Development Goals Indicators of well-being, poverty and sustainability relevant to indigenous peoples, E/C.19/2008/9; Permanent Forum Recommendations: 2nd Sesión, recommendation 68; 5th Session, recommendations 92, 101, 102, 110, 165, ; 6th Session, recommendation 57, 60, 61, 101, 119, 124, 127; 7th Session, recommendations 63, 78, 111; 11th Session, recommendation 21; 12th Session, recommendation 110.

[271] "Elementos para la incorporación del enfoque étnico en los sistemas de información en salud (SIS). Guía básica", Ana María Oyarce, Malva-marina Pedrero, Octubre 2012.

[272] "Mortalidad infantil y en la niñez de pueblos indígenas y afrodescendientes de América Latina: inequidades estructurales, patrones diversos y evidencia de derechos no cumplidos", CEPAL y CELADE, Naciones Unidas, Santiago de Chile 2010 http://www.eclac.cl/Celade/publica/bol62/BD6206.html.

Table 1: Latin America: Overview of the process of incorporation of variables for the ethnic identification in continuous data registration regarding health

Country	Policy/ Program	Ethnic Identification (need to footnote short forms)	Registers/registries	Variables
Argentina	Yes	Yes (Pi)	Case history Perinatal case history	Self-identification
Bolivia	Yes	Yes (Pi)	Case history model SNIi Perinatal case history Snis Certificate for the recently born	Self-affiliation Spoken language Mother tongue
Brazil	Yes	Yes (Pi Y A)	Unified public health system	Ethnic and racial self-identification
		Si (Pi)	Family registry Forms for those seeking medical treatment Personal records Registration log book Monthly consolidated report of activities Forms for referral and cross-referral Vaccination registers	Territorial
Colombia	Yes	Yes (Pi Y A)	Case history Certificate for the recently born Death certificate Other registers (violence)	Self-identification
Costa Rica	Yes	N/A		
Chile	Yes	Yes	Registry of discharges from hospital	Self-identification of peoples
			Medical treatment agenda (South Arau-canía SS)	Self-identification Last names

Ecuador	Yes	Yes (Pi Y A)	Form 001 for admittance and discharge MSP	Cultural Group
			Form 051 Perinatal case history MSP	Ethnic group
			Daily register of people seeking medical treatment MSP	Ethnic affiliation
			Live births/deaths statistical report INEC	Mother ethnic group Mother self-identification
			Foetal death INEC	Mother self-identification
			Death in general INEC	Ethnic self-identification
El Salvador	No	Yes	Family registry	
Guatemala	Yes	Yes (Pi)	Daily register of people seeking medical treatment in hospitals and centres	Self-affiliation to peoples Self affiliation to linguistic community Mother tongue
			Daily register of people seeking medical treatment and follow-up	Self-affiliation to peoples Self-affiliation to linguistic community Mother tongue
			Registry of births	Self-affiliation to peoples Self-affiliation to linguistic community Mother tongue
			Registry of deaths	Self-affiliation to peoples Self affiliation to linguistic community Mother tongue
Honduras	Yes	N/A	Registry of births	Self-affiliation to peoples
Mexico	Yes	Yes	Complete these blank boxes	

Nicaragua	Yes	Yes		
Panama	Yes	N/A		
Paraguay	Yes	Yes	Basic case history	Ethnic group
			Registry of discharges from hospital	Ethnic group
			Daily register of people seeking medical treatment	Ethnic group
Peru	No	Yes	HIS system Daily register of people seeking medical treatment	Ethnic group
Bolivarian Republic of Venezuela	Yes	Yes	Primary care Immunization Epidemiologic records Register of people seeking medical treatment	Ethnic self-identification Race Ethnic group Indigenous peoples

Source: Ana María Oyarce, 2012.

In the case of surveys, variables for ethnic identification have been incorporated in demographic and health surveys, as well as in home surveys in 11 countries. On the other hand, regarding vital statistics, there are only recent experiences of incorporating variables of this type in registries of birth and death in 8 countries in Latin America.[273]

Various advances are also observed in continuous health registers and registries. Based on their coverage, recent experiences of national scope are identified (such as in Bolivia, Brazil, Colombia, Chile, Ecuador, Guatemala and Paraguay), as well as other experiences focused on specific territories of concentrations of indigenous peoples (such as Argentina, El Salvador, Honduras, Mexico, Nicaragua, Peru and Bolivia).

Recommendations regarding the systems for registration are: 1) to incorporate health registers as well as registers of ethnically pertinent benefits; 2) to indicate an ethnic variable in health and epidemiologic data; 3) to include quantitative and qualitative indicators; 4) to ensure high-quality information by enhancing the processes for collection and consolidation of data; and 5) to guarantee that the information is used for analysis, as well as to have a decision-making process based on that information.

---

[273] "Elementos para la incorporación del enfoque étnico en los sistemas de información en salud (SIS). Guía básica", Ana María Oyarce, Malva-marina Pedrero, Octubre 2012.

Conclusion

International and national frameworks exist for the protection of the rights of indigenous peoples, which authorize signatory states to ensure the application of the right to health by policy actions that promote health with an intercultural approach, providing health services with intercultural management and care, and fostering citizen participation of indigenous peoples in the analysis and decision-making on health.

However, despite the existence of international and national legal norms for the protection of indigenous peoples, health inequalities persist, which are characterized by 1) the prevalence of preventable diseases and illnesses easily solvable when addressed in a timely way; 2) barriers to both geographic and sociocultural access to high-quality and culturally relevant health services; 3) scant recognition of the wisdom and practices of the traditional medicines of indigenous peoples in the process health, disease, care and healing.

Health experiences for indigenous peoples have focused on culturally adequate birth care (Bolivia, Peru, Ecuador, Guatemala and Mexico), and only in limited cases on the strengthening of traditional/ancestral medicine as a part of the health services (Mexico, Chile). Regarding the strengthening of ancestral/traditional medicine, it is necessary to discuss the pertinence of being a part of health services (Mexico and Chile) and/or if they should rather be preserved and strengthened within the indigenous peoples' territories.

The epidemiological profiles do not incorporate the sociocultural profile, which includes ethnocultural diseases or diseases with a cultural affiliation, as part of the analysis of the health situation of indigenous peoples for policy decision making and action regarding health.

Plans for training health human resources with an intercultural approach are still in a preliminary stage in Latin America, which has impacts with regard to 1) development of an intercultural relation, dialogue and negotiations between health providers and those seeking their services; 2) the intercultural management and care are not provided according to the sociocultural needs in health; and 3) the articulation and complementary action between ancestral health knowledge and conventional medicine.

Some of the important strategies that need to be considered include:

≡ Apply mechanisms and instruments to implement national and international legal frameworks for compliance with the health rights of indigenous peoples.

≡ Recognize, strengthen and protect the ancestral health wisdom and practices of indigenous peoples, and to articulate them within the national health systems.

≡ Implement spaces for intercultural dialogue for the exchange of wisdom and practices, as well as their mutual enrichment from the various health and health care approaches.

≡ Strengthen, consolidate and replicate successful and validated intercultural health experiences, both at the national and international levels, acknowledging their local sociocultural contexts.

≡ Institutionalize in the national health systems and in the curriculum plans of the institutions educating human resources in health, both the approach to and the concept of intercultural health.

≡ Organize conferences, seminars and forums to allow for the understanding of the situation of health among indigenous peoples and the holistic process of connecting health, disease, care and healing from the perspective of different world views to strengthen wisdom about traditional medicine and to define mechanisms for the interaction and complementary nature of traditional medicine and conventional medicine.

≡ Support processes of community legitimization for traditional/ancestral physicians and to develop registers for indigenous therapists at the Ministry of Health, in coordination with indigenous organizations and indigenous peoples in each country.

≡ Establish an intercultural epidemiological profile incorporating traditional diseases and health determinants for indigenous peoples.

≡ Diasggregate data from databases to include analysis using the indigenous identifiers and ethnic variables in health registers for national information systems, to produce regular reports of the health situation according to the epidemiological profile of indigenous peoples and indicators for intercultural health management and care, information on the services provided by traditional/ancestral physicians and traditional midwives as part of the process of integral health information and the interaction of traditional/ancestral medicine, conventional medicine and other types of medicine existent in the territory.

≡ Strengthen by specific and targeted capacity building measures the participation of indigenous peoples in the ongoing analyses of their health status, intercultural health management and care, articulation and harmonization of traditional/ancestral medicine with alternative medicine, conventional medicine and health promotion.

≡ Promote research and systematic organization of ancestral wisdom and practices in health and traditional/ancestral medicine.

Bibliography

Arriagada, Irma, "Políticas y programas de salud en América Latina. Problemas y Propuestas", CEPAL, N.U. http://www.eclac.org/publicaciones/xml/7/23777/sps114_lcl2450.pdf.

Banco Interamericano de Desarrollo; "Salud de la mujer indígena; Intervenciones para reducir la muerte materna".

http://www.iadb.org/es/publicaciones/detalle,7101.html?id+13108#.Umrz8XCshNc.

Campos, Roberto, "Salud e Interculturalidad en América Latina: Avances y Estancamientos"; http://www.cirsociales.uady.mx/pdf/eventos/roberto-campos.pdf.

CELADE, "Los pueblos indígenas y la pobreza en América Latina: un análisis empírico", Estudios socio demográficos en pueblos indígenas, Serie E, No. 40 (LC/DEM/G.146), Santiago de Chile, División de Población, Centro Latinoamericano y Caribeño de Demografía (CELADE).

CELADE-CEPAL, "Mortalidad infantil y en la niñez de pueblos indígenas y afro descendientes de América Latina: inequidades estructurales, patrones diversos y evidencia de derechos no cumplidos". http://www.eclac.cl/publicaciones/xml/1/41581/LCW.348Oct_2010.pdf.

CEPAL/CELADE, "La identificación de poblaciones indígenas en los censos de América Latina", in: América Latina: aspectos conceptuales de los censos del 2000, CEPAL/CELADE, Santiago de Chile.

CEPAL/CELADE", Mortalidad infantil y en la niñez de pueblos indígenas y afro descendientes de América Latina: inequidades estructurales, patrones diversos y evidencia de derechos no cumplidos", CEPAL and CELADE, Naciones Unidas, Santiago de Chile 2010 http://www.eclac.cl/Celade/publica/bol62/BD6206.html.

Cevallos, Rodrigo, "Prestación de servicios de salud en zonas con pueblos indígenas", http://www2.paho.org/hq/dmdocuments/2009/servicios%20salud%20zonas%20indigenas.pdf.

Convention on the Rights of the Child http://www.ohchr.org/en/professionalinterest/pages/crc.aspx.

Convention on the Elimination of all Forms of Discrimination against Women http://www.ohchr.org/Documents/ProfessionalInterest/cedaw.pdf.

Fifth Technical Meeting of the Sponsoring Committee for Safe Maternity in Mexico [5ª Reunión Técnica del Comité Promotor por una Maternidad Segura en México] https://www.google.com.ec/url?sa=t&rct=j&q=&esrc=s&source=web&cd=2&cad=rja&ved=0C-DUQFjAB&url=http%3A%2F%2Fmaternidadsinriesgos.org.mx%2Freuniones%2F5taReunionTecnica%2F5a_Reunion_Tecnica_CP_Maternidad_Segura_CARE_Elena_Esquiche.ppt&ei=aORJUuzDNKbl4AONm4HgBw&usg=AFQjCNFMQL_j2d9x3uWjNzLvZ5q77mvx-6A&sig2=BkMt_aYkdE6QcE7JE3cwMA&bvm=bv.53217764,d.dmg.

Indigenous Peoples in Latin America - a general overview, International Work group for Indigenous Affairs http://www.iwgia.org/regions/latin-america/indigenous-peoples-in-latin-america.

International Covenant on Economic, Social and Cultural Rights http://www.ohchr.org/EN/ProfessionalInterest/Pages/CESCR.aspx.

ISAGS, Health Systems in South America: challenges to the universality, integrality and equity, [Sistemas de Salud en Suramérica: desafíos para la universalidad, integralidad y la equidad], 2012.

Mescco, Jahve, Perú: "Hacia una salud intercultural efectiva para los pueblos indígenas, http://caio.uy.over-blog.com/article-peru-hacia-una-salud-intercultural-efectiva-para-los-pueblos-indigenas-71294354.html.

Ministerio de Salud Pública del Ecuador", Parto en libre posición con pertinencia Intercultural como política del Ministerio de Salud Pública del Ecuador, 2013".

Ministerio de Salud Pública del Ecuador",Política Pública de Salud Intercultural", 2013.

Minorities Rights Group International State of the World's Minorities and Indigenous Peoples 2012.

 "Mujer indígena: Salud y derechos", Participatory Diagnosis with CIDOB, CNAMIB, CNMCIOB-BS, Executive Report from the Workshop, Bolivia 2008.

Montenegro, Raul and Stephens, Carolyn "Indigenous health in Latin America and the Caribbean" www.thelancet.com, Vol 367, June 3, 2006.

Organización Panamericana de la Salud, "Derechos Humanos y Salud: Pueblos Indígenas" http://www.paho.org/hq/dmdocuments/2009/tool%20box%2010069_pueblos.pdf.

Oyarce, Ana María, Pedrero Malva-marina, "Elementos para la incorporación del enfoque étnico en los sistemas de información en salud (SIS). Guía básica", Octubre 2012.

Pan American Health Organization (PAHO) "Human Rights and Health: Indigenous Peoples" 2008.

PAHO/WHO honors efforts to improve gender equity in health in Latin America, 7 June 2013: http://www.paho.org/hq./index.php?option=com_content&view=article&id=8769%3Apahow ho-honors-efforts-to-improve-gender-equity-in-health-in-latin-america&catid=740%3Anews-press-releases&Itemid=1926&lang=en.

Permanent Forum on Indigenous Issues, Follow-up to the recommendations of the Permanent Forum: (a) Economic and Social Development Report of the international technical expert meeting on "Keeping track—indicators, mechanisms and data for assessing the implementation of indigenous peoples' rights", E/C.19/2011/11.

Ruiz, Bocos, "Situación de las Mujeres en los Pueblos Indígenas de América Latina. Obstáculos y Retos".

"Sistematización de servicios de salud con pertinencia cultural", Guatemala, 2010, pág. 23 http://unfpa.org/webdav/site/lac/shared/DOCUMENTS/2011/Peru%202011%20AECID/Siste-matizaci%C3%B3n%20de%20Servicios%20de%20Salud%20con%20Pertinencia%20Cultural.%20 Guatemala%202010.pdf.

Social Panorama of Latin America, 2012 [Panorama Social de América Latina 2012] ECLA, Santiago de Chile, 2012.

Terra, Consuelo, "El aporte del parto aimara", http://www.paula.cl/tendencia/el-aporte-del-parto-aymara/.

The Universal Declaration of Human Rights http://www.un.or/en/documents/udhr/.

U.N. Committee on the Elimination of Racial Discrimination (CERD), General Recommendation XXIII: Indigenous Peoples, UN Doc. CERD/C/51/misc 13/Rev 4, at 3 (1997) [hereinafter CERD General Recommendation on Indigenous Peoples].

Vaca, Karina, "Sistematización de la experiencia en salud de Médicos del Mundo en el Hospital de Patacamaya", http://www.saludintegralincluyente.com/ftp/saludintegralincluyente/DOCUMENTOS/PDF/ sistematizacion/Sistematizacion%20Patacamaya%20Bolivia.pdf.

Internet sites

http://celade.cepal.org/redatam/PRYESP/SISPPI.

http://www.inei.gob.pe/biblioineipub/bancopub/Est/Lib0001/capit003.htm.

http://websie.eclac.cl/sisgen/ConsultaIntegrada.asp?idAplicacion=14.

http://celade.cepal.org/redatam/PRYESP/SISPPI/.

http://www.opsecu.org/jspui/bitstream/123456789/130/1/130.pdf.

http://www.ilo.org/indigenous/Activitiesbyregion/LatinAmerica/lang--en/index.htm.

Millennium Summit Declaration http://www.un.org/millennium/declaration/ares552e.htm.

http://ssj.jalisco.gob.mx/sites/ssj.jalisco.gob.mx/files/programapueblosindigenasfinal_1.pdf.

http://guerrero.gob.mx/programas/programa-de-salud-y-nutricion-para-los-pueblos-indigenas-prosani/.

Special documents

"Antecedentes, situación actual y perspectivas de la salud intercultural en América Latina". Universidad Indígena Intercultural-URACCAN, 2008.

"Atención de salud con pertinencia intercultural: modulo técnico y teórico". UNFPA. 2010.

"Competencias interculturales para el personal de salud", Secretaría de Salud de México, 2009.

"Del dicho al hecho...los avances de un primer nivel de atención en salud incluyente". Comisión Europea, Consorcio MMN-CORDAID, 2008.

"Desarrollo de un Sistema de Información Integral de Salud Intercultural". Rakin Mongen Filu Lawen Puche. CEPAL, 2010.

"Determinantes sociales de la salud de los pueblos indígenas: informe del encuentro regional". OPS, 2009.

"El enfoque intercultural: herramienta para apoyar la calidad de los servicios de salud". Secretaría de Salud de México, 2003.

International Labor Organization Convention No. 169, 1989 [Convenio No. 169 de la Organización internacional del Trabajo. OIT, 1989], http://www.ilo.org/indigenous/Conventions/no169/lang--en/index.htm.

"Los pueblos indígenas y la pobreza en América Latina: un análisis empírico", Estudios socio demográficos en pueblos indígenas, Serie E, No. 40 (LC/DEM/G.146), Santiago de Chile, División de Población, Centro Latinoamericano y Caribeño de Demografía (CELADE).

"Mortalidad infantil y en la niñez de pueblos indígenas y afrodescendientes de América Latina: inequidades estructurales, patrones diversos y evidencia de derechos no cumplidos". CELADE-CEPAL, Santiago de Chile 2010.

"Prestación de servicios de salud en zonas con pueblos indígenas: recomendaciones para un sistema de licenciamiento y acreditación de servicios interculturales de salud en el marco de la renovación de la Atención Primaria de Salud". OPS, 2009.

"Pueblos indígenas de América Latina: políticas y programas de salud, ¿cuánto y cómo se ha avanzado?: informe de seminario taller". CELADE, 2008.

"Salud de los pueblos indígenas de las Américas: evaluación de los logros en salud en el marco del decenio internacional de los pueblos indígenas del mundo". OPS 2008.

"Salud materno infantil de los pueblos indígenas y afrodescendientes de América Latina: una relectura desde el enfoque de derechos". CEPAL, 2010.

"Segunda reunión de la Sub-red de Salud Intercultural: informe de la reunión". UII-OPS-Fondo Indígena, 2009.

"Sistematización experiencia en salud proyecto: Salud familiar comunitaria con interculturalidad y fortalecimiento de los servicios de salud en 12 municipios de la Mancomunidad de Municipios de la Cuenca del Río Caine y Chimore, Departamentos de Potosí, Cochabamba y Chuquisaca". Comisión Europea, Médicos del Mundo Navarra, 2011.

"Transformando el Sistema Público de Salud desde el Primer Nivel de Atención". Medicus Mundi Navarra, Guatemala, 2012.

CHAPTER FIVE

Access to Health Services by Indigenous Peoples in North America

Chapter Five

Access to Health Services by Indigenous Peoples in North America

Introduction

This chapter on North America applies to the United States of America and Canada as per the Permanent Forum's seven sociocultural regions which gives broad representation to the world's indigenous peoples. In the United States, indigenous peoples are collectively known as Native Americans, which include American Indians and Alaska Natives as well as the people indigenous to Hawaii, or Native Hawaiians.[274] In Canada, the collective term aboriginal peoples refers to three groups namely, First Nations, Métis and Inuit defined by section 35 (2) of the Canadian Constitution Act 1982.

Many indigenous peoples are geographically dispersed across North America. Some live on their traditional territories or other Native-controlled land areas while others live in urban and rural areas beyond the boundaries of their indigenous controlled regions. Indigenous peoples living in urban areas maintain often close ties to their communities and the tribes with which they are affiliated, as well as develop bonds with other indigenous peoples in their urban settings. According to the 2006 census in Canada more than 50 per cent of indigenous peoples[275] live in urban areas. According to the Office of Minority Health, 60 per cent of the indigenous peoples in the USA[276] now live in cities.

Indigenous peoples living in border areas face unique challenges when traditional territories cross national boundaries including tribes living along the United States-Mexico border, the United States-Canadian border, Alaska Natives living along the borders of Eastern Russia and Canada. Heightened border security measures implemented in recent years have increasingly made cross-border contact between members of the same tribes very difficult.[277]

United States of America

The United States presently recognizes and maintains what it refers to as government-to-government relations with approximately 566 American Indian and Alaskan native tribes and villages, around 230 of these being Alaskan native groups. Most of the tribes and villages determine

---

[274] The health issues of Native Hawaiians are covered in the chapter on the Pacific in this report.

[275] http://www.aadnc-aandc.gc.ca/eng/1100100014265/1369225120949.

[276] http://minorityhealth.hhs.gov/templates/browse.aspx?lvl=2&lvlID=52.

[277] James Anaya Report of the Special Rapporteur on the rights of indigenous peoples, The situation of indigenous peoples in the United States of America A/HRC/21/47/Add.1 30 August 2012 p. 6.

their own membership. Federally recognized tribes have reservations or other lands that have been left or set aside for them, over which they exercise their own powers of self-government.[278]

Many other groups in the United States that identify as indigenous peoples have not been federally recognized, although some of these have achieved recognition at the state level.[279] Today, according to the United States census, people who identify as Native American represent approximately 1.7 per cent of the overall population of the United States, with 5.2 million persons identifying as American Indian or Alaska Native.[280] It should be noted that this number significantly exceeds the number of those who are enrolled or registered members of federally recognized indigenous groups.

Canada

Membership and identification as an indigenous person in Canada is complex. Given limited space here, this chapter will briefly describe an overview of the membership categories. In the context of health services these categories determine access by government jurisdiction to a range of health services and program eligibility in areas including health and beyond health.

According to Statistic Canada's National Household Survey (NHS) in 2011, the total number of people who self-identified as indigenous peoples in Canada was 1.4 million, representing 4.3 per cent of the total Canadian population of 30 million inhabitants.[281] First Nations represent 60.8 per cent of the total aboriginal population and 2.6 per cent of the total Canadian population. Of the aboriginal population, 33 per cent are Métis and 4 per cent are Inuit. The greatest numbers of First Nations peoples live in Ontario and the western provinces including British Columbia, Alberta, Sasketchewan and Manitoba. The regions with the largest proportion of indigenous peoples in the total population are the Nunavut, the Northwest Territories, the Yukon Territory and the Provinces of Manitoba and Saskatchewan.

First Nations

Today, there are more than 600 federally recognized First Nations, 2,787 First Nation reserves (land set apart and designated as a reserve for the use and occupancy of an Indian group or band) across the country.[282] A significant number of indigenous peoples are not registered Indians under the Federal Government's 1876 Indian Act, which defines who is considered a "status Indian" or not, and the law stipulates specific criteria which must be met to determine whether an individual is eligible to receive a range of services and benefit from a range of programmes offered by federal and provincial government agencies.[283]

---

[278] James Anaya Report of the Special Rapporteur on the rights of indigenous peoples, The situation of indigenous peoples in the United States of America A/HRC/21/47/Add.1 30 August 2012 p. 5.

[279] James Anaya Report of the Special Rapporteur on the rights of indigenous peoples, The situation of indigenous peoples in the United States of America A/HRC/21/47/Add.1 30 August 2012 p. 5.

[280] U.S. Census Bureau, the American Indian and Alaska Native Population: 2012, pp. 1-3.

[281] "An Overview of Aboriginal Health in Canada", National Collaborating Centre for Aboriginal Health p. 1.

[282] Aboriginal Peoples in Canada in 2006: Inuit, Métis and First Nations, p. 9.

[283] "An Overview of Aboriginal Health in Canada", National Collaborating Centre for Aboriginal Health p. 1.

In 2011, some 637,660 First Nations people were reported as Registered Indians, representing 74.9 per cent of all First Nations peoples, the remainder were non-status First Nations peoples who identify with a specific First Nations but do not meet the Indian Act membership criteria and they represent one-quarter of First Nations people (213,900), 15.3 per cent of the total aboriginal population and less than 1 per cent of the total Canadian population.[284] Registered Indians are estimated to be 45.5 per cent of the total aboriginal population and 1.9 per cent of the total Canadian population. Due to an amendment of the Indian Act in 1985, a large number of indigenous peoples who had lost their status under the Act's old provisions were able to regain status and more recently Bill C-3 changed membership criteria of the Indian Act (2011) to address discrimination against First Nations women. A minority of status Indians in Canada now live on reserves and settlements, with greater than 50 per cent now living off-reserve, with most residing in urban metropolitan cities. As mentioned, residency is fluid because people live off reserve to find employment however it does not mean they have relinquished their First Nations community membership or tribal membership status.

Inuit

In 2011, 59,445 people identified as Inuit. They represented 4.2 per cent of the total aboriginal population and 0.2 per cent of the total Canadian population.[285] The Inuit of Canada's Arctic regions are closely related to the Inuit of Greenland, Alaska and Russia. For many centuries, outsiders have called Inuit "Eskimos". This term is no longer considered acceptable. The Inuit prefer the name by which they have always known themselves, Inuit, which means "the people" in their language, Inuktitut.[286] The Inuit inhabit vast areas of Nunavut, Yukon and the Northwest Territories, Nunavik in northern Quebec and Labrador. Together these regions comprise just less that 40 per cent of Canada. Population density is extremely low, and the total population of this region is less that 50 per cent indigenous. Inuit people also live in urban Canadian cities and towns.

Métis

The 1982 constitutional amendments included the Métis peoples as one of the three indigenous groups of Canada. The Métis are the descendents of French-Canadian fur traders and native women, mainly Cree, Ojibwa, or Saulteaux women. In 2011, 451,795 people identified as Métis. They represented 32.3 per cent of the total aboriginal population and 1.4 per cent of the total Canadian population. Although the Métis represented just 1.4 per cent of the total population of Canada, they accounted for larger shares of the population in the West. Métis represented 8 per cent of the total population of the Northwest Territories, 6.7 per cent of Manitoba's population and 5.2 per cent of Saskatchewan's population. Among census metropolitan areas, Winnipeg had the highest population of Métis, 46,325 people, or 6.5 per cent of its total population. It was followed by Edmonton with 31,780, Vancouver with 18,485 and Calgary with 17,040. In addition, 11,520 Métis lived in Saskatoon, and 9,980 resided in Toronto.[287]

---

[284] Aboriginal Peoples in Canada: First Nations People, Métis and Inuit (2011).

[285] Aboriginal People in Canada: First Nations People, Métis and Inuit (2011).

[286] http://www.arcticinuksuk.com/inuit-culture.html.

[287] Aboriginal Peoples in Canada: First Nations People, Métis and Inuit (2011).

Historically, distinct Métis communities developed along the routes of the fur trade and across the Canadian Northwest within the Métis Nation Homeland. As stated above, this Homeland includes the three Prairie Provinces (Manitoba, Saskatchewan, Alberta), as well as, parts of Ontario, British Columbia, the Northwest Territories and the Northern United States. Today, many of these historic Métis communities continue to exist along rivers and lakes where forts and posts were hubs of fur trade activity from Ontario westward. The Métis have their own language and unique culture, and large numbers of Métis citizens now live in urban centres within the Métis Nation Homeland.

International frameworks

Health is a fundamental human right. Every human being is entitled to the enjoyment of the highest attainable standard of health conducive to living a life in dignity. It was first articulated in the 1946 Constitution of the World Health Organization (WHO), whose preamble defines health as "a state of complete physical, mental and social well-being and not merely the absence of disease or infirmity".[288] The preamble further states, "the enjoyment of the highest attainable standard of health is one of the fundamental rights of every human being without distinction of race, religion, political belief, economic or social condition".[289] The 1948 Universal Declaration of Human Rights also mentions health as part of the right to an adequate standard of living (art. 25). The right to health is also recognized as a human right in the 1966 International Covenant on Economic, Social and Cultural Rights (art. 10 and 12).[290] The Convention on the Elimination of All Forms of Discrimination against Women (1979) and the Convention on the Rights of the Child (1989) have traditionally provided the legal framework for the foundation of international human rights, including the right to health. These instruments include provisions for the right to life and for the "right of everyone to enjoy the highest attainable standard of physical and mental health",[291] with some specifically recognising the rights of individuals from marginalized populations, including indigenous peoples as follows.

ILO Convention No. 169

Article 3 of ILO Convention 169 (1991), states that indigenous peoples "must fully enjoy fundamental human rights without obstacles or discrimination".[292] Article 2 gives governments responsibility for ensuring that all indigenous peoples have the same rights and opportunities as non-indigenous peoples. Article 7 specifically refers to the obligation that states parties have with regard to the improvement of the conditions of life, work, levels of health and education as a matter of priority in national plans. Article 25 enshrines the obligations of states parties with regard to the right to social security and health which in summary include: availability of health services to indigenous peoples; implementation of community-based services which shall take into account traditional preventive care and healing practices and medicines; and the training of local community health workers.

---

[288] Constitution of the World Health Organization http://www.who.int/governance/eb/who_constitution_en.pdf.

[289] Constitution of the World Health Organization http://www.who.int/governance/eb/who_constitution_en.pdf.

[290] E/C.12/2000/4, 11 August 2000.

[291] International Covenant on Economic, Social, and Cultural Rights, Article 12.1.

[292] http://www.ilo.org/dyn/normlex/en/f?p=NORMLEXPUB:12100:0::NO::P12100_ILO_CODE:C169#A3.

United Nations Declaration on the Rights of Indigenous Peoples (2007)

The right to health is also recognized specifically for indigenous peoples in the United Nations Declaration on the Rights of Indigenous Peoples (2007). The United Nations Declaration on the Rights of Indigenous Peoples articulates several health rights and incorporates the concept of collective rights. It also includes government obligations to provide indigenous peoples' access to health services and to respect indigenous health systems. In particular Articles 23 and 24 state that indigenous peoples have the right to the enjoyment of the highest standard of physical and mental health and that indigenous peoples have the right to be actively involved in developing and determining health programmes affecting them and to administer such programmes through their own institutions.[293] Further, indigenous peoples have the right to their traditional medicines and to maintain their health practices, including the conservation of their vital medicinal plants, animals and minerals. Indigenous individuals also have the right to access, without any discrimination, to all social and health services.[294] In accordance with Article 29, "States shall also take effective measures to ensure, as needed, that programmes for monitoring, maintaining and restoring the health of indigenous peoples, as developed and implemented by the peoples affected by such materials, are duly implemented".[295]

National Frameworks

It is a noted irony that indigenous peoples living in the richest countries of United States and Canada are among their poorest citizens. In terms of addressing indigenous peoples' health situation there are structural issues that require consideration because in many instances, governments worldwide are willing to address issues of inequality for indigenous peoples but at the same time are unwilling to address issues of difference. Many governments seek to end any distinct political or legal status of indigenous peoples and many are reluctant to directly address certain indigenous agendas, which impact the health of indigenous peoples.[296]

As mentioned, at the national level, the federal government in both the United States and Canada have responsibility for indigenous health for those who meet the national registration criteria. Health services were originally provided for federally recognized indigenous tribes living on reservations. However, there is jurisdictional ambiguity and a lack of clarity on the respective roles and responsibilities between the federal, provincial, territorial and state government vis-à-vis health and social services to indigenous peoples in North America.

United States of America

In the United States, the Indian Health Service (IHS) provides services to Members of 566 federally recognized American Indian and Alaska Native Tribes and their descendants. The IHS is an agency within the federal Department Health and Human Services. The provision of health services

[293] United Nations Declaration on the Rights of Indigenous Peoples, Article 23.

[294] United Nations Declaration on the Rights of Indigenous Peoples, Article 24.1.

[295] United Nations Declaration on the Rights of Indigenous Peoples, Article 29.3.

[296] Stephen Cornell "Indigenous peoples, poverty and self-determination in Australia, New Zealand, Canada and the United States" in Indigenous Peoples and Poverty: An International Perspective eds. Eversole, McNeish and Cimadore (2005) pp. 199, 203.

to members of federally recognized tribes grew out of the special government-to-government relationship between the federal government and Indian tribes. This relationship, established in 1787, is based on Article I, Section 8 of the Constitution, and has been given form and substance by numerous treaties, laws, Supreme Court decisions, and Executive Orders. The IHS operates a comprehensive health service delivery system for approximately 2 million American Indians and Alaska Natives. The majority of those who receive IHS services live mainly on reservations and in rural communities in 36 states, mostly in the western United States and Alaska.[297]

Since 1972, the IHS has embarked upon a series of initiatives to fund health-related activities in off-reservation settings, which will make health care services accessible to urban Native Americans including Indians and Alaska Natives. Currently, the IHS funds 33 urban Indian health organizations, which operate at sites located in cites throughout the United States. Approximately 600,000 American Indians and Alaska Natives are eligible to utilize this program. The 33 programs administer medical services, dental services, community services, alcohol and drug abuse prevention, education and treatment, AIDS and sexually transmitted disease education and prevention services, mental health services, nutrition education and counselling services, pharmacy services, health education, optometry services, social services, and home health care.[298]

Canada

In Canada, the federal government established the Health Canada's role in First Nations and Inuit health in 1945, when Indian health services were transferred from Indian Affairs to Health Canada. By 1962, Health Canada was providing direct health services to First Nations people on reserve and to Inuit communities in the north. By the mid 1980s, work began to have First Nations and Inuit communities control the administration of community health services by implementing the health transfer policy. The First Nations and Inuit Health Branch (FNIHB) within the Department of Health Canada has headquarters in Ottawa, Ontario, the capital city of Canada and regional offices in every province and supports the delivery of public health and health promotion services on reserve and in Inuit communities. It also provides drug, dental and ancillary health services to First Nations and Inuit people regardless of residence. Within FNIHB are the community programme directorate, primary health care and public health directorate, non-insured health benefits directorate, the office of nursing services, and the office of community medicine, business planning and management directorate, strategic policy, planning and analysis directorate and the chief advisor of First Nations and Inuit relations. The Health Transfer Policy acknowledges the special relationship between First Nations and the federal government but does not recognize health as an aboriginal treaty right. While it transfers a range of services to First Nations and Inuit communities, it retains the major decision-making powers. For example, First Nations proposals for community health plans must be approved by the federal government. Further, the Health Transfer Policy does not recognize the role of traditional healers, nor does it fund the training of First Nations health care professionals.[299] However, First Nations can fund education assistance to members from the limited education and training resources available to the community.

---

[297] http://www.ihs.gov/aboutihs/.

[298] http://minorityhealth.hhs.gov/templates/browse.aspx?lvl=2&lvlID=52.

[299] Naomi Adelson, "The embodiment of Inequality: Health Disparities in Aboriginal Canada", Canadian Journal of Public Health, Vol. 96 (2005), p. 558.

First Nations, Inuit and Métis living in urban centres often find themselves excluded from many of the benefits and services that arise from the FNIHB. Indigenous peoples moving into or living in urban areas are faced with having to negotiate a range of health care provisions as they exit their community health networks and enter the provincially funded public health care system. While there are various successful, culturally appropriate urban initiatives across Canada, there remains a problem of inadequate assessment of health care needs and often there are very few resources to offer appropriate services to the urban, and particularly the poor, women, men and children. Aboriginal women continue to search for services that are gender-sensitive, culturally appropriate and at the same time inclusive of their children.[300] For the northern territories of Nunavut, the Northwest Territories and the Yukon health services funding are allocated by the territorial governments.

Analysis of the Health Situation for Indigenous Peoples in USA and Canada

Overview

The appropriation and displacement of indigenous peoples from their lands and their subsequent marginalization from the rest of society is a historical reality with continuing repercussions today in the United States and Canada.[301] Indigenous peoples current social inequalities results from a combination of socioeconomic deficits that are ongoing such as colonization, globalization, and migration, loss of language and culture and disconnection from land. The severance of ties to their lands, can affect indigenous peoples' associated cultural practices and participation in traditional economies, all of which are essential for health and well-being.[302]

One of the most devastating consequences of colonialism in both the United States and Canada which are still felt today, was the forced assimilation policy involving the systematic removal of indigenous children from their families to place them in government or church-run residential or boarding schools, with the objective of expunging their indigenous identities. The Indian boarding or residential school policy which began in the 1880s continued well into the mid-1900s. That emotional, physical and sexual abuse occurred in boarding schools, as well as punishment for speaking their languages and practicing their cultures has been well documented, has been acknowledged and has tarnished the human rights record of Canada and the United States. The effects of boarding schools on generations of indigenous peoples, including generations still living and future generations, cuts deep in indigenous communities throughout the United States and Canada, where many believe are the root cause of pervasive social problems such as alcoholism and sexual abuse and the widespread loss of indigenous languages.[303] Negative memories of this institutionalization are thought to have created a social climate of distrust of other government-funded institutions such as hospitals and clinics, resulting in avoidance until an illness is advanced.

---

[300] Cecilia Benoit, Dena Carroll, Munaza Chaudhry "In search of a Healing Place: Aboriginal women in Vancouver's Downtown Eastside" Social Science & Medicine 56 (2003) 821-833, p. 831.

[301] Carolyn Stephens, John Porter, Clive Nettleton, Ruth Willis " Disappearing, displaced and undervalued: a call to action for indigenous health worldwide", www.thelancet.com, Vol 367, June 17, 2006, p. 2023.

[302] Malcolm King, Alexandra Smith, Michael Gracey " Indigenous Health part 2: the underlying causes of the health gap", www.thelancet.com, Vol 374, July 4, 2009, p. 76.

[303] James Anaya Report of the Special Rapporteur on the rights of indigenous peoples, The situation of indigenous peoples in the United States of America A/HRC/21/47/Add.1 30 August 2012 p. 5.

Urbanization is part of the continuing transformation of indigenous peoples' culture; however, it can also affect residential instability, which is also marked by frequent migration back and forth from cities and towns to reserves, as well as high mobility within the cities and towns. This instability affects indigenous peoples in a number of ways especially where there is high proportion of female lone-parent families with low incomes. These families often face many challenges in their efforts to deal with urban living. Other marginalized indigenous groups also suffer poor health and social exclusion and/or exploitation such as women, elders, youth, two-spirited people,[304] and persons with disabilities. The push factors that determine the patterns of rural to urban migration include unemployment, poor social and economic conditions, boredom and low quality of life, overcrowding due to scarcity of housing, health facilities and educational opportunities.

The relationship between HIV/AIDS and indigenous peoples has not received due international attention despite the fact that indigenous peoples have particular vulnerabilities to acquiring HIV/AIDS. Many indigenous cultures have traditionally understood sexuality as part of creation, connected to ancestry and cultural traditions and the cycle of life. In some indigenous cultures, sexual diversity was accepted and celebrated. Unfortunately, stigma and discrimination exists in many indigenous communities against lesbians, gay, bisexual and transgender or two-spirited persons which makes it hard for them to access services and support programmes. Likewise, women and girls can also be vulnerable to HIV infection, particularly in situations of racialized and sexual violence or where their daily survival strategies include trading unsafe sex for money, food, shelter or drugs and where needle sharing occurs. The rate of HIV infection among indigenous youth is also increasing.[305]

In addition to concerns such as land loss, and control over resources there are other emerging health issues. The Arctic regions of the United States (Alaska) and Canada (Northern Canada) have the highest levels of persistent organic pollutants (POPs) on earth. POPs are artificially created organic compounds that resist natural breakdown and can persist for many years. The toxic health-threatening substances are transported over long distances by rivers, oceans and air currents from warmer parts of the world to the colder polar regions. They also accumulate in the fatty tissue of seals and whales which traditionally play a key role in Arctic indigenous peoples' diet and can be passed directly to infants through maternal breast milk, causing disruption of the hormone and immune systems and affecting postnatal growth.[306]

United States

The indigenous peoples of the United States are diverse and geographically dispersed, and the large majority are economically disadvantaged. Disease patterns among American Indians and Alaska Natives are strongly associated with the adverse consequences of poverty, limited access to health services, and cultural dislocation. Inadequate education, high rates of unemployment, discrimination, and cultural differences all contribute to unhealthy lifestyles and disparities in access to health care for many indigenous peoples. Despite the funding appropriated by the United States Congress to deliver health care services, indigenous peoples continue to suffer disproportionately from a variety of illness and diseases. While the incidence and prevalence of infectious

---

[304] Indigenous lesbian, gays, bi-sexual and transsexuals (LGBT).

[305] HIV/AIDS and Indigenous Peoples: Final Report of the 5th International Policy Dialogue, International Affairs Directorate, Health Canada, October 21-23, 2009 Ottawa, Canada, pp. 7-8.

[306] State of the World's Minorities and Indigenous Peoples 2013, p. 115.

diseases have been dramatically reduced through increased clinical care and public health efforts such as vaccinations for infectious diseases and the construction of sanitation facilities, newer threats such as diabetes and other chronic conditions mean that indigenous peoples continue to experience health disparities and higher death rates than the rest of the population.[307]

The data on health disparities provided by the Indian Health Service's own fact sheets presents enormous health issues for Native Americans and Alaska Natives. Indigenous peoples born today have a life expectancy that is 5.2 years less than the US population of all races (72.6 years to 77.8 years, respectively). They also die at higher rates than other Americans from tuberculosis (500 per cent higher), alcoholism (514 per cent higher), diabetes (177 per cent higher), unintentional injuries (140 per cent higher), homicide (92 per cent higher) and suicide (82 per cent higher).[308]

Mortality disparity rates for American Indians and Alaska Natives (AI/AN) in the IHS Service Area 2005-2007 and U.S. All Races 2006 (age-adjusted mortality rates per 100,000 population)

	AI/AN rate 2005-2007	U.S. All-race rate 2006	Ratio: AI/AN to U.S. all races
All causes	953.7	776.5	1.2
Alcohol induced	45	6.9	6.5
Breast cancer	19.6	23.5	0.8
Cerebrovascular	43.8	43.6	1
Cervical cancer	2.8	2.4	1.2
Diabetes	65.6	23.3	2.8
Heart disease	191.7	200.2	1
HIV infection	3.2	4	0.8
Homicide (assault)	11	6	1.8
Infant Deaths [1]	7.3	6.7	1.1
Malignant neoplasm	170.1	180.7	0.9
Maternal deaths	20.2	13.3	1.5
Pneumonia/influenza	24.3	17.8	1.4
Suicide	19	10.9	1.7
Unintentional injuries*	94.8	39.8	2.4

[1]Infant deaths per 1,000 live births.
* Unintentional Injuries include motor vehicle crashes.

Note: Rates are adjusted to compensate for misreporting of American Indian and Alaska Native race on state death certificates. American Indian and Alaska Native death rate columns present data for the three-year period specified. U.S. All Races columns present data for a one-year period. ICD-10 codes were introduced in 1999; therefore, comparability ratios were applied to deaths for years prior to 1999. Rates are based on American Indian and Alaska Native alone; 2000 census with bridged-race categories.

---

[307] American Indians and Alaska Natives: Health Disparities Overview http://itepsrv1.itep.nau.edu/itep_course_downloads/AQ-Alaska_Resources/HealthEffects/AIAN_Disparities_Overview.pdf.

[308] http://www.ihs.gov/newsroom/factsheets/disparities/.

Suicide is the second leading cause of death behind unintentional injuries among indigenous children and young adults, according to the IHS. Native Americans aged 15-24 years commit suicide 3.5 times higher than the national average and incidence is rising. Moreover, 40 per cent of indigenous suicides occur within this age group. Suicide figures vary by community however, suicide rates have consistently been higher among Alaska Natives than any other racial/ethnic group in the United States. Suicide ranked fourth among the leading causes of death among Alaska Natives in 2008.[309] Alaska has the highest rate of suicide per capita in the country. A 1983-1984 study noted that although Alaska Natives represented 14 per cent of the population in Alaska, they accounted for 33 per cent of the suicides.[310] During 2003-2006, Alaska Natives comprised 16 per cent of Alaska's total population, and accounted for 38 per cent of the suicides.[311] In 2008, the suicide rate among Alaska Natives (42.9 per 100,000) was 1.9 times higher than the rate for Alaska's total population (24.6 per 100,000) and 3.7 times that for the U.S. total population (11.6 per 100,000).[312] Suicide rates among Alaska Natives have been consistently the highest among adult males under 35 years of age.[313] A more recent study by the Alaska Native Tribal Health Consortium showed that during 2004-2008, the median age of suicide among Alaska Whites was 43 years, while the median age among Alaska Natives was 26 years.[314]

Some researchers also mentioned that self-destruction and suicide may also be hidden in some instances. For example, accidental death from motor vehicle crashes is higher among indigenous peoples than the general population of the United States. Fatal single vehicle crashes involving indigenous peoples were found to be a higher risk group for self-destruction than either Native American fatal multiple vehicle crashes or non-Native fatal crashes. Single-vehicle crashes among indigenous youths may hide some forms of self-destruction and/or suicide as they do in other populations.[315] In some indigenous communities in North America, there are certain rituals and customs around death so suicide is regarded as taboo and as a result, suicides often go unreported or get classified by police as accidental death.[316]

There have been profound changes over the last 75 years among Alaska Natives; in the past, males aged 20-29 years would have had families of their own and would have been involved in subsistence activities in order to support their families. According to studies, there are likely to be a multitude of psychosocial factors that contribute to the extremely high suicide rates among Alaska Natives. For example, mental health disorders (particularly depression and substance abuse) are associated with more than 90 per cent of all cases of suicide. At the same time, suicide is thought to be a consequence stemming from many complex sociocultural factors and is more

---

[309] Jessica Craig, MPH, Alaska Native Tribal Health Epidemiology Center, and Deborah Hull-Jilly, MPH, Alaska Section of Epidemiology ", Characteristics of Suicide Among Alaska Native and Alaska non-Native People, 2003-2008", (2012) p. 3.

[310] Hlady W.G., Middaugh J.P., The epidemiology of suicide in Alaska, 1983-1984. Alaska Med. Nov-Dec 1987;29(5):158-164.

[311] Perkins R., Sanddal, T.L., Howell M., Sanddal N.D., Berman A., Epidemiological and follow-back study of suicides in Alaska. Int J Circumpolar Health. 2009;68(3):212-223.

[312] Web-based Injury Statistics Query and Reporting System (WISQARS). 2007. http://www.cdc.gov/ncipc/wisqars.

[313] Perkins R., Sanddal T.L., Howell M., Sanddal N.D., Berman A. Epidemiological and follow-back study of suicides in Alaska. Int J Circumpolar Health. 2009;68(3):212-223.

[314] Day G., Holck P., Provost E., Alaska Native Mortality Update: 2004-2008: Alaska Native Epidemiology Center; October 2011.

[315] Philip A. May, "Suicide and Self-Destruction among American Indian Youth", American Indian and Alaska Native Mental Health Research, 1(1), June 1987, p. 68.

[316] Laurel Morales "Native Americans Have Highest Rate of Suicide", August 31, 2012 http://www.fronterasdesk.org/content/native-americans-have-highest-rate-suicide.

likely to occur during periods of socioeconomic, family and individual crisis (e.g. loss of a loved one, unemployment, sexual orientation, difficulties with developing one's identity, disassociation from one's community or other social/belief group and honour). Other factors include alcohol and drug abuse, access to firearms, exposure to domestic/family violence, physical health problems and less access to suicide prevention and intervention programs.[317]

The prevalence of diabetes is higher among the American Indian and Alaska Native population (16.5 per cent) than any other major racial or ethnic group in the United States, and the prevalence of diabetes has been increasing.[318] Diabetes kills roughly four times as many American Indians and Alaska Natives as it does members of the mainstream United States population.[319] In general, people are more likely to develop type 2 diabetes and die from its complications as they grow older, a pattern that is even more pronounced among American Indians and Alaska Natives.[320] Many people do not know they have type 2 diabetes until the symptoms of complications appear.[321] Indigenous peoples with diabetes are six times more likely than the general population to have kidney disease and between three to four times more likely to require lower-limb amputations. In this way, diabetes not only contributes to early mortality but it is among one of the leading causes of disability, contributing to unemployment and poverty. Gestational diabetes is also of great concern and is noted to occur more frequently among American Indian and Alaska Native women than women in other minority groups. Women who experience gestational diabetes have a 20 to 50 per cent chance of developing type 2 diabetes in 5 to 10 years after pregnancy.[322] Children whose mothers had diabetes during pregnancy are at increased risk of developing type 2 diabetes themselves.

In April 2007, Amnesty International issued a report entitled Maze of Injustice: The failure to protect Indigenous women from sexual violence in the United States. The report confirmed what Native American and Alaska Native advocates have long known: that sexual violence against indigenous women is at epidemic proportions and that survivors are frequently denied justice. The United States Department of Justice's own statistics indicate that Native American and Alaska Native women are more than two and a half times more likely to be raped or sexually assaulted than women in the United States in general and that 86 per cent of the reported crimes are committed by non-Native men. Health Service providers have a key role to play in providing survivors with medical attention they may need. However, many IHS facilities do not consistently provide forensic sexual assault

---

[317] Jessica Craig, MPH, Alaska Native Tribal Health Epidemiology Center, and Deborah Hull-Jilly, MPH, Alaska Section of Epidemiology "Characteristics of Suicide Among Alaska Native and Alaska non-Native People", 2003-2008 (2012), p. 7 http://www.epi.hss.state.ak.us/bulletins/docs/rr2012_01.pdf.

[318] Patricia M. Barnes, M.A.; Patricia F. Adams; and Eve Powell-Griner, "Health Characteristics of the American Indian or Alaska Native Adult Population: United States, 2004-2008" http://www.cdc.gov/nchs/data/nhsr/nhsr020.pdf.

[319] Indian Health Service. Trends in Indian Health, 2000-2001. Washington, DC: U.S. Department of Health and Human Services. http://www.ihs.gov/NonMedicalPrograms/IHS_Stats/files/Trends00-01_Part4.pdf.

[320] Indian Health Service. Trends in Indian Health, 2000-2001. Washington, DC: U.S. Department of Health and Human Services. http://www.ihs.gov/NonMedicalPrograms/IHS_Stats/files/Trends00-01_Part4.pdf.

[321] Centers for Disease Control and Prevention. National Diabetes Fact Sheet: General Information and National Estimates on Diabetes in the United States. Atlanta, Georgia: U.S. Department of Health and Human Services, Centers for Disease Control and Prevention, 2005. http://www.cdc.gov/diabetes.

[322] Centers for Disease Control and Prevention. National Diabetes Fact Sheet: General Information and National Estimates on Diabetes in the United States. Atlanta, Georgia: U.S. Department of Health and Human Services, Centers for Disease Control and Prevention, 2005. http://www.cdc.gov/diabetes.

examinations. IHS also lack clear protocols for treating victims of sexual violence, are severely underfunded and lack personnel trainers to provide services in the event of sexual violence.[323]

Age-adjusted percentages of persons 18 years of age and over with diabetes, 2004-2008

	American Indian/ Alaska Native	White	American Indian/ Alaska Native/white ratio
Men and women	17.5	6.6	2.7
Men	18.2	7.2	2.5
Women	16.2	6.2	2.6

Source: CDC 2010. Health Characteristics of the American Indian and Alaska Native Adult Population: United States, 2004-2008.

Radioactive tailings are one of the major concerns for many indigenous peoples living near abandoned uranium mines on tribal lands. The first major uranium mine in the United States was started in 1953 near Laguna Pueblo, New Mexico.[324] Since that time there have been over 15,000 uranium mines with a majority of those being on indigenous peoples' lands. Most of the other mines lay abandoned with radioactive tailings and dust present at almost all of them. Most of the mining has been on the Colorado Plateau, but other areas in Washington State and the Dakotas have also been impacted. Indigenous peoples have had their water sources impacted by the radioactive tailings from the mine operations. A large part of the workforce for these mines included a large number of indigenous peoples. A few decades after uranium mining began in the Navajo Nation, increased numbers of cancer cases, lung cancer in particular, began to show up in the miners.[325] The area where most of the mines are located is typically dry, and the dust that comes off of the wasted rock tailings is radioactive. This dust, mixed with the air, is thought to cause lung cancer and other breathing ailments. Elevated radon levels have also been associated with these abandoned mines. The effect of long-term radiation exposure in the levels associated with these mines is largely unknown. Despite the obvious need, there have not been to date any comprehensive studies of radiation and heavy metal contamination in the United States.[326]

Food security remains an issue for indigenous peoples. This is especially so in Alaska where Alaskan Natives are subject to a particular legal regime under the Alaska Native Claims Settlement Act 1971 which extinguished all claims of aboriginal title including any aboriginal hunting and fishing rights that may exist, throughout Alaska. The act set up a system of Native-run corporations. Since then, indigenous hunting and fishing rights are subject to the same regulatory regime that applies to non-indigenous activities. Subsistence hunting and fishing remains crucial both for cultural purposes and for food security. Subsistence activities are also subject to a state regulatory regime

---

[323] Amnesty International *Maze of Injustice*: One Year Update, 2008, pp. 1, 10.

[324] Philip Sittnick, Uranium Mining and Its Impact on Laguna Pueblo: A Study Guide for an Interdisciplinary Unit, July 1998, p. 17, http://www.miningwatch.ca/sites/www.miningwatch.ca/files/umine_0.pdf.

[325] Kevin Zeese/Margaret Flowers America's "Secret Fukushima": Uranium Mining is Poisoning the Bread Basket of the World, The Fourth Media 17 June 2013 http://www.4thmedia.org/.

[326] Kevin Zeese/Margaret Flowers America's "Secret Fukushima": Uranium Mining is Poisoning the Bread Basket of the World, The Fourth Media 17 June 2013 http://www.4thmedia.org/.

that allows for, competing land and resource uses, such as mining and other activities, including hunting and fishing for sport, which also threatens the natural environments and food sources.[327]

Canada

Prior to European contact indigenous peoples in Canada practiced their own systems of health knowledge. However, the traditional health systems were devastated during colonization as diseases and conflicts impacted indigenous peoples.

Today, health care for indigenous peoples in Canada continues to be a complex and diverse issue. While the health of indigenous peoples in Canada has seen improvement in recent years, they continue to experience considerably lower health outcomes than non-indigenous Canadians. Comparing the wider society to indigenous peoples on many health indicators, indigenous peoples continue to experience higher infant and young-child mortality rates; higher maternal morbidity and mortality rates; a heavy infectious disease burden; malnutrition; shortened life expectancy; diseases and death associated with cigarette smoking; social problems, illnesses and deaths linked to misuse of alcohol and other drugs; accidents, poisonings, interpersonal violence, homicide and suicide; obesity, diabetes, hypertension, cardiovascular, and chronic renal disease (lifestyle diseases); and diseases caused by environmental contamination (for example, heavy metals, industrial gases and effluent wastes).[328]

The disparities in health between the indigenous and non-indigenous populations are linked to the underlying causes that sit largely outside of the constituted health domain and are referred to as the determinants of health. Health disparities are directly and indirectly associated with or related to social, economic, cultural and political inequities; the end result of which is a disproportionate burden of ill health and social suffering. There are major differences in the socioeconomic circumstances and lived world experiences of First Nations, Inuit, and Métis peoples, between status and non-status, on-reserve and off-reserve, as well as urban and rural indigenous peoples. At the same time, census data and other research show a persistent gap in socioeconomic status and well-being between indigenous and non-indigenous peoples in Canada.[329] For example, Canada's 2006 statistics indicated that fewer indigenous peoples between the ages of 25 and 34 obtained high school diplomas (68.1 per cent) than non-indigenous people (90 per cent).[330] The 2005 median income for indigenous peoples was CAN$ 16,752 which is almost CAN$ 10,000 (or 35 per cent) lower than for non-indigenous people (CAN$ 25,955),[331] and despite a 10 per cent increase in aboriginal employment between 1996 and 2006 (compared to a 4.1 per cent increase in non-indigenous employment during the same time period), the unemployment rate for indigenous peoples in 2006

[327] James Anaya Report of the Special Rapporteur on the rights of indigenous peoples, The situation of indigenous peoples in the United States of America A/HRC/21/47/Add.1 30 August 2012 p. 6.

[328] An Overview of Aboriginal Health in Canada, National Collaborating Centre for Aboriginal health, p. 3.

[329] Naomi Adelson, "The Embodiment of Inequity: Health Disparities in Aboriginal Canada" Canadian Journal of Public Health, March-April, 2005), p

[330] A Demographic and Socio-Economic Portrait of Aboriginal Populations in Canada, Indian and Northern Affairs Canada, 2009, p. 4, http://publications.gc.ca/collections/collection_2010/ainc-inac/R3-109-2009-eng.pdf.

[331] A Demographic and Socio-Economic Portrait of Aboriginal Populations in Canada, Indian and Northern Affairs Canada, 2009, p. 4, http://publications.gc.ca/collections/collection_2010/ainc-inac/R3-109-2009-eng.pdf.

was still 13.0 per cent which was more than 2.5 times higher compared to non-indigenous people (5.2 per cent).[332]

Indigenous peoples in Canada face many urgent health issues. For example, indigenous Canadians are overrepresented in HIV infection rates. Indigenous peoples are especially vulnerable to HIV infection when compared the general Canadian population due to poor access to health services, high rates of poverty, substance abuse, intravenous drug use and also tattooing. While indigenous peoples account for 4.3 per cent of the total Canadian population, they account for 8 per cent of people living with HIV and 12.5 per cent of new infections in 2008. Indigenous peoples also experience disproportionate rates of tuberculosis at 26.4 times the rate of Canadian borne non-indigenous peoples. While there are limited data on the rates of diabetes in Métis and Inuit communities, type 2 diabetes is considered to have reached epidemic level in First Nations communities.[333] In some First Nations communities, youth suicide occurs at a rate of 800 times the national average.[334] The suicide rate among Inuit communities in Arctic Canada is 10 times that of the general Canadian population.[335]

The 2008-2010 First Nations Regional Health Survey (RHS) indicated that household overcrowding and poor housing conditions (dwellings in need of major repair) in indigenous communities show some improvement, but regional statistics indicate that this remains a major concern in some areas. The rates of household overcrowding remained steady in Canada's non-indigenous population at 1.4 per cent, the rates of overcrowding in the total indigenous population went from 7.6 per cent in 1996 to 4.3 per cent in 2006.[336] At the same time, overcrowding rates reached 23 per cent in Nunavut and 8 per cent in Saskatchewan (Indian and Northern Affairs Canada, 2009). Similarly, indigenous peoples were three times as likely as non-indigenous people to live in houses in need of major repair, and over 22 per cent of dwellings in indigenous communities in 5 provinces and 3 territories (Manitoba, Saskatchewan, Northwest Territories, Yukon, and Nunavut) were in need of major repair in 2006, compared with an average of 7.0 per cent in non-indigenous communities in Canada.[337]

More than half of Canada's aboriginal population live in urban centres, and the two-thirds of this population lives in Western Canada.[338] Canada's urban aboriginal people today comprise a

[332] A Demographic and Socio-Economic Portrait of Aboriginal Populations in Canada, Indian and Northern Affairs Canada, 2009, p. 6,. http://publications.gc.ca/collections/collection_2010/ainc-inac/R3-109-2009-eng.pdf.

[333] H.V. Thommasen, J. Patenaude, N. Anderson, A. McArthur and H. Tildesley "Differences in diabetic co-morbidity between Aboriginal and non-Aboriginal people living in Bella Coola, Canada" Rural and Remote Health 4:319 (online) 2004 http://www.rrh.org.au/publishedarticles/article_print_319.pdf.

[334] Chandler, M.J. and Lalonde, C. (1998) "Cultural continuity as a hedge against suicide in Canada's First Nations". Transcultural Psychiatry, 35: 191-219.

[335] Kral, M.J. (2012). "Postcolonial Suicide among Inuit in Arctic Canada". Culture, Medicine, and Psychiatry. 36(2): 306-325.

[336] A Demographic and Socio-Economic Portrait of Aboriginal Populations in Canada, Indian and Northern Affairs Canada, 2009, p. 7, http://publications.gc.ca/collections/collection_2010/ainc-inac/R3-109-2009-eng.pdf.

[337] A Demographic and Socio-Economic Portrait of Aboriginal Populations in Canada, Indian and Northern Affairs Canada, 2009, p. 7, http://publications.gc.ca/collections/collection_2010/ainc-inac/R3-109-2009-eng.pdf.

[338] Hanselmann, C. (2001). Urban Aboriginal people in Western Canada: Realities and policies. Calgary, Alberta: Canada West Foundation.

diverse, youthful and growing population.[339] Despite their growing numbers, urban aboriginal people in Canada continue to earn far below the median average income for non-urban counterparts. Urban aboriginal people also tend to have comparatively higher rates of homelessness, greater housing needs and higher rates of suicide and are particularly at risk of substance abuse, contracting tuberculosis and/or HIV or developing diabetes. This indicates that many aboriginal people, especially those residing in urban areas, are in danger of falling through the cracks of the Canadian health care system and social security safety net.[340]

Other examples where the underlying causes or determinants of health are most felt is the experience of the Indian residential school system survivors. In Canada and the United States, as well in other colonized nations, many generations of indigenous children were sent away from parents and their communities to residential schools. The effect of this experience is collective trauma, consisting of, the structural effects of disrupting families and communities; the loss of parenting skills as a result of institutionalization; patterns of emotional response resulting from the absence of warmth and intimacy in childhood; the carryover of physical and sexual abuse; the loss of indigenous knowledge, languages and traditions; and the systemic devaluing of indigenous peoples' identity. The legacies of these and other policies of forced assimilation are also seen in the present relationships of indigenous peoples with the larger society.

The situation of indigenous women in Canada remains a serious social issue and a major concern. According to Canadian government statistics, indigenous women are five times to seven times more likely than other women to die as the result of violence. The Native Women's Association of Canada, through its own hard work, documented more than 582 cases of missing and murdered indigenous women in Canada, most within the last three decades. Due to the gaps in police and government reporting, the actual numbers may be much higher.[341]

Vulnerable and marginalized women are exposed to a higher risk of violence including sexual assault, murder and serial predation. The phenomenon of missing and murdered women is one stark example of this exposure and is seen as part of a broader pattern of marginalization and inequality. The increased vulnerability of certain groups of women, such as women involved in the sex trade, play an important role in providing victims for serial killers.

The loss of the missing women and the unsatisfactory police, government and public response has resulted in widespread physical and emotional distress, particularly within families but extending to other important relationships. One dimension of this distress is the guilt and shame at having failed to protect loved ones. In some cases, these emotions have caused what appears to be irreparable damage to families. Some described personal struggles with addiction, some described the agony of watching other family members using alcohol or drugs to cope with their pain, and some experienced both of these situations. Health problems and the practical require-

---

[339] Dion Stout, M., Kipling, G. and Stout, R. (2001). Aboriginal Women's Health Research Synthesis Paper: Final Report. Centres of Excellence for Women's Health. Ottawa, Women's Health Bureau.

[340] Cecilia Benoit, Dena Carroll, Munaza Chaudhry, "In search of a Healing Place: Aboriginal women in Vancouver's Downtown Eastside" Social Science & Medicine 56 (2003) 821-833, p. 822.

[341] Native Women's Association of Canada. (2010). What their stories tell us: Research findings from the Sisters in Spirit initiative, Ottawa, ON, http://www.nwac.ca/sites/default/files/reports/2010_NWAC_SIS_Report_EN.pdf.

ments of dealing with surviving children have meant that family members have been unable to work; these financial concerns have sometimes caused further health impacts on families.[342]

Discrimination and marginalization of indigenous women in Canada is not new; it has a long colonial history. In 1857, indigenous men were allowed to renounce their indigenous status and the right to live on reserve lands in order to assimilate into non-indigenous society. Indigenous women, on the other hand were not given the same choice. In fact, in contrast to traditional indigenous matriarchal family structure the post colonial indigenous women's status was determined by the choices made by her husband or father. A second law passed in 1869, stripped women of their indigenous status and their place in their community if they married a man from another community, even if he was also indigenous. In addition, children born to an indigenous woman who married a non-indigenous man would also be denied status. This was not true for Indian men, whose non-Indian wives gained status as Indians upon marriage. These laws remained in place for more than a century.

In 1985, after a long, hard struggle by indigenous women, which included bringing a successful complaint to the UN Human Rights Committee, 35 the policies were repealed for being incompatible with protections against discrimination in the new Canadian Charter of Rights and Freedoms. While Bill C-31 (1985) addressed many of these problems, it did not reduce discrimination against women. Under the new Act, anomalies can develop where the children of a status Indian woman can pass on status to their children only if they marry registered Indians, whereas the grandchildren of a status male will have full status, despite the fact that one of their parents does not have status.[343] While a person may be a Status Indian, it is up to a Band whether she or he is considered a Band member. Entitlements reinstated under Bill C-31 do not necessarily translate into Band membership. This can be problematic for women and their families who have had their Status reinstated through Bill C-31. Women may not have many connections to a Band, or there may be a shortage of resources for such things as housing, education programs or health care on the reserve, so that Bands can be reluctant to accept new members.[344]

Poverty has clear outcomes on health because, in part, it determines what kinds of foods households have available to them and what they can afford to purchase. Thus, families at lower incomes are subject to the stress of food insecurity from a compromised diet that results when food is no longer available. In 1998-1999, indigenous peoples living off reserve were almost three times more likely to be living in households experiencing food insecurity than was the case for all Canadians (27 per cent to 10 percent). This condition is strongly related to low incomes as well as single parent status, both of which are more likely to occur in aboriginal households.

In 2012, the Special Rapporteur on the right to food, Mr. Olivier De Schutter, undertook a country visit to Canada. In his report[345] he stated he was disconcerted by the deep and severe food insecurity faced by aboriginal peoples living both on- and off-reserve in remote and urban areas. In the Yukon, the Northwest Territories and Nunavut, where the greatest concentration of Inuit

---

[342] Forsaken: the Report of the Missing Women Commission of Inquiry (2012) Vol. 111, p. 41.

[343] Report of the Aboriginal Justice Inquiry of Manitoba (1999)http://www.ajic.mb.ca/volumel/chapter13.html#4.

[344] Kathy Bent, Joanne Havelock, Margaret Haworth-Brockman, "Entitlements and health services for First Nations and Métis women in Manitoba and Saskatchewan", The Prairie Women's Health Centre of Excellence, August 2007, http://www.pwhce.ca/pdf/entitlementsHealthServices.pdf.

[345] A/HRC/22/50/Add.1.

populations resides, food insecurity in 2007-2008 was 11.6 per cent, 12.4 per cent and 32.6 per cent respectively. Health Canada,[346] The Special Rapporteur also stated that First Nations Regional Longitudinal Health Survey (RHS 2008-2010) indicates that 17.8 per cent of First Nations adults (ages 25-39) and 16.1 per cent of First Nations adults (ages 40-54) reported being hungry, but did not eat due to lack of money for food in 2007-2008.[347] Though the situation of food insecurity is monitored through surveys such as the Canadian Community Health Survey, the Inuit Health Survey and the First Nations Food, Nutrition and Environment Study, Canada, the Special Rapporteur found there were no data on food insecurity in Métis population.[348]

The Special Rapporteur also stated that despite programmes such as the Canada Prenatal Nutrition Program (including the First Nations and Inuit component); Aboriginal Head Start (includes on-reserve and urban and northern component); the Aboriginal Diabetes Initiative; and Nutrition North Canada, discussed in greater detail below, research conducted by the University of Manitoba noted that in 2008-2009, nearly 60 per cent of First Nations children in northern Manitoba households were food insecure.[349] The Inuit Health Survey reported that 70 per cent of adults living in Nunavut were food insecure. This is six times higher than the national average and represents the highest documented food insecurity rate for any aboriginal population in a developed country.[350] Among off-reserve aboriginal households, approximately one in five households was food insecure, including 8.4 per cent severely food insecure.[351] These rates are three times higher than among non-aboriginal households, where 7.7 per cent were food insecure, including 2.5 per cent with severe food insecurity.[352] In March 2011, one in 10 of the 851,014 who relied on food banks across Canada self-identified as an aboriginal person.[353]

Families in remote and isolated indigenous communities frequently lack access to affordable nutritious foods, particularly perishables such as fruits, vegetables and meats, due to limited food selections, high food prices and poor quality of fresh produce. Expensive transport costs and difficult logistics (e.g., air freight charges, and uncertainty of travel on winter roads, where they exist, or air travel subject to weather conditions), high poverty rates and a continuing decline in the use of traditional foods result in few healthy food choices.[354] The high prevalence of food insecurity for aboriginal people is not surprising. In the literature, food insecurity is related to health outcomes that include multiple chronic conditions, obesity, distress and depression.

---

[346] Health Canada, "Household Food Insecurity in Canada in 2007-2008: Key Statistics and Graphics", http://www.hc-sc.gc.ca/fn-an/surveill/nutrition/commun/insecurit/key-stats-cles-2007-2008-eng.php.

[347] A/HRC/22/50/Add.1.

[348] A/HRC/22/50/Add.1.

[349] Children's Food Insecurity poster, http://home.cc.umanitoba.ca/~thompso4/Poster_ CHILDRENfinalagconference.ppt.pdf.

[350] R. Rosol et al., "Prevalence of affirmative responses to questions for food insecurity: International Polar Year Inuit Health Survey, 2007-2008" and International Journal of Circumpolar Health, vol. 70, No. 5 (2011), pp. 488-497; G.M. Egeland, IPY Inuit Health Survey speaks to need to address inadequate housing, food insecurity and nutrition transition. International Journal of Circumpolar Health, vol. 70, No. 5 (2011), pp. 444-446.

[351] Health Canada, "Household Food Insecurity in Canada in 2007-2008: Key Statistics and Graphics", http://www.hc-sc.gc.ca/fn-an/surveill/nutrition/commun/insecurit/key-stats-cles-2007-2008-eng.php#fn-np8.

[352] Health Canada, "Household Food Insecurity in Canada in 2007-2008: Key Statistics and Graphics", http://www.hc-sc.gc.ca/fn-an/surveill/nutrition/commun/insecurit/key-stats-cles-2007-2008-eng.php#fn-np8.

[353] Food Banks Canada, "Hungercount 2011", p. 7, www.foodbankscanada.ca/hungercount.

[354] A/HRC/22/50/Add.1.

Access to health services in the United States and Canada

Indigenous peoples in the United States and Canada do not have easy access to basic western health care when needed. Access is constrained by financial, geographical and cultural barriers. Indigenous peoples tend to be low on Government priority lists, especially when they live in remote areas where services are difficult and costly to provide. When services are available, indigenous peoples are often reluctant or afraid to use them because staff can be insensitive, discriminatory and unfriendly.

In Canada, within the fly-in or isolated communities, some indigenous women are required to fly over a thousand kilometres to reach a hospital in order to give birth, have a tooth extracted or treat and illness. Many have never left their community before and there is a reluctance to do so in many cases. Even when affordable health services do exist within indigenous communities, they are often of lower quality than services available for non-indigenous peoples. While health care priorities may be set by the Government may do not match the priorities of indigenous communities, there has been some progress made in terms of indigenous peoples and their communities' managing and administering their own health care systems.[355]

In Canada, there is long-standing jurisdictional conflict between the provincial and federal governments over responsibility for health services which has negatively impacted indigenous peoples who have had to cope with a patchwork of fragmented services. To a large degree, jurisdictional issues which impact on accessibility to health services stem from the decades of a "tug of war" over which level of government is responsible for provision of services. Although provincial governments are required to provide equal access to health care services under the Canada Health Act for all residents of the province including indigenous peoples living on reserves, the provincial governments often take the position that the federal government is responsible for certain health services to indigenous peoples who are registered as Status Indians under the Indian Act. As a result, some health services not covered by the Canada Health Act but otherwise provided by the provinces through the Regional Health Authorities may or may not be provided to indigenous communities. The provincial government's position is that the federal government has responsibility for certain health services to indigenous peoples as Indians under the Indian Act. On the other hand, the federal government's position is that provincial services should extend to reserves under the cost-sharing arrangements that apply to the general population. This fundamental disagreement translates in a very real way into program fragmentation, problems with coordinating programs, underfunding, inconsistencies, service gaps, and lack of integration. Critics argue that the federal government routinely tries to rid itself, or limit, indigenous programs and services by continuing to diminish what it determines as discretionary health services.

Barriers to accessing health care services in the United States include the unavailability of public and private transportation and given the low income levels of most residents, procuring transportation to IHS services can be a significant burden. Also, when specialty care is required, IHS referrals often send patients to larger contracted hospitals in urban areas, significantly far away from the patient's home and family. For individual patients from the tight-knit communities that serve as the center of tribal culture in many rural regions, travelling to a distant region to receive

---

[355] Interagency coalition on Aids and Development "HIV/AIDS and Indigenous Populations in Canada and Sub-Saharan Africa" http://www.icad-cisd.com/pdf/HIV_and_Indigenous_Populations_EN.pdf.

specialty care causes a significant loss in the community support systems one would typically rely on during times of need.[356]

As stated previously, the IHS-funded health services are provided through a network of hospitals, clinics, and health stations that are managed directly by IHS, by tribes or tribal organizations, and urban Indian health programs. Some services are provided through contract with non-Indian providers. In general, services provided through IHS and tribally operated facilities are limited to members of and descendants of members of federally recognized tribes that live on or near federal reservations. Urban Indian health programs serve a wider group of American Indians and Alaska Natives, including those who are not able to access IHS or tribally operated facilities because they do not meet eligibility criteria or reside outside the service areas. IHS funding is limited and must be appropriated by Congress each fiscal year. In 2013, total program funding was $5.46 billion. Although the IHS budget has increased over time, funds are not equally distributed across facilities and they remain insufficient to meet health care needs. As such, access to services through IHS varies significantly across locations, and American Indians and Alaska Natives who rely solely on IHS for care often lack access to needed care.[357]

Addressing health gaps

Indigenous peoples in North America like elsewhere in the world, view health and well-being far more broadly than merely physical health and the absence of disease. Indigenous peoples often use their own words that translate roughly to "living well' which combines beliefs in the importance of balance. The four elements of life: physical, emotional, mental and spiritual are all are intricately woven together and interact to support a strong and healthy person. Balance also requires the need for an individual to live in harmony with others, their community and the spirit world. Hence, indigenous peoples' idea of sickness or illness tends to refer to an absence of well-being. The connection to family and relatives are essential components of well-being.[358]

Government-sponsored social and health services have made efforts to become more culturally sensitive and to respond more effectively to the needs of indigenous clients. Indigenous liaison and caseworkers are able to offer more culturally sensitive services and are working hard to impact the policies and practices of their organizations to be more responsive to indigenous clients. As well, a growing number of indigenous organizations in urban centres have been developing innovative programs to address the gaps in services provided by mainstream government departments and agencies and to offer more culturally sensitive alternatives.

There are still a large number of gaps, where the health system is failing indigenous peoples. These include the protection and safety of children. Too often children must leave their homes and, in many instances their communities, in order to be safe and more often than not are placed in non-indigenous foster care which results in children having no contact with extended family

---

[356] Tshona Reneé Corbin Barriers to health care access among American Indian and Alaska Native populations (2008) http://d-scholarship.pitt.edu/7075/1/TRCorbin2010.pdf.

[357] Henry J Kaiser Foundation "Health Coverage and Care for American Indians and Alaska Natives" October 2013 | Issue Brief http://kaiserfamilyfoundation.files.wordpress.com/2013/10/8502-health-coverage-and-care-for-american-indians-and-alaska-natives.pdf.

[358] Malcolm King, Alexandra Smith, Michael Gracey " Indigenous Health part 2: the underlying causes of the health gap", www.thelancet.com, Vol 374, July 4, 2009, p. 77.

and for this reason do not have a strong connection to their language, culture, sense of identity and sense of belonging. In later years some become alienated from their families and communities resorting to negative behaviours such as alcohol and drug use, gang affiliation and patterns of violence. Social assistance provisions for women, even those with children, who are leaving abusive situations, are not adequate for women to re-establish themselves and sustain their daily needs. Women end up trapped in poverty without the resources to get the urgent counselling and other supports they may need or to improve their circumstances through further education and training.

Social and mental health services are fragmented, forcing people to interact with many different agencies, each with its own narrow eligibility criteria and range of services. Clients end up demoralized, confused and frustrated as they attempt to negotiate a maze of departments and agencies in order to get the financial, legal and psychological help they need. This task is, of course, particularly difficult for individuals who are traumatized by the abuse to which they have been subjected. As well, this situation results in critical gaps between their needs and available services.

Many small communities have virtually no services for the victims of abuse and no means for ensuring their safety. Also, they have very little to offer the perpetrators of abuse. In instances like these, indigenous peoples are forced to go to larger centres to get help, where they are cut off from family and friends and may have virtually no support system.

The role of colonialism in diminishing indigenous peoples' identity is seen as a root cause to a myriad of mental health problems. The wounds of the past continue to fester and often in silence. The path to healing is voicing the abuse and receiving validation from culture. The high suicide rates indicate a crisis in mental health and may be due to underservicing of indigenous communities' mental health systems. Mental health strategies should be a priority in any current mental health initiatives within Canada and the United States.[359] Indigenous peoples' mental health issues are best understood in the context of colonialism.

Positive indigenous representations and role models and authority figures are needed to facilitate the development of healthy identities based on cultural strengths, not on disadvantage, disease burden and discrimination. Traditional teachings and knowledge provide a basis for positive self-image and healthy identity. Elders are widely seen to be pivotal for indigenous societies to regain their positive identity. Assaults on identity contribute to a self-perpetuating circle that keeps indigenous peoples where they are. Language is crucial to identity, health and relations. It is especially important as a link to spirituality, an essential component of indigenous health. Throughout the world, indigenous languages are being lost, and with them an essential part of indigenous identity. Language revitalization can be seen, therefore, as a health promotion strategy.

One of the major areas of concerns are the gaps in data information. Public health assessments and interventions depend on accurate statistical data. Unfortunately in both the United States and Canada there are serious deficits in the availability of accurate disaggregated data for indigenous peoples. For example, in Canada health data initiatives have not been collected for non-registered First Nations peoples or Inuit and Métis peoples living in urban areas. There are also inconsistencies in First Nation Inuit and Métis ethnic identifiers in provincial health data collected through vital statistics registrations systems, hospital administration databases and acute and

---

[359] Warry, 2000.

chronic disease surveillance systems. As a result, these populations are often invisible in health statistics.[360] It is important to acknowledge differences in the socioeconomic circumstances and lived world experiences of First Nations, Inuit, and Métis peoples, between status and non-status, on-reserve and off-reserve, as well as urban and rural aboriginal populations[361] in order for data to be accurate, complete and up-to-date.

Research based on existing administrative, survey, population and other data sets is limited by how populations were included. For example Statistics Canada uses several methods for identifying aboriginal ancestry, most often using a broad definition, allowing survey and census respondents to self-identify as having aboriginal ancestry. However some First Nation reserves refused to take part in some national surveys (Census Canada, for instance), and in other cases survey design did not include residents of the northern territories, most of whom are aboriginal (e.g., Canadian Community Health Surveys).[362]

British Columbia's tripartite Transformative Change Accord are steps in the right direction. The Transformative Change Accord commits the Government of British Columbia to improving the mental health and addictions problems of aboriginal peoples through the establishment of mental health programs, as well as through concerted efforts to equalize the socioeconomic differences (that underlie many of the health problems facing aboriginal peoples) between aboriginal and non-aboriginal people in British Columbia.[363] The British Columbia Tripartite Framework Agreement on First Nation Health Governance was made in October 2011 between the Federal Minister of Health, the Provincial Minister of Health for the Province of British Columbia and the First Nations Health Authority as endorsed by the First Nations Health Council of British Columbia.[364] Federal funding for British Columbia First Nations health care services has been transferred to the First Nations Health Authority and the transition is being implemented.[365] This is an important and exciting development that could have global implications as an innovative model for indigenous peoples health system governance administered at the provincial level and mandated by indigenous peoples themselves.

Traditional healing

Despite considerable health issues, indigenous peoples in North America continue to demonstrate resilience and strive for wellness based on indigenous peoples' knowledge and well-being. Indigenous peoples are reclaiming traditional tribal spirituality and rituals to cleanse the bodies and

[360] Smylie, J., and M. Anderson, 2006, "Understanding the health of Indigenous peoples in Canada: key methodological and conceptual challenges", Canadian Medical Association Journal 175(6): 602-605.

[361] Reading, C. and Wien, F., 2009, Health inequalities and social determinants of Aboriginal Peoples' health. Prince George, BC: National Collaborating Centre for Aboriginal Health.

[362] Kathy Bent, Joanne Havelock, Margaret Haworth-Brockman, "Entitlements and health services for First Nations and Métis women in Manitoba and Saskatchewan", The Prairie Women's Health Centre of Excellence, August 2007. http://www.pwhce.ca/pdf/entitlementsHealthServices.pdf.

[363] Government of British Columbia, Government of Canada and Leadership Council Representing the First Nations of British Columbia (2005). Transformative Change Accord. Retrieved July 16, 2010 from http://www.gov.bc.ca/arr/social/down/transformative_change_accord.pdf.

[364] http://www.hc-sc.gc.ca/fniah-spnia/pubs/services/tripartite/framework-accord-cadre-eng.php.

[365] http://www.fnhc.ca/index.php/news/article/interim_health_plan_overview/.

souls of their community members. Sweat lodge ceremonies have been used to treat alcoholism, post-traumatic stress disorder in both white and Native veterans. Prisons in several states have allowed indigenous inmates to practice sweat lodge and other tribal religious ceremonies as part of their rehabilitation.

Traditional medicine is a very important part of First Nations health that is almost always overlooked by the health care system. Traditional medicine uses a holistic model of well-being through the integration of emotional, physical, mental and spiritual aspects of being. Even though specific practices vary between different tribes, all traditional medicine is based on the understanding that humans are part of nature and health is a matter of balance. Therefore, there is respect for the land and all of her offerings. Traditionally, elders understood the importance of respecting and using their environment for foods, medicines, and ceremonies for overall health.

In September 2009, the First Nations Health Society, on behalf of the First Nations Health Council conducted an environmental scan to gather information from the 123 First Nations Health Centres in British Columbia Canada, on traditional models of wellness (or traditional practices and medicines). This project is aimed at providing background information for the FN Health Society to undertake further work, if needed, on promoting traditional models of wellness within British Columbia for First Nations.

During the environmental scan on traditional models of wellness, such models of wellness were defined as having a healthy mind, body and spirit and that wellness from a traditional perspective encompassed a person feeling well emotionally, physically and spiritually and leading a healthy lifestyle, which involved connection to the land and one's culture and beliefs. Maintaining wellness involved carrying out traditional practices of the community such as fishing, hunting, berry gathering and participating in healing circles, sweats, drumming and learning the language. Identity and connection to culture were seen as integral to maintaining wellness from a traditional perspective.

Conclusion

Indigenous peoples in North America have long experienced lower health status when compared with the rest of the population. Lower life expectancy and the disproportionate disease burden exist because of inadequate education, disproportionate poverty, discrimination in the delivery of health services, and cultural differences. These are broad quality of life issues rooted in economic adversity and poor social conditions.

Indigenous health is at a crisis and there is an urgent need for a more holistic vision of health and health intervention driven by indigenous peoples' own vision of health and well-being. Further research and action, driven by indigenous peoples themselves is required at the international and national levels but most importantly at the local levels as well.

Commentators and Scholars across all sectors of the health studies of indigenous peoples concur that, despite inadequacies in the health care delivery system and regardless of peoples' relative access to or use of the biomedical system, the problems are entrenched in the history of relations between indigenous peoples and the nation state.

Restoring traditional healing practices and knowledge is an important pathway to both empowerment and health for indigenous communities. The traditional knowledge once practiced in historical indigenous societies needs to be restored as an intervention to begin to addictions and the epidemics of preventable conditions facing indigenous peoples.

In spite of the considerable health issues and challenges outlined above, indigenous peoples continue to demonstrate resilience and strive for wellness based in indigenous ways of knowing and being. Indigenous peoples' approaches to health are often rooted in a healthy balance of four elements or aspects of wellness: physical, emotional, mental and spiritual. These four elements are sometimes represented in the image of the medicine wheel.[366]

Bibliography

A Demographic and Socio-Economic Portrait of Aboriginal Populations in Canada, Indian and Northern Affairs Canada, 2009, http://publications.gc.ca/collections/collection_2010/ainc-inac/R3-109-2009-eng.pdf.

Aboriginal Peoples in Canada in 2006: Inuit, Métis and First Nations.

Aboriginal People in Canada: First Nations People, Métis and Inuit (2011).

Adelson, Naomi "The embodiment of Inequality: Health Disparities in Aboriginal Canada" Canadian Journal of Public Health, Vol. 96 (2005).

American Indians and Alaska Natives: Health Disparities Overview http://itepsrv1.itep.nau.edu/itep_course_downloads/AQ-Alaska_Resources/HealthEffects/AIAN_Disparities_Overview.pdf.

Anaya, James Report of the Special Rapporteur on the rights of indigenous peoples, The situation of indigenous peoples in the United States of America A/HRC/21/47/Add.1 30 August 2012.

"An Overview of Aboriginal Health in Canada", National Collaborating Centre for Aboriginal Health.

Carolyn Stephens, John Porter, Clive Nettleton, Ruth Willis " Disappearing, displaced and undervalued: a call to action for indigenous health worldwide", www.thelancet.com, Vol 367, June 17, 2006.

Cecilia Benoit, Dena Carroll, Munaza Chaudhry "In search of a Healing Place: Aboriginal women in Vancouver's Downtown Eastside" Social Science & Medicine 56 (2003).

Centers for Disease Control and Prevention. National Diabetes Fact Sheet: General Information

and National Estimates on Diabetes in the United States. Atlanta, Georgia: U.S. Department of Health and Human Services, Centers for Disease Control and Prevention, 2005.

Chandler, M.J. and Lalonde, C. (1998) "Cultural continuity as a hedge against suicide in Canada's First Nations". Transcultural Psychiatry, 35: 191-219.

Constitution of the World Health Organization.

Cornell, Stephen "Indigenous peoples, poverty and self-determination in Australia, New Zealand, Canada and the United States" in Indigenous Peoples and Poverty: An International Perspective eds. Eversole, McNeish and Cimadore (2005).

---

[366] King, M., Smith, A. and Gracey, M. (2009). Indigenous health part 2: The underlying causes of the health gap. The Lancet, 374(9683): pp. 76-85.

Craig, Jessica MPH, Alaska Native Tribal Health Epidemiology Center, and Deborah Hull- Jilly, MPH, Alaska Section of Epidemiology "Characteristics of Suicide Among Alaska Native and Alaska non-Native People, 2003-2008", (2012).

Day G, Holck P, Provost E. Alaska Native Mortality Update: 2004-2008: Alaska Native Epidemiology Center; October 2011.

Dion Stout, M., Kipling, G. and Stout, R. (2001). Aboriginal Women's Health Research Synthesis Paper: Final Report. Centres of Excellence for Women's Health. Ottawa: Women's Health Bureau.

Forsaken: the Report of the Missing Women Commission of Inquiry (2012) Vol. 111

Food Banks Canada, "Hungercount 2011", www.foodbankscanada.ca/hungercount

G.M. Egeland, IPY Inuit Health Survey speaks to need to address inadequate housing, food insecurity and nutrition transition. International Journal of Circumpolar Health, vol. 70, No. 5 (2011).

Government of British Columbia, Government of Canada and Leadership Council Representing the First Nations of British Columbia (2005). Transformative Change Accord. Retrieved July 16, 2010 from http://www.gov.bc.ca/arr/social/down/transformative_change_accord.pdf.

Hanselmann, C. (2001). Urban Aboriginal people in Western Canada: Realities and policies. Calgary, Alberta: Canada West Foundation.

Health Canada, "Household Food Insecurity in Canada in 2007-2008: Key Statistics and Graphics", http://www.hc-sc.gc.ca/fn-an/surveill/nutrition/commun/insecurit/key-stats-cles-2007-2008-eng.php#fn-np8.

HIV/AIDS and Indigenous Peoples: Final Report of the 5th International Policy Dialogue, International Affairs Directorate, Health Canada, October 21-23, 2009 Ottawa, Canada.

Henry J Kaiser Foundation "Health Coverage and Care for American Indians and Alaska Natives" October 2013 | Issue Brief http://kaiserfamilyfoundation.files.wordpress.com/2013/10/8502-health-coverage-and-care-for-american-indians-and-alaska-natives.pdf.

Hlady WG, Middaugh JP. The epidemiology of suicide in Alaska, 1983-1984. Alaska Med. Nov-Dec 1987;29(5):158-164.

H.V. Thommasen, J. Patenaude, N. Anderson, A. McArthur and H. Tildesley "Differences in diabetic co-morbidity between Aboriginal and non-Aboriginal people living in Bella Coola, Canada" Rural and Remote Health 4:319 (online) 2004,
http://www.rrh.org.au/publishedarticles/article_print_319.pdf.

Indian Health Service. Trends in Indian Health, 2000-2001. Washington, DC: U.S. Department of Health and Human Services,
http://www.ihs.gov/NonMedicalPrograms/IHS_Stats/files/Trends00-01_Part4.pdf.

Interagency coalition on Aids and Development "HIV/AIDS and Indigenous Populations in Canada and Sub-Saharan Africa"
http://www.icad-cisd.com/pdf/HIV_and_Indigenous_Populations_EN.pdf.

Jilly, MPH, Alaska Section of Epidemiology "Characteristics of Suicide Among Alaska Native and Alaska non-Native People", 2003-2008 (2012).

Kathy Bent, Joanne Havelock, Margaret Haworth-Brockman "Entitlements and health services for First Nations and Métis women in Manitoba and Saskatchewan", The Prairie Women's Health Centre of Excellence, August 2007. http://www.pwhce.ca/pdf/entitlementsHealthServices.pdf.

King, M., Smith, A. and Gracey, M. (2009). Indigenous health part 2: The underlying causes of the health gap. The Lancet, 374(9683).

Kral, M.J. (2012). "Postcolonial Suicide among Inuit in Arctic Canada". Culture, Medicine, and Psychiatry. 36(2): 306-325.

Malcolm King, Alexandra Smith, Michael Gracey "Indigenous Health part 2: the underlying causes of the health gap", www.thelancet.com, Vol 374, July 4, 2009.

May, Philip A. "Suicide and Self-Destruction among American Indian Youth", American Indian and Alaska Native Mental Health Research, 1(1), June 1987.

Morales, Laurel "Native Americans Have Highest Rate of Suicide", August 31, 2012 http://www.fronterasdesk.org/content/native-americans-have-highest-rate-suicide.

Native Women's Association of Canada. (2010). What their stories tell us: Research findings from

the Sisters in Spirit initiative. Ottawa, ON: http://www.nwac.ca/sites/default/files/reports/2010_NWAC_SIS_Report_EN.pdf.

Patricia M. Barnes, M.A.; Patricia F. Adams; and Eve Powell-Griner, "Health Characteristics of the American Indian or Alaska Native Adult Population: United States, 2004-2008" http://www.cdc.gov/nchs/data/nhsr/nhsr020.pdf.

Perkins R, Sanddal TL, Howell M, Sanddal ND, Berman A. Epidemiological and follow-back study of suicides in Alaska. Int J Circumpolar Health. 2009;68(3).

Prince George, BC: National Collaborating Centre for Aboriginal Health.

Reading, C. and Wien, F. (2009). Health inequalities and social determinants of Aboriginal Peoples' health.

R. Rosol et al., "Prevalence of affirmative responses to questions for food insecurity: International Polar Year Inuit Health Survey, 2007-2008" and International Journal of Circumpolar Health, vol. 70, No. 5 (2011).

Report of the Aboriginal Justice Inquiry of Manitoba (1999) http://www.ajic.mb.ca/volumel/chapter13.html#4.

State of the World's Minorities and Indigenous Peoples 2013.

Smylie, J., and M. Anderson. 2006. "Understanding the health of Indigenous peoples in Canada: key methodological and conceptual challenges", Canadian Medical Association Journal 175(6).

Tshona Reneé Corbin Barriers to health care access among American Indian and Alaska Native populations (2008) http://d-scholarship.pitt.edu/7075/1/TRCorbin2010.pdf.

U.S. Census Bureau, the American Indian and Alaska Native Population: 2012.

Warry, Wayne Unfinished Dreams: Community Healing and the Reality of Aboriginal Self-Government, University of Toronto Press, Toronto, Canada 2000.

Web-based Injury Statistics Query and Reporting System (WISQARS). 2007. http://www.cdc.gov/ncipc/wisqars.

Chapter Six

Access to Health Services by Indigenous Peoples in the Pacific Region

Dr. Collin Tukuitonga

CHAPTER SIX

ACCESS TO HEALTH SERVICES BY INDIGENOUS PEOPLES IN THE PACIFIC REGION

DR. COLLIN TUKUITONGA

Introduction

This chapter addresses indigenous peoples' access to health services in the Pacific region. It provides a background of the historic, political and cultural factors which have shaped events in the various countries, and influenced the health status of indigenous peoples in the Pacific region. It describes the current health situation, social determinants of health, health service funding and delivery, major challenges as well as the initiatives that have been shown to be effective in improving indigenous peoples' access to all levels of health care.

The Working Group on Indigenous Populations Working paper on the concept of "indigenous people" lists the following factors that have been considered relevant to the understanding of the concept of "indigenous" by international organizations and legal experts:[367]

≡ Priority in time, with respect to the occupation and use of a specific territory;

≡ The voluntary perpetuation of cultural distinctiveness, which may include the aspects of language, social organization, religion and spiritual values, modes of production, laws and institutions;

≡ Self-identification, as well as recognition by other groups, or by state authorities, as a distinct collectivity;

≡ An experience of subjugation, marginalization, dispossession, exclusion or discrimination, whether or not these conditions persist.

Self-identification as indigenous or tribal is considered as a fundamental criterion and this is the practice followed by the United Nations. Article 33 of the United Nations Declaration on the Rights of Indigenous Peoples refers to the right of indigenous peoples to decide their own identities and procedures of belonging.

The Pacific region includes indigenous peoples of the Pacific Ocean which stretches between the Southern Ocean, Asia, Australia, and North and South America. Thousands of islands are spread across this expanse, which adds to the region's considerable geographical, cultural, and linguistic diversity. For example, the region accounts for only a tiny fraction of the global population, but it

---

[367] http://www.ohchr.org/EN/Issues/IPeoples/Pages/WGIP.aspx.

contains close to a quarter of the world's languages.[368] Some of the indigenous peoples of the Pacific are well known e.g. Maori in Aotearoa/New Zealand, but the needs of others are less well recognized e.g. Kanaks of New Caledonia. According to the sociocultural regions of the United Nations Permanent Forum on Indigenous Issues, the Pacific is seen to include Australia, New Zealand, Papua New Guinea, the province of West Papua, the small island states of the Pacific region, including the Federated States of Micronesia, the Northern Mariana Islands and Marshall Islands, the indigenous peoples of Hawaii as well as indigenous peoples of Rapa Nui (Easter Island). For the purposes of this chapter the regions of Asia and North America are covered elsewhere in this publication.

Colonized by European powers relatively late in global terms, the Pacific indigenous peoples were also among the last to be decolonized. Since the early 1960s the process of decolonization has created independent small island States (Fiji, Kiribati, Nauru, Papua New Guinea, Samoa, Solomon Islands, Tonga, Tuvalu, Vanuatu). It should be noted that Tonga is the only Pacific island country not formally colonized by a foreign power. Other countries remain as territories or self-governing states in "free association" with a former colonial power (American Samoa, Cook Islands, Federated States of Micronesia, French Polynesia, Guam, Marshall Islands, New Caledonia, Niue, Northern Mariana Islands, Palau and Tokelau).[369]

The Pacific islands are a culturally diverse region and indigenous peoples have distinct cultures that have existed for thousands of years and have unique systems of knowledge and understanding, such as those related to ocean navigation, vessel construction and traditional medicines. Pacific peoples, especially those who still live in the islands are more likely to speak their mother tongue and view their culture as something that is lived and continuously demonstrated. In contrast, political and economic transformations have displaced large numbers of Pacific people who have moved away from their home islands to inhabit a diaspora spanning the globe, from Australia and New Zealand to Europe and North America. There are also communities of Pacific peoples living on other islands, creating further cultural diversity in an already complex region. Pacific peoples today as in the past have adopted a number of creative survival strategies in the face of rapid cultural, social, political, and economic transitions. Among these are abilities to navigate multiple worlds that might include both Christian and indigenous spiritual practices, western and indigenous lifestyles, and western and "traditional" political and economic structures, while still maintaining a commitment to family and community relations.

Indigenous peoples in the Pacific region have unique characteristics that reflect their local situations but they also share a number of characteristics with other indigenous peoples globally, such as:

≡   The diversity of languages and cultural practices, although some similarities are seen where indigenous peoples share common origins e.g., the Maori of New Zealand, Native Hawaiians in Hawaii and Maori in the Cook Islands.[370]

---

[368]   Ian Anderson, Sue Crengle, Martina Leialoha Kamaka, Tai-Ho Chen, Neal Palafox, Lisa Jackson-Pulver "Indigenous health in Australia, New Zealand, and the Pacific" www.thelancet.com Vol 367 May 27, 2006

[369]   Howe, K. R., Robert C. Kiste, and Brij V. Lal. Tides of history: the Pacific Islands in the twentieth century. Honolulu: University of Hawaii Press, 1994.

[370]   Greenhill, S, and Russell D. Gray. "Testing Population Dispersal Hypotheses Pacific Settlement". In. The Evolution of Cultural Diversity: Phylogenetic Approaches. Ed. Ruth Mace et al. London: UCL Press, 2005. 31-52.

≡ The proportion of the total population of these countries that identify as indigenous ranges from 2.9 per cent in Australia to 15 per cent in New Zealand. There are also differences and distinctions in definitions of who is indigenous and who is not, who are counted and who are not. Overall, indigenous peoples in all Pacific countries are enjoying a revival in their culture and languages.[371]

≡ Populations of indigenous peoples in all the Pacific countries are growing rapidly and have lower median ages in direct contrast to the ageing, non-indigenous populations which presents challenges for the future of local economies and the workforce. Unfortunately younger ages have higher death rates and higher child to adult dependency ratio, in comparison to the non-indigenous populations.

The total population estimate of the 22 nations and territories (see list in Annex) in this area is just under 12 million, with approximately 8 million people in Papua New Guinea alone. In New Zealand, there are 682,200 people claiming to be indigenous descent (Maori or Pacific Islander) which comprises 15 per cent out of a total population. In Australia there are 669,736 which is 2.9 per cent of a total population.[372] The Native Hawaiian population is 527,077 which comprise 0.17 per cent of the total population of the USA.[373]

Fiji and New Caledonia are interesting and unique situations in the Pacific. Historically, in Fiji, the indigenous Melanesian Fijians and indentured Indians and now have almost equal numbers in the total population of approximately 850,000 people. Between 1879 and 1916, when Fiji was under British rule, Fijian Indians were brought to Fiji by the British as to work as labourers in the cane fields. Recently, several military coups, have led to significant out-migration by the Indian people and indigenous Melanesian Fijians now have resumed political dominance in the country although the Indian population continues to dominate the economic and business sectors and academia.[374]

In New Caledonia, the Kanak people are the indigenous Melanesian inhabitants that constitute 44 per cent of the total population of 260,166. Europeans make up 34 per cent of the total population, while Polynesian people (mainly Wallisians) and Asians make up the remainder. New Caledonia is an overseas territory (collectivity) of France and remains within the French Republic. While the total number of indigenous peoples in New Caledonia is a majority in the country, the European population has political or economic dominance.

Indigenous peoples of the Pacific region experience poorer health for many indicators compared to the non-indigenous general populations. The gap in life expectancy at birth between indigenous and non-indigenous population was estimated to be 19-21 years in Australia, 8 years in New Zealand. Rates of avoidable deaths among indigenous people are generally higher than for non-indigenous people. Diabetes prevalence is increasing among all indigenous populations as

---

[371] Denoon, Donald et al., The Cambridge History of the Pacific Islanders. Cambridge, U.K.: Cambridge University Press, 1997.

[372] Estimates of Aboriginal and Torres Straight Islander Australians, retrieved 29/09/1023 from http://www.abs.gov.au/ausstats/abs@.nsf/Latestproducts/3238.0.55.001Media%20Release1June%202011?opendocument&tabname=Summary&prodno=3238.0.55.001&issue=June%202011&num=&view=Australian Bureau of Statistics.

[373] U.S. Census Bureau, 2010 Census.

[374] Veitayaki, J. "Breaking Fiji's Coup Culture through Effective Rural Development". In 1987: Fiji TwentyYears On. Ed. Lal B V et al. Lautoka, Fiji: Fiji Institute of Applied Studies, 2008.

part of increased incidence of non-communicable diseases (NCDs). Cardiovascular diseases are central to the high mortality among indigenous people in all three countries.[375]

While some improvements are being made in the overall health situation of indigenous peoples in the Pacific region, their health needs are greater, and indigenous peoples generally have lower access to and use of health care services at all levels of the health system. Indigenous people also tend to received substandard care for many of the common conditions.[376,377] For example, non-indigenous women are overscreened for cervical cancer while indigenous women are under-screened, despite higher incidence of cervical cancer among them.[378]

Determinants of health

Like all people, the health status of indigenous peoples is influenced by the social, economic and cultural determinants such as education, income, food supply, housing and availability of health and medical care services. Social determinants of health (SDH) are shaped by more distal factors such as the prevailing political ethos, local environment and historical factors, such as colonialism. Indigenous peoples tend to be more susceptible to these factors which partly explain the significant health inequalities that exist. Figure 1 outlines the social determinants of health for all populations, including indigenous peoples, and the influence of colonization, Christianity, urbanization and globalization on health.[379]

The interactions between various social determinants of health are complex and the potential impacts can be indirect. With higher levels of educational attainment, individuals have increased income but are also more likely to have better working conditions with less hazardous jobs that reduce their risks associated with workplace injuries. Education attainment improves access to employment that is more secure, better retirement policies and comprehensive health care insurance for services that that may not covered by government health programs. Education is also associated with health literacy, which refers to the understanding that individuals have about their health and how to access health services and health information. Thus, individuals are better able to understand the health information they are provided and to take control of their health.[380]

---

[375] Ring I, Brown N. The health status of indigenous peoples and others BMJ 2003 23; 327 (7412): 404-405.

[376] Medical Council of New Zealand (2010). Best health outcomes for Pacific peoples; practice implications.

[377] Tukuitonga C. (Chapter 6) in Coles Medical Practice in New Zealand 2013 Edition. Medical Council of New Zealand

[378] Tracking Disparity: trends in ethnic and socioeconomic inequalities in mortality, 1981-2004. NZ Ministry of Health, 2007.

[379] Adapted from Lehane, L., Mary J Ditton (2012) Health challenges for Burmese migrants in Thailand. 8 January 2012, viewed 27 February 2014, http://asiapacific.anu.edu.au/newmandala/2012/01/08/health-challenges-for-burmese-migrants-in-thailand/.

[380] Pulver LJ, Haswell MR, Ring C et al. Indigenous Health—Australia, Canada, Aotearoa New Zealand and the United States - Laying claim to a future that embraces health for us all. World Health Report 2010. World Health Organisation.

Figure 1: Social Determinants of Health

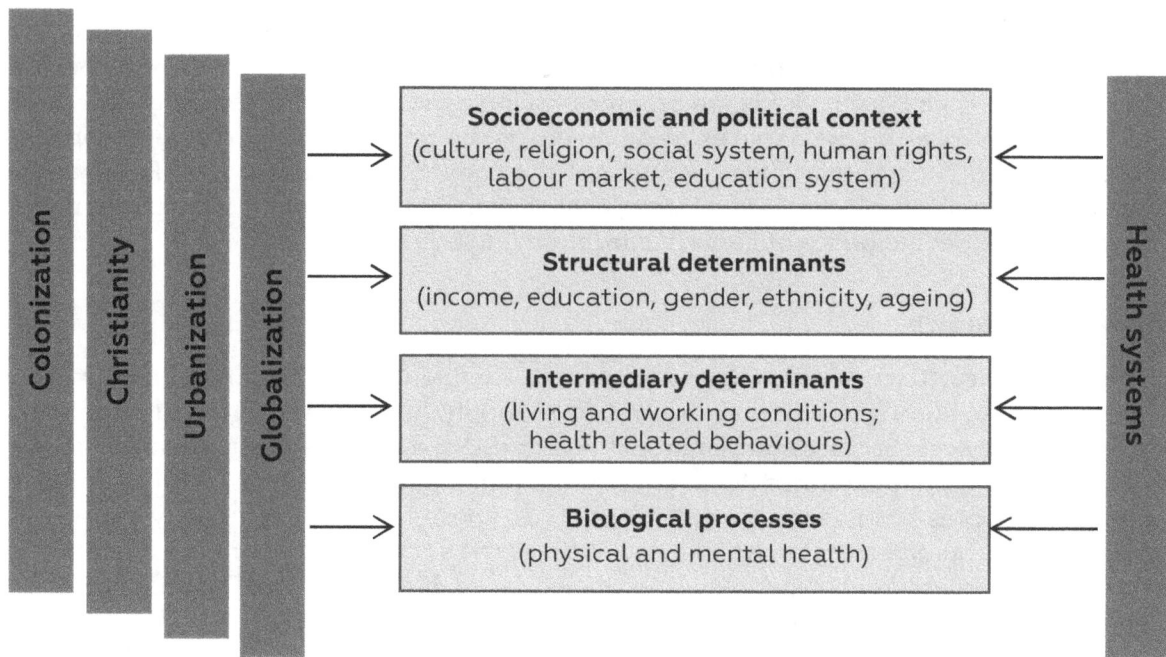

Colonization

Indigenous peoples share similar histories dating back to the colonial era through to the modern influences and socioeconomic determinants of health, including urbanization and globalization. Colonization has had a profound impact on the lives of indigenous peoples and is an important determinant of the health status of indigenous peoples and their descendants. Direct effects of colonialism or colonial policies on indigenous health include the introduction of contagious diseases for which indigenous peoples had no or little resistance. The impact was profound because introduced diseases decimated much of the local populations, drastically impacting local communities and their social structures.

The suppression of traditional medicine was achieved in New Zealand through legislation. The Tohunga Suppression Act 1907 (repealed in 1962) was intended to stop traditional Maori healing practices which were believed to have relied upon a supernatural or spiritual element. Thus the act was designed to replace traditional Maori healers with "modern" science based medicine. Tohunga were the holders of the knowledge of most rites, including health matters (or rongoa) as they were experts in the use of medicinal plants and herbs.[381]

Colonization has also been shown to have residual effects across generations through the protracted effects of land dispossession, marginalization, discrimination, personal and institutional racism and other factors that limit the ability of indigenous peoples to participate fully in the major institutions of the societies in which they live. Indigenous peoples in the Pacific region continue to have limited representation in their national parliaments and other institutions such as the

---

381 Tohunga Suppression Act, retrieved (04/11/2013) from http://www.teara.govt.nz/en/document/28223/tohunga-sup-pression-act.

judiciary. Indigenous peoples are underrepresented in most professions although there are several affirmative action training programmes with encouraging results in New Zealand.[382,383] In the majority of instances, indigenous peoples have limited financial capital needed to participate fully in the private sector and are often employed in low-paid jobs. The health effects of colonization have been described in a number of studies in New Zealand, Australia, Hawaii and elsewhere.[384,385,386]

Christianity

Christianity as a function of colonization and assimilation has also had a profound effect on Pacific cultures and peoples. Early missionaries systematically destroyed all forms of local religious symbols and convinced indigenous communities that their spirituality was false and had no power. Indigenous peoples' religious structures were disrespected in many ways thus breaking all forms of cultural taboo. Once established, church doctrine was integrated into local customs and use of local clergy ensured that Christian principles dominated most cultures of the Pacific. Protestant churches were established early to be self-financing, self-governing as well as self-propagating.[387] Indigenous clergy were the ideal state of affairs. Tonga was so heavily missioned that historians and anthropologists conclude that Christianity has reworked Tongan culture into a missionary framework.[388] The integration of Christian traditions and practices into local Pacific cultures has been so successful that it is often difficult to differentiate local culture from introduced Christian traditions.

The London Missionary Society (LMS) was particularly influential in the Pacific region from 1830 onwards. The LMS established the Malua Theological College in the village of Malua, Samoa in 1844, where several hundred missionaries were subsequently sent to a number of other Pacific islands.[389] Pacific churches continue to be influential forces in the migration and establishment of Pacific communities in Pacific Rim countries and beyond. The impact of Christianity on Pacific .cultures included significant impact on attitudes related to health and illness, which are often described as traditional cultural practices. Colonization and Christianity destroyed many local healing and other customary health practices so effectively that many of the traditional methods have been lost, and indigenous peoples are struggling to reclaim some of these ancient healing practices. Indigenous knowledge has been slowly eroded over the course of subsequent generations because most Pacific societies transmit knowledge and information orally.

---

[382] Curtis E., Reid P., Indigenous Health Workforce Development: challenges and success of the Vision 20:20 programme. ANZ J Surg 83 (2013) 49-54.

[383] Curtis E., Wikaire E., Stokes K., Reid P., Addressing indigenous health workforce inequities: a literature review exploring "best" practice for recruitment into tertiary programmes. Int J. Equity Health 2012; 11:1-15.

[384] Effects of colonisation on Maori, retrieved (14/10/2013) from http://www.teara.govt.nz/en/death-rates-and-life-expectancy/page-4.

[385] Social determinants and the health of indigenous peoples in Australia—a human rights based approach, retrieved (14/10/2013) from http://www.humanrights.gov.au/.../social-determinants-and-health-indigenous-peoples.

[386] Liu D, Alameda A. "Social determinants of health for Native Hawaiian children and adolescents" Hawaii Med J 2011 November, 70(11 Suppl 2): 9-14.

[387] Hezel F. Christianity in Micronesia, Introducing World Christianity Edited by Charles Farhadian, London: Blackwell Press, 2010.

[388] Christianity in the Pacific, retrieved 10/10/2013 from http://epress.anu.edu.au/austronesians/austronesians/mobile_devices/ch17s03.html.

[389] Samoan and London Missionary Society Church History, retrieved 04/10/2013 from http://www.scncucc.org/voices/2009/11/ucc-conference-church-life/samoan-london-missionary-society-church-history/.

Urbanization

Rapid industrialization of New Zealand and Australia following the Second World War saw increased migration from rural areas to cities and urban areas for work. Maori peoples in New Zealand best exemplify the urban migration by indigenous peoples in the Pacific. Before the Second World War (pre 1939), over 80 per cent of Maori were living in rural areas, primarily within their own tribal districts. For most Maori it was a deliberate migration in search of what has been described as "the Big Three": work, money and pleasure. In the beginning, the majority of migrants were unmarried young Maori looking for a more "modern" life. By the 1960s families had begun to migrate in significant numbers. The government had also realized that the economic future of most Maori lay in the larger towns and cities. The Hunn Report of 1961, made recommendations for social reforms of the Maori as "relocation" of Maori became official policy and rural Maori families were encouraged to move to the cities with the provision of accommodation, employment and general assistance in adjusting to a new life. The urban migration of Maori has been described as the most rapid movement of any population in the world. In 1945, 26 per cent of the Maori population lived in the towns and cities. By 1956 this had increased to 35 per cent. The urban population grew to 62 per cent in 1966, and reached nearly 80 per cent by 1986. Today, 84 per cent of Maori live in urban areas.[390]

Urbanization is a two-edged sword with risks and benefits. Migration to urban areas is usually associated with increased isolation from family, land, language, traditions and cultures but urbanization also improves education, employment prospects and socioeconomic circumstances of many indigenous families. While urbanization can improve the socioeconomic circumstances of many people, it can often be difficult to find employment with an adequate level of income needed for city living. When indigenous peoples migrate to urban areas, links with the "home area" remain but may weaken over time as families develop new lifestyles in urban areas. In recent times, some indigenous people have returned "home" to their tribal lands, partly in response to increased unemployment in the cities as a result of the global financial crisis.

Globalization

Globalization is an important influence on the health status of indigenous peoples especially since the mid-1990s. New Zealand, Australia and the United States are among the world leaders in promoting free trade. In simple terms, globalization is the free flow of goods, ideas and services across national borders. Globalization is a process by which national and regional economies, societies, and cultures have become integrated through the global network of trade, communication, immigration and transportation.[391] Globalization was often primarily focused on the economic side, such as trade, foreign direct investment and international capital flows but more recently the term has been expanded to include a broader range of areas and activities such as culture, media, technology, sociocultural and political factors.[392]

---

[390] "Urbanisation—Urban Māori —". Te Ara Encyclopedia of New Zealand. http://www.teara.govt.nz/en/urban-maori/page-1 (accessed 04/10/2013).

[391] Globalisation and Trade, retrieved 04/10/2013 from http://www.wto.org/english/res_e/booksp_e/anrep_e/wtr08-2b.

[392] "Definition of globalisation". Financial Times Lexicon. http://lexicon.ft.com/Term?term=globalisation (accessed 4/10/2013).

While globalization has resulted in many social and economic benefits for indigenous people and mainstream populations globally, it has also led to increased unemployment and job losses in some countries. Inevitably, indigenous peoples are usually the most affected by job losses due to shifts in manufacturing, food production etc. as the unskilled workers in developed countries are displaced from their livelihoods. In addition to the indirect effects of globalization on the health status of indigenous peoples, they are also more directly impacted by the free trade in food, sugar-sweetened beverages, alcohol and other factors that contribute to the rising incidence of non-communicable diseases (NCDs) such as diabetes, heart disease and some cancers. People in many Pacific islands import half of all the foods they consume, which are often highly processed foods that contain usually high levels of salt, sugar, fats and other additives which are regarded as not part of a healthy diet. Indigenous peoples now have some of the highest rates of obesity, diabetes and heart disease in the world. Indigenous peoples also have higher rates of smoking and alcohol abuse compared with non-indigenous peoples in New Zealand, Australia and Hawaii. Alcohol is a major cause of health and social problems among indigenous people in the Pacific and is partly responsible for child abuse, violence against women, road traffic injuries and other problems.[393]

Globalization has also led to increased migration of skilled health workers from small islands and rural areas to the cities and beyond. This is one of the major weaknesses for health systems in the Pacific region where there is a shortage of human resources. In general, skilled health workers migrate from the small island states to New Zealand, Australia and Hawaii, as well as to Europe and the mainland United States, thus reducing the availability of trained indigenous health care workers locally.[394] Migration of indigenous health workers is a global phenomenon linked to the movement of people across borders as part of the broader migration and globalization process.[395]

In figure 2, the table reproduced from Negin (2008) shows the brain drain of Pacific-trained doctors, nurses and midwives who migrate to Australia and New Zealand, diminishing the health workforce of the smaller Pacific nations.

[393] Alcohol and Harm, retrieved 04/10/2013, from http://www.lawcom.govt.nz/sites/default/files/publications/2010/04/Publication_154_464_Part_8_Chapter%203%20-%20Alcohol%20and%20harm.pdf.

[394] University of New South Wales. Human Resources for Health Knowledge Hub. Migration of Health Workers in the Asia-Pacific Region. Dec. 2010. http://www.hrhhub.unsw.edu.au/HRHweb.nsf/resources/1_HWMig_Summary_Dec2010.pdf/$file/1_HWMig_Summary_Dec2010.pdf.

[395] World Health Organization Commission on Social Determinants of Health. Globalization Knowledge Network. Globalization and Health Worker Crisis. Aug. 2007, http://www.who.int/social_determinants/resources/gkn_packer_al.pdf.

Table 1 and 2: Pacific-born doctors and nurses in Australia and New Zealand by country to the domestic workforce

Doctors	Aus. and NZ	Domestic	Per cent in Aus. and NZ relative to domestic	Nurses and Midwives	Aus. and NZ	Domestic	Per cent in Aus. and NZ relative to domestic
Niue	7	4	175	Niue	47	22	213.6
Fiji	361	380	95	Fiji	469	310	151.3
Tonga	26	30	86	Tonga	421	350	120.3
Samoa	42	50	84	Samoa	1828	1660	110.1
Cook Islands	12	20	60	Cook Islands	77	80	96.3
Papua New Guinea	160	275	58.2	Papua New Guinea	12	63	19
Nauru	4	10	40	Nauru	441	2841	15.5
Kiribati	6	20	30	Kiribati	7	50	14
Tuvalu	3	10	30	Tuvalu	30	360	8.3
Solomon Islands	12	60	20	Solomon Islands	18	260	6.9
Vanuatu	4	30	13.3	Vanuatu	37	653	5.7
Timor-Leste	8	79	10.1	Timor-Leste	48	1795	2.7
Micronesia	0	60	0	Micronesia	0	250	0
Palau	0	30	0	Palau	0	152	0
Marshall Islands	0	24	0	Marshall Islands	0	121	0

Source: Negin, J (2008) "Australia and New Zealand's contribution to the Pacific Island health worker brain drain".

Health services of indigenous peoples in the Pacific Region

Some of the countries of the Pacific region are very small, geographically isolated from the rest of the world by vast amounts of ocean and heavily dependent on development assistance and remittances.[396] Consequently, they are often forgotten or simply ignored by other nations of the world.[397] Such invisibility is just one of the significant barriers that these tiny nations face as they struggle to ensure the health of their citizens in the new millennium. Indigenous peoples of the

---

[396] United Nations Development Programme. Subregional Programme Document for the Pacific Island Countries and Territories (2013-2017). Nov. 2012. http://www.undp.org/content/dam/rbap/docs/programme-documents/FJ-SRP-2013-2017.pdf.

[397] Reilly, B., and Elsina Wainwright. "The South Pacific". In. Making States Work: State Failure and the Crisis of Governance. Ed. Simon Chesterman et al. Tokyo: United Nations University Press, 2005. 122-142.

Pacific region are in worse health than the general population in both the developed and developing countries alike.

Malnutrition and undernutrition are common within the region with more than one fifth of children and pregnant women being anemic. Iron deficiency anemia affects more than 25 per cent of the general population. This has a direct impact on the productivity of the workforce as well as an immediate effect on one's sense of well-being and stamina and yet can easily be rectified. In Fiji, Papua New Guinea and Vanuatu, iodine deficiency and related goitre are endemic although, in Fiji and Papua New Guinea, great progress has been made recently through salt iodization. About 40 per cent of the Pacific island region's population has been diagnosed with a non-communicable disease, notably cardiovascular disease and hypertension and cancers, which are on the increase and are being diagnosed in younger people.[398] These diseases account for three-quarters of all deaths across the Pacific archipelago and 40-60 per cent of total health care expenditure. Infectious diseases such as malaria, leprosy, filariasis, tuberculosis, hepatitis and sexually transmitted infections including HIV/AIDS in some islands are major health issues. These can be controlled through environmental and public health measures.[399]

In many areas of the Pacific region, the inadequacy of communication and infrastructure and lack of access to health care also result in indigenous women dying from the complications of pregnancy and childbirth at rates which approach those in sub-Saharan Africa. However, despite this, birth rates in the region are high. Coupled with greater infant and childhood survival, population growth rates are high. Furthermore between 40 per cent and 50 per cent of the population of some countries are less than 15 years old. Young people in some societies are sexually active early, but this occurs in the absence of informed choices about behaviour and responsibility. Consequently, there are high rates of sexually transmitted infections and teenage pregnancy with its consequential physical and social risks including HIV.

Maori peoples have the poorest health of any population group in New Zealand. In 2012, life expectancy at birth for Maori men was 72.8 years, while life expectancy at birth for non-Maori men was 80.2 years. Life expectancy at birth for Maori women was 76.5 years, while life expectancy at birth for non-Maori women was 83.7 years. Avoidable death rates are almost double for Maori than for other New Zealanders, and Maori die, on average, eight-ten years earlier. Maori have a higher mortality rate than non-Maori as well as higher rates of illness. For example, excess cancer deaths among Maori account for two-thirds of the excess male cancer deaths and one-quarter of the excess female cancer deaths in New Zealand, compared to Australia.[400]

Inequalities in overall Maori health persist even when confounding factors such as poverty, education and location are eliminated, demonstrating that cultural or biological factors or something about the lived social experiences, seemingly specific to Maori theoretically exert an independent influence as an indigenous determinant of health. It is also likely that part of the cause if unequal access to health services and medical treatment and care.

---

[398] "Pacific Islanders Pay Heavy Price for Abandoning Traditional Diet". Bulletin of the World Health Organization 88 (7 July 2010): 484-485.

[399] http://www.who.int/bulletin/volumes/88/7/10-010710/en/

[400] Jansen P, Jansen D 2013. Māori and Health. Chapter 5 in St George IM (ed.). Cole's medical practice in New Zealand, 12th edition. Medical Council of New Zealand, Wellington.

Maori women have rates of breast, cervical and lung cancer that are several times those of non-Maori women. There is high incidence of obesity in the Maori community, which contributes to the higher incidence of diabetes, and the younger age of diagnosis. Maori have lower access to medical care and rehabilitation services when compared with non-Maori. Even though Maori turn up for general practitioner appointments at the same rate as non-Maori, they obtain fewer diagnostic tests, less effective treatment plans and are referred for secondary or tertiary procedures at significantly lower rates than non-Maori patients.[401]

In Australia, indigenous peoples are a much younger population. According to estimates from the 2011 Census, about 36 per cent of indigenous peoples were less than 15 years of age, compared with 18 per cent of their non-Indigenous counterparts in that age group.[402] In 2011 the Census showed a 21 per cent increase in the population of indigenous peoples compared with the 2006 Census. A number of reasons contributed to the growth of the indigenous population;

- ≡ higher fertility rates of indigenous women compared with the rates of other Australian women;

- ≡ the significant numbers of indigenous babies born to indigenous fathers and non-indigenous mothers;

- ≡ this increase may also be due to a higher rate of self-reported boriginal identity and the way identity was collected and analysed, possibly reflecting increasing pride with identifying as an indigenous person.

The majority of indigenous peoples live in cities and towns. Overall, slightly more than one-half of the indigenous population lived in areas classified as "major cities" or "inner regional" areas, compared with almost nine-tenths of the non-indigenous population. Almost one-quarter of indigenous peoples lived in areas classified as "remote" or "very remote" in relation to having "very little access to goods, services and opportunities for social interaction".[403] In Australia, most of the indigenous peoples live in low socioeconomic circumstances with low educational achievement, high unemployment and low income and overcrowded housing. Many are located in areas with inadequate social support services.[404]

During the early colonial period in Australia, introduced diseases was certainly the major cause of death for indigenous peoples but direct conflict and occupation of their lands also contributed substantially to indigenous mortality. Conflict escalated in many places, in some instances resulting in overt massacres of indigenous peoples. Prior to arrival of the British colonizers in 1788, indigenous peoples were able to define their own sense of being through control over all aspects of their lives, including ceremonies, spiritual practices, medicine, social relationships, manage-

---

[401] Davis P., Suaalii-Sauni T., Lay-Yee R., Pearson J., 2005, Pacific Patterns in Primary Health Care: A comparison of Pacific and all patient visits to doctors: The National Primary Medical Care Survey (NatMedCa): 2001-2002. Report 7. Wellington: Ministry of Health

[402] Gray C, Brown A, Thomson N. Review of cardiovascular health among Indigenous Australians. Australian Indigenous HealthBulletin 12(4), http://healthbulletin.org.au/articles/review-of-cardiovascular-health-among-indigenous-australians.

[403] Australian Indigenous HealthInfonet (2013) summary of Australian Indigenous health, retrieved (15/10/2013) from http://www.healthinfonet.ecu.edu.au/health-facts/summary.

[404] "Social determinants and the health of Indigenous peoples in Australia: A Human Rights Based Approach". Australian Human Rights Commission, N.p., n.d. Web. 27 Feb. 2014, https://www.humanrights.gov.au/news/speeches/social-determinants-and-health-indigenous-peoples-australia-human-rights-based.

ment of land, law and economic activities. In addition to the impacts of introduced diseases and conflict, colonization of indigenous peoples' lands undermined the ability of indigenous peoples to lead healthy lives by devaluing their culture, destroying their traditional food base, separating families and dispossessing whole communities. This loss of autonomy undermined social vitality, which, in turn, affected the capacity to meet life's challenges, including maintaining health as a vicious cycle of dispossession, demoralization and poor health was established.

These impacts on indigenous peoples eventually forced colonial authorities to try to "protect" remaining indigenous people. This pressure led to the establishment of Aboriginal "protection" boards, the first established in Victoria by the Aboriginal Protection Act of 1869. A similar Act established the NSW Aborigines Protection Board in 1883, with the other colonies also enacting legislation to "protect" indigenous populations within their boundaries. The "protection" provided under the provisions of the various Acts imposed enormous restrictions on the lives of many indigenous peoples. These restrictions meant that, as late as 1961, in eastern Australia "nearly one-third of all Australians recorded as being of Aboriginal descent lived in settlements". The provisions of the Acts were also used to justify the forced separation of indigenous children from their families "by compulsion, duress or undue influence". The National Inquiry into the separation of the children concluded that "between one in 3 and one in 10 Indigenous children were forcibly removed from their families and communities in the period from approximately 1910 until 1970". It was the 1960s, at the earliest, when the various "protection" Acts were repealed.[405]

The health status of Australia's indigenous peoples is poor in comparison to the remainder of the Australian population.[406] There remains a large inequality gap in Australia across all health and social statistics. For example, for all age groups below 65 years, the age-specific death rates for indigenous Australians are at least twice those experienced by the non-indigenous population. The causes of death with the largest contribution to excess mortality among indigenous males are circulatory diseases, cancers, injuries, respiratory diseases and endocrine, metabolic and nutritional disorders. The indigenous male death rates due to external causes (injuries) were more than three times those for non-indigenous males aged 25 to 44 years.[407]

Between 2004 and 2008, two-thirds (66 per cent) of indigenous deaths occurred before the age of 65 years compared with 20 per cent of non-indigenous deaths. In that same period, endocrine, metabolic and nutritional disorders contributed to raise indigenous mortality up to six to seventimes the non-indigenous rates. For indigenous females, the causes of death with the largest contribution to excess mortality are circulatory diseases, endocrine, metabolic and nutritional disorders, digestive diseases, neoplasms and respiratory diseases. The indigenous infant mortality rate declined between 1991 and 2008, though it remains twice that of non-indigenous infants. A range of risk factors contribute to excess indigenous mortality, including tobacco smoking, excessive alcohol consumption, high overweight/obesity, poor nutrition and lower utilization of

---

[405] "Aboriginal Societies: The Experience of Contact", Australian Law Reform Commission. N.p., n.d. Web. 27 Feb. 2014. http://www.alrc.gov.au/publications/3.%20Aboriginal%20Societies%3A%20The%20Experience%20of%20Contact/changing-policies-towards-aboriginal.

[406] Australian Insitute of Health and Welfare 2011. The health and welfare of Australia's Aboriginal and Torres Strait Islander people, an overview 2011. Cat. no. IHW 42 Canberra: IHAW.

[407] Australian Institute of Health and Welfare 2011. The health and welfare of Australia's Aboriginal and Torres Strait Islander people, an overview 2011. Cat. no. IHW 42. Canberra: AIHW.

health services relative to need.[408] The 2012-2013 National Australian Aboriginal and Torres Strait Islander Health Survey (NATSIHS) is the largest survey of indigenous Australians health status, and results are being released progressively during 2013-2014.

While there have been improvements on some measures of indigenous health status, they have not matched the rapid health gains made in the general population in Australia. For example, death rates from cardiovascular disease in the general population have fallen 30 per cent since 1991, and 70 per cent in the last 35 years, whereas indigenous peoples do not appear to have made any reduction in death rates from cardiovascular disease over this period.[409]

Important determinants of indigenous health inequality in Australia include the lack of equal access to primary health care and inadequate infrastructure and support services in indigenous communities compared to other Australians.

A clear relationship exists between the social disadvantages experienced by indigenous peoples and their current health status. Whereas the health disparities and vulnerabilities experienced by indigenous peoples in Australia can be considered as having their roots in the history of colonization, present-day perpetuation of indigenous peoples disadvantage owes much to contemporary civil society turning a blind eye to the disparities. Education, employment, income, housing, access to health services, social networks, connection to land, racism, and incarceration are issues where indigenous peoples are experience substantial disadvantage.

Holistic Health

It is also important in considering indigenous health to understand how indigenous people themselves conceptualize health. Like most indigenous peoples in the world, indigenous Australians' perspective of health is holistic. It encompasses everything important in a person's life, including land, environment, physical body, community, relationships, and law. Health is the social, emotional, and cultural well-being of the whole community and the concept is therefore linked to the sense of being indigenous.[410]

When Captain James Cook arrived in Hawaii in 1778, it was estimated that there were between 300,000 and 400,000 Native Hawaiians, the *kanaka maoli*. Over the course of the next century the Native Hawaiian population dropped between 80-90 per cent. This decline was due, in large part, to the diseases introduced by contact with foreigners. By 1878, the native population was estimated to be between 40,000 and 50,000 people. While drastically smaller than the population of just one hundred years previously, the Native Hawaiians still comprised over 75 per cent of the total population of Hawaii.[411]

---

[408] Ibid.

[409] National Health and Medical Research Centre, "Promoting the health of Australians, Case studies of achievements in improving the health of the population", AGPS, Canberra, 1997, Thomson, N. and Brooks, J., "Cardiovascular Disease", in Editor, Thomson, N., The Health of Indigenous Australians, Oxford University.

[410] "The context of Indigenous health". Australian Indigenous HealthInfoNet. N.p., n.d. Web. 27 Feb. 2014, http://www.healthinfonet.ecu.edu.au/health-facts/overviews/the-context-of-indigenous-health.

[411] The Native Hawaiian Population and other Pacific Islander Population (2010), retrieved 04/10/2013 from http://www.census.gov/prod/cen2010/briefs/c2010br-12.pdf.

The 1900 U.S. Census identified 37,656 residents of full or partial Native Hawaiian ancestry. Today, there are fewer than 8,000 Native Hawaiians alive who are 100 per cent blood quantum.[412] On the contrary, the number of those who identify as having part Native Hawaiian ancestry and who consider themselves to be Hawaiian, has increased steadily since the turn of the century. Today, estimates are between 225,000 and 250,000 people with Hawaiian blood living in Hawaii. According to the U.S. Census Bureau report for 2000, there were 401,162 people who identified themselves as being Native Hawaiian alone or in any combination, and 140,652 people identified themselves as being Native Hawaiian alone. Two-thirds live in the State of Hawaii while the other one-third is scattered among other states, with a high concentration in California.[413]

Today, Native Hawaiians are still fighting to regain their language, culture, rights and land. One effort under way is the move to have Native Hawaiians federally recognized as the indigenous people of the Hawaiian islands thereby allowing a government-to-government relationship between mainland Native American tribes and Alaska natives in the United States. Native Hawaiian culture has seen a revival in recent years as a consequence of decisions made at the 1978 Hawaii State Constitutional Convention. At the convention, the Hawaii state government committed itself to a progressive study and preservation of Native Hawaiian culture, history and language. A comprehensive Hawaiian culture curriculum was introduced into the State of Hawai'i's public elementary schools teaching ancient Hawaiian art, lifestyle, geography, hula and Hawaiian language vocabulary.[414]

Indigenous Hawaiians have the poorest health and socioeconomic indicators of the various ethnic groups in the State of Hawaii.[415] When compared to the U.S. all-race population, Native Hawaiians have death rates that are 44 per cent higher for heart disease, 39 per cent higher for cancer, 31 per cent higher for strokes and 196 per cent higher for diabetes The Native Hawaiian infant mortality rate was more than twice that for Whites. High Native Hawaiian infant mortality was equally due to neonatal and post-neonatal deaths. Preterm-related causes of death accounted for 43.9 per cent of the infant mortality disparity, followed by sudden unexpected infant death (21.6 per cent) and injury (5.6 per cent). Maternal educational inequality was associated with the largest portion of the neonatal mortality disparity (20.9 per cent); younger maternal age (12.2 per cent) and smoking (9.5 per cent) were the only significant contributors to the post-neonatal mortality disparity.[416]

Tobacco smoking, high-fat diet, alcohol drinking, hyperlipidemia and obesity are the major lifestyle risk factors.[417] Although cigarette smoking in the general U.S. population has decreased con-

[412] Pentaris, P. "Culture and Death: A Multicultural Perspective". Hawaii Pacific Journal of Social Work Practice 4.1 (2011): 45-84. Print.

[413] United States: Race reporting for the Native Hawaiian by Selected Categories: 2010, retrieved 10/10/2013 from http://www.ohadatabook.com/QT-P9_United%20States.pdf.

[414] Wilson, W.H."The Sociopolitical Context of Establihsing Hawaiian-medium Education" In. Indigenous Community-Based Education. Ed. Stephen May. Clavedon, UK: Multilingual Matters, 1999. 95-108.

[415] Native Hawaiian Fact Sheet 2011. Office of Hawaiian Affairs, Honolulu. HI.

[416] Hirai AH, Hayes DK, Taualii MM et al. Excess Infant Mortality Among Native Hawaiians: Identifying Determinants for Preventive Action .Am J Public Health l2013 Nov;103(11):e88-95. doi: 10.2105/AJPH.2013.301294. Epub 2013 Sep 12.

[417] Noncommunicable diseases - Fact sheet. (n.d.). World Health Organization. Retrieved February 26, 2014, from http://www.who.int/mediacentre/factsheets/fs355/en/.

siderably over the past several decades, prevalence rates among Native Hawaiians have remained elevated by comparison with other groups.

Figure 2. Current smoking among adults by demographic characteristics in Hawaii[418]

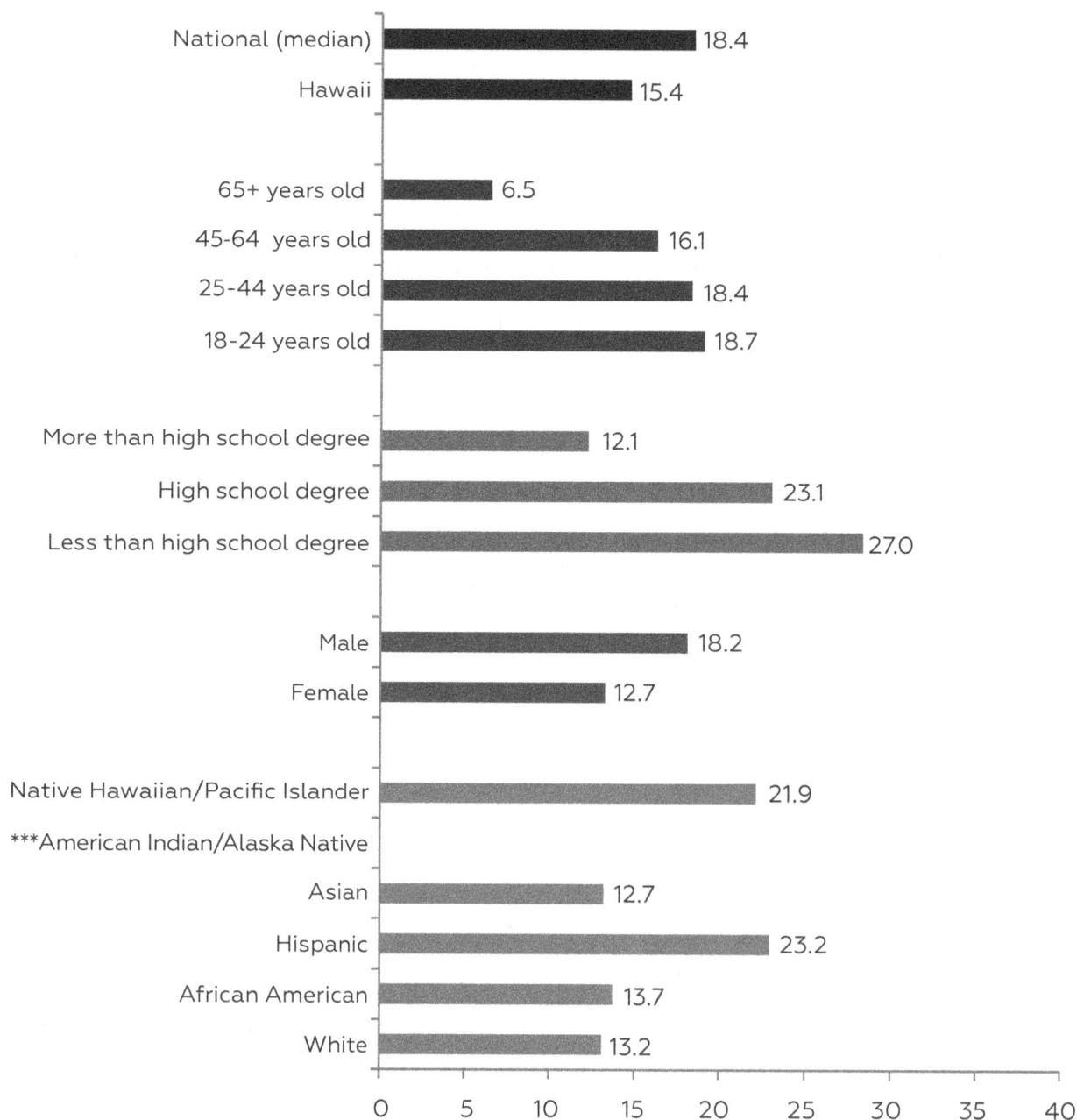

Category	Value
National (median)	18.4
Hawaii	15.4
65+ years old	6.5
45-64 years old	16.1
25-44 years old	18.4
18-24 years old	18.7
More than high school degree	12.1
High school degree	23.1
Less than high school degree	27.0
Male	18.2
Female	12.7
Native Hawaiian/Pacific Islander	21.9
***American Indian/Alaska Native	
Asian	12.7
Hispanic	23.2
African American	13.7
White	13.2

(x-axis: 0, 5, 10, 15, 20, 25, 30, 35, 40)

[418] Centers for Disease Control and Prevention, Tobacco Control State Highlights, 2010, Atlanta: U.S. Department of Health and Human Services, Centers for Disease Control and Prevention, National Center for Chronic Disease Prevention and Health Promotion, Office on Smoking and Health, 2010.

Figure 3. Current smoking among adults by demographic characteristics in California[419]

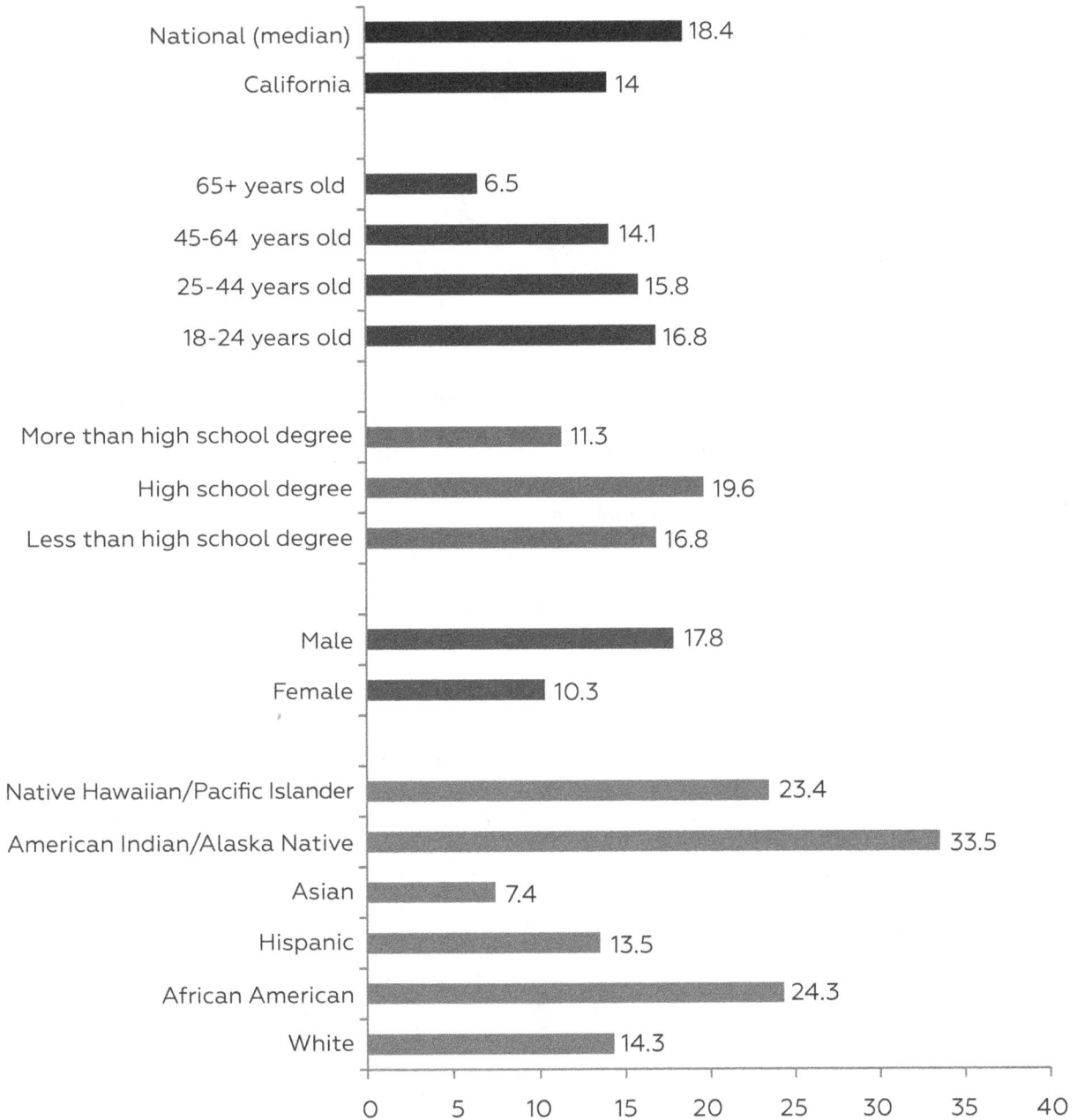

[419] Ibid.

New Zealand

The landmark Social Security Act introduced in 1938 established the "cradle to the grave" welfare philosophy and universal access to health care in New Zealand. The policy included the availability of the General Medical Subsidy (GMS), a fee-for-service arrangement, in which private general practitioners were able to claim part of the cost of treating patients at the primary care level. Hospital and other specialist services, including pharmaceuticals, were free to the user. Doctors claimed that the GMS failed to keep pace with rising costs and they were forced to introduce extra billing by patients to increase charges for physician consultations. Over the years, the system of the GMS and patient part charges led to an "oversupply" of doctors in affluent areas due to the prosperous residents' ability to pay. Conversely, less affluent and rural areas had fewer doctors with fewer services despite high levels of need. Most indigenous Maori (and other minority groups) live in less affluent areas as a result of high unemployment, low income and availability of social housing.[420]

Developments in Maori health have been strengthened by the presence of an effective political voice in the Aotearoa/New Zealand Parliament. The Maori Party was formed in 2004 as a result of the foreshore and seabed controversy, a debate about whether Maori have legitimate claim to ownership of part or all of New Zealand's foreshore and seabed. The Maori Party is formally in coalition, along with two other minor political parties, with the national party-led Government. Their presence in parliament has been widely regarded as being influential in a number of significant policy and funding that benefit Maori and other minority groups, e.g., Whanau Ora is an interagency approach that includes services and opportunities to support the aspiration of Maori *whanau* (extended families) to become more self-managing and to take responsibility for their economic, social and cultural development. They have also made significant gains in tobacco control, including substantial rises in tobacco taxes and funding for rheumatic fever and rheumatic heart disease prevention.

Indigenous health providers

The introduction of the New Zealand Health Strategy and the Primary Health Care Strategy in 2001 made major changes to the way primary health care was organized, governed and funded.[421,422] He Korowai Oranga (Maori Health Strategy) was introduced in 2002 outlining the direction for Maori health development in New Zealand.[423] These strategies led to a number of changes including capitation funding rather than a fee for service and introduced greater participation by Maori in the provision of primary health care services. The availability of a Maori Provider Development Scheme (MPDS) and additional funding for "high need" populations led to the growth of a number of Maori-owned Community Controlled Primary Health Care (PHC) clinics and related services. An independent evaluation of the MPDS showed that the scheme had made a positive

---

[420] Barwick H., "Improving access to primary care for Maori and Pacific peoples. A literature review", commissioned by the Health Funding Authority. Wellington: Ministry of Health; 2000.

[421] The New Zealand Health Strategy retrieved 10/10/2013 from http://www.health.govt.nz/publication/new-zealand-health-strategy.

[422] The Primary Health Care Strategy retrieved 10/10/2013 from http://www.moh.govt.nz/notebook/nbbooks.nsf/0/8255DFFA80749680CC2569F0006F9FF3/$file/PHCStrat.pdf.

[423] He Korowai Oranga retrieved 10/10/2013 from http://www.health.govt.nz/publication/he-korowai-oranga-maori-health-strategy.

contribution to the development of the capacity and capability of Maori health providers.[424] *Ka tika ka ora* is the Maori Health provider programme managed by the New Zealand Ministry of Health (MOH) on behalf of District Health Boards (DHBs).[425] The programme is designed to develop a comprehensive national picture of activities that the Ministry and DHBs have planned to undertake to support the Maori health provider sector and provide a foundation for building a consistent approach in supporting a solid body of Maori health providers. Maori health providers have made a big impact on health care delivery in New Zealand and increasingly accepted as an integral part of the health care landscape.[426]

Since *He Korowai Oranga* was implemented as policy in 2002, substantial progress has been made in building capacity of the Maori health and disability workforce. This policy could be considered a best practice for other health systems around the world. Key factors in successful programs to increase Maori health workforce recruitment and retention include Maori leadership, mentorship and peer support and comprehensive support within study programs and in the transitions between school, university and work. The interventions to date provide a strong basis for ongoing action to address inequities in health workforce participation, and are likely to be relevant to health workforce development approaches for other indigenous people.[427] There is an active Maori health research programme health funded by the Health Research Council of New Zealand and academic institutions.[428] The research programmes supports both the development of a Maori health research workforce and research projects into priority health issues of concern to Maori. The research programme includes investigations involving Maori research concepts and interventions.[429]

Australia

Indigenous health policy in Australia is guided by the National Aboriginal and Torres Islander Health Plan 2013-2023.[430] One of the nine guiding principles of this policy is the directive that Governments adopt a holistic approach, recognizing that the improvement of indigenous Australians' health status must include attention to physical, spiritual, cultural, emotional and social well-being, community capacity and governance.

The Indigenous Health Service Delivery Division (IHSDD) formerly known as the Office for Aboriginal and Torres Strait Islander Health (OATSIH) in the Department of Health and Ageing was established in 2013 to give greater focus to the health needs of indigenous Australians in mainstream health

---

[424] Evaluation of the Maori Provider Development Scheme retrieved 10/10/2013 from http://www.health.govt.nz/publication/evaluation-maori-provider-development-scheme.

[425] Ka tika ka ora retrieved 10/10/2013 from http://www.health.govt.nz/our-work/populations/maori-health/maori-health-providers/ka-tika-ka-ora-maori-health-provider-work-programme.

[426] Ministry of Health. 2009. Maori Provider Work Programme. Wellington: Ministry of Health.

[427] Ratima M, Brown R, Garrett N et al. Strengthening Maori participation in the New Zealand health and disability workforce. Med J Aust 2007 186 (10): 541-543.

[428] Māori Health Research. (n.d.). Health Research Council of New Zealand. Retrieved February 27, 2014, from http://www.hrc.govt.nz/funding-opportunities/maori-development.

[429] Jones, B., Ingham, T.R., Cram, F., Dean, S. & Davies, S. (2013). An Indigenous approach to exploring health-related experiences among Māori parents: The Pukapuka Hauora asthma study. BioMed Central 13:228 (15 March 2013).

[430] National Aboriginal and Torres Strait Islander Health Plan 2013-2023, retrieved 09/11/2013 from http://www.health.gov.au/internet/main/publishing.nsf/content/B92E980680486C3BCA257BF0001BAF01/$File/health-plan.pdf.

programmes, and to administer funding to Aboriginal and Torres Strait Islander community controlled clinics. IHSDD funds a comprehensive range of services for indigenous Australians with the aim to close the gap in health outcomes within the 2013-2023 decade. The aim is to provide coordinated clinical care, population health and health promotion programs for disease prevention, early intervention and effective disease management. The IHSDD pursues a three way approach, namely;

- ☰ to improve access to, and responsiveness of the mainstream health system;

- ☰ to ensure complementary actions through Aboriginal and Torres Strait Islander specific health initiatives;

- ☰ to increase collaboration across governments and the health sector to improve service delivery and health outcomes.

The National Aboriginal Community Controlled Health Organization (NACCHO)

NACCHO was established in 1992 and is a peak body on Aboriginal health representing the interests of Aboriginal Community Controlled Health Services (ACCHSs). ACCHSs deliver a range of services to meet the complex health needs of indigenous Australians. ACCHSs plays a central role due to the religious, cultural, spiritual and social needs including provision of culturally appropriate primary health care services specific to the needs of local communities. ACCHSs aims to respond to the unique needs of indigenous Australians through a network of centres throughout Australia. Examples of ACCHSs initiatives include the Aboriginal Health Worker Forum, the Kimberley Aboriginal Medical Services Council Inc., Nunkuwarrin Yunti of SA Inc., Wu Chopperen Social Health Programme in Cairns and others. In 2013, NACCHO launched the HEALTHY FUTURES 10-point plan 2013-2030, which outlines priorities and strategies for ACCHSs, government and other stakeholders for improving the health of indigenous Australians.[431] The plan includes a range of measures including research, funding and support for the workforce to deliver innovative and comprehensive primary health care.[432]

Like most indigenous societies, indigenous Australians have a rich and sophisticated system of traditional medicine and healing practices. Traditional medicine practice (TMP) by indigenous Australians encompasses a holistic world view, which recognizes good health as a complex system involving interconnectedness with the land, spirit and ancestry and the connectedness of social, mental, emotional and physical well-being of the individual and community. A recent review of the role of TMP in primary care within Aboriginal Australia showed that the practices were used concurrently or sequentially with conventional health care services.[433]

---

[431] Investing in Healthy Futures for Generational Change, retrieved from 10/10/2013 from http://www.naccho.org.au/download/naccho_health_futures/NACCHO%20Healthy%20Futures%2010%20point%20plan%202013-2030.pdf.

[432] "Aboriginal Male Healthy Futures for Generational Change". National Aboriginal Community Controlled Health Organisation. N.p., 1 Aug. 2013. Web. 28 Feb. 2014. http://www.naccho.org.au/download/naccho_health_futures/A%20Blueprint%20for%20Aboriginal%20Male%20Healthy%20Futures%20.pdf.

[433] Oliver S. The role of traditional medicine practice in primary health care within Aboriginal Australia: a review of the literature. Journal of Ethnobiology and Ethnomedicine 2013, 9:46 doi:10.1186/1746-4269-9-46.

Hawaii

Until recently, the United States of America does not have a purposeful national publically system of health care as much as a laissez fare practices that have developed over time. The central element is a financial arrangement that pays for health care services through employer-purchased insurance. Historically, patients have had the right to choose any physician, and physicians have been free to choose among specialties and to practice where and how they like. New managed care plans increasingly restrict both of these choices. Market incentives encourage the development of new drugs and high-tech treatments. For some of the uninsured, the government pays for health care through Medicare, Medicaid, the military, Native American Health Service, the Veterans Administration, and other programs. This leads to great complexity, since all of these plans follow different eligibility, underwriting, benefit, and reimbursement policies. Hawaii's health care plan makes a basic package of health benefits available to all residents through employer-mandated insurance, supports health promotion and disease prevention, and controls health care expenditures.

Hawaii was the first state in the USA to enact laws creating a near universal health care coverage system, with the Hawaii Prepaid Health Care Act which was passed in 1974.[434] The Act required employers to provide health insurance to employees. Legislation in 1989 added those not covered by Medicare, Medicaid, or private insurance and emphasized comprehensive, preventive care. In 1994, health care programs for Medicaid and other low-income groups were converted into managed care plans. Managed care plans are financing systems that control health care costs in two ways. First, they lock in consumers to specific lists of providers (physicians, hospitals, nursing homes, etc.) who agree to accept reduced fees. Second, many require the insurance company's approval before providing benefits. The first managed care plans were started in the 1940s, with the development of several health maintenance organizations (HMOs). Their purpose was to provide comprehensive health care for a set monthly fee, rather than fee for service. Considered radical at the time, HMOs and other managed care products are now mainstream. Many have demonstrated cost savings and quality outcomes by emphasizing preventive care and conservative use of treatments.[435]

In Hawaii, there have been several health initiatives implemented to address the needs of Native Hawaiians. Na Pu'uwai, Inc. is a community-based Native Hawaiian organization on the island of Molokai, dedicated to the betterment of the health conditions of Native Hawaiians.[436] It was founded in 1985 as an advisory committee to the Molokai Heart Study in collaboration with the University of Hawaii, WHO and OHA. In 1987, in collaboration with the University of Oregon, Na Pu'uwai conducted the Ho'oke 'Ai—Molokai Diet Study which laid the foundation, and served as the catalyst to renewed interest in the benefits of the traditional Hawaiian diet.[437] The results of these research projects and the ongoing information that Na Pu'uwai has gathered through the Cardiovascular Risk Clinics have had a major impact on the understanding and management of

---

[434] Hawaii Prepaid Health Care Act, retrieved 10/10/2013 from http://labor.hawaii.gov/dcd/home/about-phc/.

[435] Cooper, E, and Liz Taylor. "Comparing Health Care Systems". Context Institute. N.p., 9 Sept. 1994. Web. 28 Feb. 2014. http://www.context.org/iclib/ic39/cooptalr/.

[436] Na Pu'uwai Native Hawaiian Health Care System, retrieved 10/10/2013 from http://www.napuuwai.com/page2.html

[437] "Our History". Na Pu´uwai, Inc. N.p., n.d. Web. 28 Feb. 2014. http://www.napuuwai.com/.

risk factors and cultural barriers affecting the health conditions of Native Hawaiians.[438] The Molokai Diet study has served as a model for current traditional Hawaiian Diet Programs such as the Waianae Diet Program and the Waimea Diet Program.[439]

The aggregation of Native Hawaiian smoking data with that of Asians has drawn attention away from the serious smoking problems that Native Hawaiians experience, thus, limiting funding, programs, and policies to reduce tobacco-related health disparities in their respective communities. In California, community-based organizations (CBOs) have played a major role in supporting the state's comprehensive tobacco control program, which is arguably one of the most successful in the nation. One study described the tobacco control activities of five Native Hawaiian serving CBOs in Southern California and how they have provided anti-tobacco education for thousands of Native Hawaiians, Chamorros, Marshallese, Samoans, Tongans, and other Pacific Islander subgroups, and used advocacy and coalition building to promote smoke-free environment policies in their communities. The concerted efforts of the CBOs and their community members have made vital contributions to the reduction of tobacco-related disparities for indigenous populations in California.[440]

Small islands of the Pacific

In most of the small islands of the Pacific, governments are the main funders and providers of health services.[441] Several small island states spend less than 5 per cent of GDP on health care services. It is generally accepted that health expenditure above this threshold is required in order to ensure the availability of basic health care services.[442] Rural areas and outer islands tend to have lower availability of health care services and residents need to travel to cities and urban areas for health care.[443] Most small island states are struggling to fund and provide health care services as a result of a growing and ageing population as well as the demands caused by people with NCDs, including costly complications such as kidney failure needing dialysis. NCDs have become the major causes of costly off-island referrals.[444]

Discussion

Indigenous peoples in the Pacific region have similar health status, due in large part to their shared colonial history and health determinants. Socioeconomic determinants of health are part of the environmental causes of ill health that affect population health. They point to evidence that highlights higher susceptibility to illness and disease as a product of particular socioeco-

---

[438] Ibid.

[439] Ibid.

[440] Palmer P.H., Lee C., Sablan-Santos L. et al., Eliminating tobacco disparities among Native Hawaiian pacific islanders through policy change: the role of community-based organizations. Health Promot Pract. 2013 Sep;14(5 Suppl):36S-9S. doi: 10.1177/1524839913486150. Epub 2013 May 10.

[441] Anderson, I. The World Bank. East Asia and Pacific Regino. Economic Costs of Non-Communicable Diseases in the Pacific Islands. Washington, DC: The World Bank, 2012. Print. http://www.worldbank.org/content/dam/Worldbank/document/the-economic-costs-of-noncommunicable-diseases-in-the-pacific-islands.pdf.

[442] World Health Organization. Western Pacific Region. Health in Asia and the Pacific: Chapter 10. Health Systems. Print. Health in Asia and the Pacific.

[443] Enhancing the Role of Government in the Pacific Island Economies. Washington, DC: World Bank, 1998.

[444] Anderson, I. Economic Costs of Non-Communicable Diseases in the Pacific Islands.

nomic and physical environments. The social determinants of health are the conditions in which people are born, grow, live, work and age. These circumstances are shaped by the distribution of wealth, power and resources at global, national and local levels.[445,446] "The inequity is systematic, produced by social norms, policies and practices that tolerate or actually promote unfair distribution of and access to power, wealth and other necessary social resource(s)".[447] This statement by Michael Marmot acknowledges that there are larger "causes of causes", or distal determinants, of unhealthy life conditions. At an International Symposium on the Social Determinants of Indigenous Health,[448] it was demonstrated that the determinants of indigenous health differ from those of the mainstream population. This is in part due to how health is conceptualized amongst indigenous peoples compared to Western, biomedical definitions

Indigenous populations were relatively large prior to contact with European settlers but conflict and diseases led to sharp declines in the numbers of indigenous peoples, especially those living in New Zealand, Australia and Hawaii, threatening the very existence of indigenous peoples. The increase in population numbers has led to the revival of interest in their languages and cultures and interest from the wider society within all three countries. Loss of languages and cultures were a result of intentional and unintentional actions by the colonizers, often with oppressive regulations and legislations aimed at assimilation into the body politic of the developing nation states. While some aspects of indigenous cultures are being celebrated, they continue to experience the poorest health status with higher rates of preventable disease and disability and premature death in the Pacific region.

Universal access to health care services in New Zealand is an integral part of the welfare and health policies but the Maori peoples have had generally low access to health care at all levels. Successive New Zealand Health Surveys have shown that Maori generally have lower access to health care despite having higher health needs. The establishment of Maori health care providers has improved the availability of primary and community health care services, but the impact on health outcomes remains unclear and needs to be carefully evaluated. Most Maori peoples continue to receive health care from mainstream health care providers. Early indications are encouraging in that 65 per cent of the caseload for Maori health providers is regarded as high need compared with mainstream providers where their "high needs" population base is 26 per cent. There is evidence of improved access to primary and community health care services primarily as a result of the changes to the criteria for universal access and availability of low-cost clinics, for example; Maori health providers also have a strong presence in rural communities where the majority of the resident population tends to be Maori.[449]

[445] Commission on Social Determinants of Health retrieved 10/10/2013 from http://www.who.int/social_determinants/the commission/en/index.html.

[446] Social determinants of health, retrieved 10/10/2013 from http://www.who.int/social_determinants/B_132_14-en.pdf.

[447] Commission on Social Determinants of Health retrieved 10/10/2013 from http://www.who.int/social_determinants/the commission/en/index.html.

[448] Social determinants and Indigenous health, retrieved 10/10/2013 from http://www.who.int/social_determinants/resources/indigenous_health_adelaide_report_07.pdf.

[449] Ellison-Loschmann L, Pearce N. Improving access to health care among New Zealand's Maori population. American Journal of Public Health. 2006;96:612-617.

The relatively profound socioeconomic disadvantage experienced by indigenous peoples in Australia compared to non-indigenous people places them at greater risk of exposure to behavioural and environmental health risk factors. Indigenous peoples also do not enjoy equal access to primary health care services and health promotion and disease prevention public health community level infrastructure including safe drinking water, effective sewerage systems, rubbish collection services and healthy housing. The Royal Australasian College of Physicians describes these health inequities as "both avoidable and systematic".[450]

The Native Hawaiian Health Care Improvement Act (NHHCIA), as amended is a Congressional Special Initiative with the purpose of improving provision of comprehensive disease prevention, health promotion, and primary care services to Native Hawaiians in Hawaii. The NHHCIA authorizes funding opportunities for the following activities:

≡ Service grant to Papa Ola Lokahi (POL) for the activities described in the NHHCIA, including the coordination of the health care program and services provided to Native Hawaiians;

≡ Service grants to the five recognized community-based Native Hawaiian Health Care Systems (NHHCS) to provide a full range of services identified by the legislation and tailored to fit the needs of their respective island communities.

The Hawaii Health Authority (HHA), which was established by the Hawaii Legislature as part of the state's Department of Budget and Finance and tasked with being "responsible for overall health planning for the state", in 2011.[451] The HHA is expected to demonstrate how to get from the present health care situation in Hawaii to an efficient, cost-effective universal health care system, and is intended to provide health policy guidance to both the administration and legislature over the next several years.

In addition to the health status and health services for indigenous peoples in the developed countries in Pacific region, there are targeted programmes for advanced health research in Australia, New Zealand and USA (Hawaii). There are clear national, state and local policies and programmes designed to improve access to health services by and for indigenous peoples in these countries. Indigenous peoples are also actively involved in research, policy development and service delivery incorporating traditional health concepts into ways of explaining health phenomenon and service delivery. In some programs, affirmative action policies operate, particularly at training institutions[452] and research funds are available for research by indigenous and non-indigenous people into the health issues of indigenous peoples. At the same time, while the data and information are available and policies are offered, indigenous people continue to have the poorest health indicators and social conditions.

In all settings, including small island nations of the Pacific, colonialism seems to be universally identified as having a profound and long-lasting influence on the health status of indigenous peoples. In the past and continuing to the present day, colonialism impacts negatively on many

---

[450] Inequity and Health: A Call to Action—addressing health and socioeconomic inequality in Australia. Royal Australasian College of Physicians 2005.

[451] "About Hawaii Health Authority". Department of Budget and Finance. N.p., n.d. Web. 28 Feb. 2014. http://hawaii.gov/budget/hha/hha-meetings-and-minutes.

[452] Sowell, Thomas, Affirmative action around the world: an empirical study. New Haven: Yale University Press, 2004. Print.

aspects of the health and well-being of indigenous peoples, including a dramatic decline in population numbers at first contact with settlers, due to the introduction of unfamiliar diseases, loss of languages and cultures, marginalization and discrimination often supported by legislation. It seems the forces of missionary-style religion, pursuit of trade and commerce and fueled by the European expansionist doctrine of Manifest Destiny converged in the Pacific region, as it did across the globe, to marginalize indigenous peoples in their homelands. The Pacific region experienced myriad loss of cultures and traditions that were aggravated by the introduction of Christianity which led to the systematic destruction of Pacific cultural practices and symbols. The Pacific was also a region of intense military strategic importance thus laid claim to by a variety of European nations. It is difficult to quantify the impact of colonization and Christianity and other forces on the health status of indigenous peoples in the Pacific. Nonetheless, it is clear that the process of colonization destroyed and undermined not only the external expression of indigenous cultures, but their inner sense of self-belief and confidence as distinct cultural groups. Increased prevalence of stress and mental disorders and social problems manifested as higher incarceration rates in indigenous peoples in all regions relative to the non-indigenous people living the same environment and is further evidence of the long-lasting and pervasive negative consequences of colonization and destruction of cultures.

Government policies and programmes can perpetuate historical practices which further aggravate the inequalities that exist between indigenous and non-indigenous peoples. For example, social housing policies often create communities consisting mainly of low-income families who are located in neighbourhoods with limited access to services. These neighbourhoods often do not have good educational institutions and children do not get a good start in life. Poor educational achievement inevitably limits employment prospects for young people and many resort to antisocial behaviours, which further limits their opportunities for maintaining health and well-being. These situations often create a never-ending vicious circle where socioeconomic disadvantage becomes intergenerational and children grow up in environments into which employment prospects are limited and risks are inherited by the next generation. Promising practices need to be shared and implemented to stem this pattern of trauma.

At the present time, the most important determinant of poor health among indigenous peoples relates to their socioeconomic situation and poverty. Poor education and low income are universally associated with poor health and they are clearly connected. The evidence suggests that the income gap between the rich and poor has a far greater negative impact on health, rather than the absolute level of income. For example, studies have shown that market economies such as the USA, Australia and New Zealand have much greater income inequalities than other jurisdictions.[453] Consequently, the health inequalities and social problems between low income (including indigenous peoples) and high income groups are more pronounced.[454] Socioeconomic disadvantage is a consequent of low educational achievement by indigenous children and young people. While children and their families are often blamed for poor performance, the education system in

---

[453] Whiteford, Peter, Australia: Inequality and Prosperity and their impacts in a radical welfare State, March 2013 p. 76, https://crawford.anu.edu.au/public_policy_community/content/doc/Australia_Inequality-and-Prosperity_final-15-March-13.pdf.

[454] Rowlingson K. Does income inequality cause health and social problems? retrieved 14/10/2013 from http://www.jrf.org.uk/sites/files/jrf/inequality-income-social-problems-full.pdf.

many developed countries does not cater well for the needs of indigenous children. Improvements in educational achievement are essential for improvements in indigenous health.

Policies and programmes to improve indigenous peoples' health have been in place in developed countries (Australia, New Zealand and USA (Hawaii) in the Pacific for some years. These initiatives involve both adjustments to mainstream funding and delivery of health services as well as support for indigenous health programmes. Adjustments to mainstream provision include funding incentives to improve to health services by removing financial barriers to access as well as training for non-indigenous health workers in cultural competency. Indigenous programmes include the delivery of conventional primary health care and community services targeting indigenous peoples, which are owned, governed and managed by indigenous peoples themselves. Some of these services include complementary traditional healing practices which are incorporated into the range of services provided by the medical clinic.

While there are number of initiatives under way in developed countries deigned to improve access to and impact of health care services, there is limited information on the impact of these programmes. In New Zealand, research is under way to determine the impact of the participation of Maori health providers on access to and the quality of services received. There are encouraging signs that health initiatives provided "by indigenous for indigenous people" is improving access to services, but somewhat too early to assess the impact on their health status.

Bibliography

Anderson I, Crengle S, Kamaka M et al. Indigenous Health in Australia, New Zealand, and the Pacific The Lancet 2006; 367:1775-85.

Anderson W (2007) The colonial medicine of settler states: comparing histories of Indigenous health. Health and History; 9(2): 144-154.

Australian Indigenous HealthInfonet (2013) summary of Australian Indigenous health, retrieved (15/10/2013) from http://www.healthinfonet.ecu.edu.au/health-facts/summary.

Bramley D, Herbert P, Tuzzio L, Chassin M. Disparities in Indigenous Health: A Cross-Country Comparison Between New Zealand and the United States. Am J Public Health. 2005 Vol 95, No.5; 844-50.

Campbell J (2002) Invisible invaders: smallpox and other diseases in Aboriginal Australia 1780-1880. Melbourne: Melbourne University Press.

Carson B, Dunbar T, Chenhall RD, Bailie R, eds. (2007) Social determinants of Indigenous health. Crows Nest, NSW: Allen and Unwin.

Denoon, Donald et al. The Cambridge History of the Pacific Islanders. Cambridge, U.K.: Cambridge University Press, 1997.

Elder B (2003) Blood on the wattle: massacres and maltreatment of Aboriginal Australians since 1788. 3rd ed. Frenchs Forest, N.S.W: New Holland.

Ellison-Loschmann L, Pearce N. Improving access to health care among New Zealand's Maori population. Am J Public Health. 2006 Vol 96, No 4; 612-617.

Greenhill, S, and Russell D. Gray. "Testing Population Dispersal Hypotheses Pacific Settlement". In. The Evolution of Cultural Diversity: Phylogenetic Approaches. Ed. Ruth Mace et al. London: UCL Press, 2005. 31-52.

Howe, K. R., Robert C. Kiste, and Brij V. Lal. Tides of history: the Pacific Islands in the twentieth century. Honolulu: University of Hawaii Press, 1994.

Harrison, B (1979) The Myall Creek Massacre in McBryde, I (ed) Records of the times past: ethno-historical essays on the culture and ecology of the New England tribes, Australian Institute of Aboriginal Studies, Canberra, pp. 17-51.

Kritharides L, Brown A, Brieger D et al. Overview and Determinants of Cardiovascular Disease in Indigenous Populations. Heart, Lung and Circulation 2010; 19:337-343.

Marmot M (2004) The status syndrome: how social standing affects our health and longevity. New York: Holt Paperbacks.

Native Hawaiian Government Reorganisation Act (2009), retrieved (11/10/2013) from http://www.gop.gov/bill/111/1/hr2314.

Ring I, Brown N. "The health status of indigenous peoples and others" BMJ 2003 23; 327 (7412): 404-405.

Robson B, Harris R. (eds). Hauora: Màori Standards of Health IV. A study of the years 2000-2005. Wellington: Te Ròpù Rangahau Hauora a Eru Pòmare.

State of the World's Minorities and Indigenous Peoples 2013.

Taualii M, Delormier T, Maddock J. A New and Innovative Public Health Specialization Founded on Traditional Knowledge and Social Justice: Native Hawaiian and Indigenous Health. Hawaii Journal of Medicine & Public Health 2013; 72 (4): 143-145.

Thomson N (1991) Tuberculosis among Aborigines. In: Proust AJ, ed. History of tuberculosis in Australia, New Zealand and Papua New Guinea. Canberra, ACT: Brolga Press: 61-67.

U.S. Census Bureau, 2010 Census.

Veitayaki, J. "Breaking Fiji's Coup Culture through Effective Rural Development". In 1987: Fiji TwentyYears On. Ed. Lal B V et al. Lautoka, Fiji: Fiji Institute of Applied Studies, 2008.

World Health Organization. World Conference on Social Determinants of Health, 2011.

Whiteford, Peter Australia: Inequality and Prospersity and their impacts in a radical welfare State, March 2013 p. 76, https://crawford.anu.edu.au/public_policy_community/content/doc/Australia_Inequali-ty-and-Prosperity_final-15-March-13.pdf.

Wilkinson R, Marmot M (2003) Social determinants of health: the solid facts. Denmark: World Health Organization.

Yap M, Biddle N (2012) Indigenous fertility and family formation: CAEPR Indigenous population project: 2011 census papers. Canberra: Centre for Aboriginal Economic Policy Research.

Appendix

Pacific Island Countries and Territories (excluding Australia, New Zealand, and Hawaii):[455]

- ≡ American Samoa
- ≡ Cook Islands
- ≡ Federated States of Micronesia
- ≡ Fiji
- ≡ French Polynesia Guam
- ≡ Kiribati
- ≡ Marshall Islands
- ≡ Nauru
- ≡ New Caledonia
- ≡ Niue
- ≡ Northern Mariana Islands,
- ≡ Palau
- ≡ Papua New Guinea
- ≡ Pitcairn Islands
- ≡ Samoa
- ≡ Solomon Islands
- ≡ Tokelau
- ≡ Tonga
- ≡ Tuvalu
- ≡ Vanuatu
- ≡ Wallis and Futuna

---

[455] "Members". Secretariat of the Pacific Region. N.p., n.d. Web. 26 Feb. 2014. http://www.spc.int/en/about-spc/members.html.

CHAPTER SEVEN

ACCESS TO HEALTH SERVICES BY INDIGENOUS PEOPLES IN THE RUSSIAN FEDERATION

BY OKSANA BURANBAEVA

Chapter Seven

Access to Health Services by Indigenous Peoples in the Russian Federation

By Oksana Buranbaeva

Introduction

This chapter will focus on indigenous peoples' access to health services in the Russian Federation. First, this paper will provide background information by defining health and reviewing relevant international and national legal frameworks regarding health care guarantees. Secondly, the paper will review the analytical frameworks relevant to understanding access to health care and factors affecting indigenous health. Third, the paper will examine the overall public health situation in the Russian Federation and give a summary of the general health care access situation in the country. It will then discuss problems in indigenous peoples' health and the causes of these problems, and examine indigenous peoples' access to health services. Finally, the paper will present promising examples of practices or interventions that are helpful in alleviating barriers to health care.

What is health?

In 1948, the World Health Organization (WHO) defined health as "a state of complete physical, mental and social well-being and not merely the absence of disease or infirmity".[456] This definition was included in the Preamble to the Constitution of the WHO in 1946 and remains unchanged since 1948. The WHO has been requested to amend the definition of health by including the spiritual component. For indigenous peoples, health is a broad and holistic concept encompassing the spiritual, the intellectual, physical and emotional dimensions. Essential is the coexistence of the past, present and future, ensuring an intergenerational continuum, including both individual and communal perspectives. There is a respect for nature that seeks to achieve balance or sense of equilibrium between the needs of indigenous peoples for their health and survival with sustainable environmental stewardship, which includes "interaction with life processes and the natural laws that govern the planet, all life forms, and spiritual understanding".[457]

Health is seen by indigenous peoples as fundamental to well-being and critical to the broader idea of expanded human capabilities.[458] A healthy person is better able to attain a higher quality of life by achieving better social integration, both gaining from and giving to his or her

---

[456] WHO (1948), p. 1.

[457] WHO (1999), The Geneva declaration on the health and survival of indigenous peoples.

[458] Sen (1985, 1999), Nussbaum (2000).

community. A healthier person is preconditioned to attain better education, greater longevity and increased livelihood.[459]

International and national legal frameworks

The right to health is enshrined in international and regional human rights treaties, such as the Universal Declaration of Human Rights, the International Covenant on Economic, Social and Cultural Rights (ICESCR), the Convention on the Elimination of All Forms of Discrimination against Women (CEDAW), the Convention on the Rights of the Child (CRC), the European Social Charter and the Constitution of the Russian Federation. The right to health in these documents is applied at the level of the individual. The UN Declaration on the Rights of Indigenous Peoples (UNDRIP), adopted by the UN General Assembly in 2007, stands out for its recognition of collective rights.[460]

The WHO Constitution states that "the enjoyment of the highest attainable standard of health is one of the fundamental rights of every human being without distinction of race, religion, political beliefs, economic or social condition".[461] The right to health means that governments are responsible for creating conditions in which everybody can achieve the highest attainable standard of health. This right encompasses "access to timely, acceptable, and affordable health care of appropriate quality",[462] as well as healthy and safe working conditions, adequate housing and nutritious food.

The Universal Declaration of Human Rights (Article 25) states that "everyone has the right to a standard of living adequate for the health and well-being of himself and of his family, including ... medical care and necessary social services".[463]

ICESCR (Article 12) states that the realization of the right to health includes those actions that reduce infant mortality and ensure the healthy development of the child, improve all aspects of environmental and industrial hygiene, prevent, treat and control epidemic, endemic, occupational and other diseases, and create conditions to ensure access to health care for all.[464] In 2000, the UN Committee on Economic, Social and Cultural Rights, a body that monitors compliance with this agreement, adopted a General Comment on the Right to Health. The Comment postulates that "the right to health extends not only to timely and appropriate health care but also to the underlying determinants of health, such as access to safe and potable water and adequate sanitation, an adequate supply of safe food, nutrition and housing, healthy occupational and environmental conditions, and access to health-related education and information, including on sexual and reproductive health".[465]

According to the Comment, the right to health compels states to respect (do not harm); protect (ensure that non-state actors do not infringe upon the enjoyment of the right to health), and ful-

---

[459] Wilkinson, R. and Marmot, M. (2003). Social determinants of health: The solid facts. Geneva: World Health Organization.

[460] UNPFII (2009), p. 158.

[461] WHO (1948), p. 1.

[462] WHO (2012).

[463] The Universal Declaration of Human Rights (1948), Article 25.1.

[464] ICESCR (1966), Article 12.2.

[465] WHO (2012).

fil (take positive steps to realize the right to health, such as ensuring that proper legislation and finance mechanisms are in place). The General Comment obliges states to have a national public health strategy that addresses the health concerns of the whole population, giving particular attention to all vulnerable and marginalized groups.[466]

The United Nations Declaration on the Rights of Indigenous Peoples, which incorporates the concept of collective rights, includes government obligations to provide indigenous peoples' access to health services and to respect indigenous health systems. Article 24 states that "indigenous individuals have the right to the enjoyment of the highest attainable standard of physical and mental health" and that "states shall take the necessary steps with a view to achieving progressively the full realization of this right".[467] "Indigenous peoples have the right to their traditional medicines and to maintain their health practices, including the conservation of their vital medicinal plants, animals and minerals. Indigenous individuals also have the right to access, without any discrimination, to all social and health services".[468] In accordance with Article 29, "States shall also take effective measures to ensure, as needed, that programmes for monitoring, maintaining and restoring the health of indigenous peoples, as developed and implemented by the peoples affected by such materials, are duly implemented".[469] Furthermore, Article 23 states that indigenous peoples have the right to be actively involved in developing and determining health programmes affecting them and to administer such programmes through their own institutions.[470]

The right to health care and medical assistance is guaranteed in Article 41 of the Constitution of the Russian Federation.[471] The Article also guarantees that medical assistance shall be made available by state and municipal health care institutions to citizens free of charge, with the money from the relevant budget, insurance payments and other revenues.[472] The Article states that "The Russian Federation shall finance federal health care and health-building programmes, take measures to develop state, municipal and private health care systems, encourage activities contributing to the strengthening of human health, to the development of physical culture and sport, and to ecological, sanitary and epidemiologic welfare".[473] Article 42 guarantees everyone's right to a favourable environment, reliable information about its condition and to compensation for damage inflicted to his or her health or property by ecological violations.[474] While the Constitution does not specifically mention the right to health guarantees for people with disabilities, children and youth, it states that fundamental rights and freedoms shall be inalienable and shall belong to everyone from birth (Article 1),[475] and it contains a special clause stating that men and women shall have equal rights and freedoms as well as equal opportunities for their pursuit (Article 19).[476]

---

[466] WHO (2012).

[467] United Nations Declaration on the Rights of Indigenous Peoples, Article 24.2.

[468] United Nations Declaration on the Rights of Indigenous Peoples, Article 24.1.

[469] United Nations Declaration on the Rights of Indigenous Peoples, Article 29.3.

[470] United Nations Declaration on the Rights of Indigenous Peoples, Article 23.

[471] Russian Constitution, Article 41.

[472] Russian Constitution, Article 41.

[473] Russian Constitution, Article 41.

[474] Russian Constitution, Article 42.

[475] Russian Constitution, Article 1.

[476] Russian Constitution, Article 19.

Article 19 additionally guarantees the equality of human and citizen rights and freedoms, regardless of gender, race, nationality, language, origin, property and official status, place of residence, attitude to religion, convictions and membership of public associations or other circumstances. The Article forbids any restrictions of citizen rights on social, racial, national, linguistic or religious grounds.[477] With health care coverage in the Russian Federation being guaranteed as a constitutional right, universal and free (under mandatory medical insurance), the responsibility for enforcing this right is shared between central, regional and local authorities.[478]

With Russian as the state language throughout the territory of the Russian Federation (Article 68),[479] Article 26 of the Constitution guarantees the right to use one's native language as well as to choose freely the language of communication, upbringing, education and creative work.[480]

The Russian federal law On Fundamental Principles of Health Care in the Russian Federation (21 November 2011) states that territorial state guarantee programmes providing free medical care shall take into account the climate and geography of a particular region and the transport availability of medical organizations (Article 81).[481] This is particularly relevant for indigenous people in remote locations.

In 1999 the Russian Federation issued the federal law On Guarantees of Rights for Indigenous Numerically Small Peoples of the Russian Federation. Article 8 of this law entitles indigenous people to free medical care in state and municipal health care facilities within the framework of the Programme of state guarantees for mandatory health insurance.[482] As described above, the legal framework is comprehensive and includes specific provisions for indigenous peoples' access to health services.

Analytical frameworks

To examine indigenous peoples' access to health services in the Russian Federation, it is useful to review three existing analytical frameworks, which inform the following sections. The first framework focus is on the core elements of the right to health; the second on the core elements of health care access; and the third on the determinants of indigenous health.

Analytical framework 1: The four components of the right to health

According to the aforementioned General Comment on the Right to Health, the right to health contains four core elements, namely, availability, accessibility, acceptability and quality. Availability refers to the provision of a sufficient quantity of functioning public health and health care facilities, goods, services and programmes. Accessibility implies that health facilities, goods, services and programmes must be accessible to everyone without discrimination. They must be accessible from

---

[477] Russian Constitution, Article 19.

[478] Popovich (2011), p. 19.

[479] Russian Constitution, Article 68.

[480] Russian Constitution, Article 26.

[481] The Russian Federation (2011), On fundamental principles of health care in the Russian Federation. Article 81.4.4.

[482] The Russian Federation (1999), On guarantees of rights for indigenous numerically small peoples of the Russian Federation. Article 8.9.

a physical point of view, affordable and that information about them also must be accessible. Acceptability implies that health services, goods, services and programmes should respect medical ethics, be sensitive to gender and life-cycle requirements and be culturally appropriate. Quality refers to the medical and scientific appropriateness of health facilities, goods and services.[483]

Analytical framework 2: Access barriers to health services[484]

Table 1: Overview of identified access barriers along supply and demand sides and four dimensions of access[485]

Supply-side barriers	Demand-side barriers
Geographic accessibility	
Service location (in relation to the household)	Indirect costs to household (e.g. transport and accommodation expenses)
	Means of transport available
Availability	
Unqualified health workers, staff absenteeism, opening hours	Information on health care services/providers
Waiting times	Education
Motivation of staff	
Drugs supply and other consumables (e.g., medical supplies, assistive devices and equipment)	
Non-integration of health services	
Lack of opportunity (exclusion from services)	
Affordability	
Costs and prices of services, including informal payments	Household resources and willingness to pay
Private-public dual practices	Opportunity costs
	Cash flow within society
Acceptability	
Complexity of billing system and inability for patients to know prices beforehand	Household's expectations
Staff interpersonal skills, including trust	Low self-esteem and little assertiveness
	Community and cultural preferences
	Stigma
	Lack of health awareness

---

[483] General Comment No. 14 (2000), Normative Content of Article 12.

[484] Jacobs, et al. (2011), pp. 1-11.

[485] Jacobs, et al. (2011), p. 4.

While there is no agreed-upon definition of access to health services,[486] one way to describe such access is "the timely use of service according to need".[487] Scholars identify four dimensions of access to health care - geographic access, availability, affordability and acceptability[488] - and state that barriers to health care access can stem from both supply and demand sides.[489] Supply-side barriers (see table below) are the barriers that are inherent to the health system and have a negative effect on the uptake of health services at the individual, household or community level. Demand-side barriers (see table below) are barriers that hinder individuals', households' or communities' ability to use health services. Supply- and demand-side barriers are not necessarily mutually exclusive. They may influence each other[490] and should be addressed simultaneously.[491]

Analytical framework 3: Cultural and socioeconomic determinants of indigenous health and access to health services[492]

Indigenous peoples worldwide face challenges in achieving optimal health health that is exacerbated by inadequate access to health services due to their socioeconomic and cultural contexts as well as some distinctive factors that are specific to indigenous peoples' culture, history and political connectedness to the dominant culture. These include issues such as indigeneity, the impacts of colonial and post-colonial experience, and often a lack of government recognition. Scholars Sheikh and Islam identify the following factors affecting indigenous health and how they determine health via access, directly or indirectly:

- geographic location and rural lifestyles;
- ethnicity/indigenous identity;
- dispossession and dislocation from the land;
- housing;
- level of education;
- income;
- employment and occupation;
- environmental factor;
- lack of data.

[486] Oliver and Mossialos (2004), pp. 655-658.

[487] Peters et al. (2008), pp. 161-171.

[488] O'Donnell (2007), pp. 2820-2834.

[489] Ensor and Cooper (2004), pp. 246-256 and O'Donnell (2007), pp. 2820-2834.

[490] James et al. (2006), pp. 147-153.

[491] O'Donnell (2007), pp. 2820-2834.

[492] Islam and Sheikh (2010), pp. 263-273.

Health status and access to health services in the Russian Federation

Overall population health in the Russian Federation

Despite the stabilization trends in recent years, the health of the general population of the Russian Federation remains poor relative to other WHO European Region[493] and other G8 countries.[494] Certain indicators, such as mortality rates for men, are very high compared to countries at similar development and income levels.[495]

In the 1990s, the whole of the Russian Federation experienced a dramatic decline in life expectancy due to social and political transformation and to soaring poverty rates resulting from the economic collapse following the dissolution of the Soviet Union. Such a striking rise in Russian mortality was beyond the experience of industrialized countries, with a five-year decline in life expectancy.[496] In Moscow life expectancy decreased by 7.7 years over a period of four years from 1990 to1994; and in the whole of Russia by 6.4 years.[497] Changes in life expectancy were due to many factors including economic and social instability, high rates of tobacco and alcohol consumption, poor nutrition, depression and deterioration of the health care system.[498] For example, cigarette consumption increased by 81 per cent between 1990 and 2000.[499]

The decline was particularly sharp in the life expectancy of men of working age, especially those in lower socioeconomic groups within regions experiencing a particularly rapid economic transition.[500] Traditionally responsible for family income, men found themselves under extreme pressure, leading to soaring rates of depression, alcohol and drug use, accidents and suicide.[501]

The top three killers in Russia today are cardiovascular disease, cancer and external causes. In addition to the abovementioned problems, Russia has one of the highest vehicular fatality rates in Europe.[502] Whereas chronic conditions and external causes are leading causes of premature death and disability, communicable diseases, particularly multidrug resistant tuberculosis and the tuberculosis epidemic intersected with HIV/AIDS also pose a considerable threat to health and well being.[503] Female mortality is significantly lower than male mortality, with female rates 117 in 1990 and 144 per 1,000 in 2009, while male mortality was 318 in 1990 and 391 in 2009,[504] but disability-adjusted life expectancy data point to the fact that even though women live considerably longer, their overall quality of life and health status is poor.[505]

---

[493] Popovich et al. (2011), p. 12.

[494] Popovich et al. (2011), p. 175.

[495] Popovich et al. (2011), p. 11.

[496] Notzon et al. (1998).

[497] Leon and Shkolnikov (1998), p. 790.

[498] Notzon et al. (1998)

[499] Danishevski et al. (2007), pp. 276-83.

[500] Leon and Shkolnikov (1998) p. 790.

[501] Abryutina (2012), p. 215.

[502] Popovich et al. (2011), p. 12.

[503] Popovich et al. (2011), p. 12.

[504] WHO (2012) World Health Statistics.

[505] Popovich et al. (2011), p. 12.

Having reached 148.3 million in 1992,[506] Russian's population declined to 142.9 million in 2010[507] and increased to 143.6 million in October 2013, due to immigration.[508] The context of mainstream Russian health challenges is important for framing the health of indigenous peoples' because as will be shown indigenous peoples are among the poorest of the poor with the greatest health challenges in the country.

Overall access to health services in the Russian Federation

Universal access to primary health care, the principle guiding health care in the Soviet Union, is still central to the discourse and practices in the health care system of the Russian Federation. With independence, Russia inherited a centralized health care system boasting an extensive network of medical facilities and a high number of physicians per capita.[509] The system had substantial overcapacity and patients were largely guaranteed free treatment.[510]

While the guiding principle of universal free access to primary care has remains unchanged, the governance and the organization of the health care system have evolved.[511] Facing severe budgetary constraints, two years into independence the Russian Federation adopted a mandatory health insurance system designed to open up an earmarked stream of funding for health care.[512] Today health care financing in the Russian Federation comes more or less evenly from compulsory sources such as general taxation and payroll contributions for mandatory health insurance and out-of-pocket payments. The range of benefits covered is comprehensive and all basic care is provided free.[513] All patients except vulnerable groups, such as veterans or disabled individuals must pay for outpatient prescription drugs.[514] The comprehensiveness of the benefit package is however, undermined by the persistent scarcity of resources and reported generalized informal payments.[515]

Since 1991, the number of physicians per capita has grown and is now one of the highest in the WHO European Region,[516] though there are few indigenous doctors.[517] Since independence, as a result of budgetary constraints, as well as the policies linked to the introduction of mandatory health insurance, there has been a decrease in the number of both hospital and outpatient facilities as well as a reduction in preventive services. The vast majority of small village hospitals have closed since 2000.[518] A particular challenge is the maintenance of health facilities in some rural areas which are lacking such basic services as adequate sanitation or hot water. Poor communi-

---

[506] Popovich et al. (2011), xv.

[507] Russian Population Census 2010.

[508] Federal State Statistics (2013).

[509] Popovich et al. (2011), xviii.

[510] Popovich et al. (2011), xviii.

[511] Popovich et al. (2011), xiii.

[512] Popovich et al. (2011), xiii.

[513] Popovich et al. (2011), xvii.

[514] Popovich et al. (2011), xvii.

[515] Popovich et al. (2011), xvii.

[516] Popovich (2011), xix.

[517] Kozlov and Lisitsyn (2008), p. 99.

[518] Popovich (2011), xix.

cations including lack of telephone connections contributes to undermine the development and maintenance of information systems.[519] According to the OECD, enhancing access, restoring the capacity of the health care system to provide quality care, and reducing mortality through preventative interventions are among the top five policy priorities at the national level.[520]

Indigenous peoples' health status and access to health services in the Russian Federation

Data availability

According to the Federal law On Guarantees of Rights for Indigenous Numerically Small Peoples of the Russian Federation, the indigenous are the numerically small peoples living on the territories of traditional residence of their ancestors, adhering to their original way of life, trades and crafts, and believing themselves to be independent ethnic entities; their total number in Russia is less than 50,000 people.[521] Nearly all the peoples currently recognized as indigenous live in the North.[522]

Between 1926 and 1993 the official list of indigenous peoples included 26 peoples occupying the vast territory of over 9 million square kilometres stretching from the Kola Peninsula to Chukotka. The government has been expanding the list since 1993. Forty groups were recognized by 2000,[523] many of the newly recognized indigenous groups were residing in the southern parts of Siberia. At the same time, some of the groups that had been previously recognized as distinct indigenous groups were merged.[524] The current official list of indigenous peoples living in the Russian Federation consists of 47 groups;[525] almost all of them live in the northern regions of the country. They are highly diverse in their origins, cultures and languages.[526] According to the census conducted in 2010, there are 316,000 indigenous people living in 23 subjects of the Russian Federation.[527] In the period between the two most recent censuses (2002 and 2010) the number of indigenous peoples of the North increased by 5.7 per cent.

However, the censuses showed a reduction in the absolute population numbers of some indigenous peoples. For example, the census conducted in 2002 revealed that 10 groups of indigenous peoples decreased in numbers and the census conducted in 2010 showed that 24 groups of peoples decreased in numbers.[528] The North is also home to ethnic minorities that are not considered numeri-

---

[519] Popovich (2011), p. 20.

[520] OECD (2012), p. 59.

[521] Russian Federation, On Guarantees of Rights for Indigenous Numerically Small Peoples of the Russian Federation, Article 1.

[522] Russia's southern Republic of Dagestan, one of the most ethnically diverse places on earth, is developing a list of indigenous peoples for inclusion in the official list of indigenous peoples compiled by the government of the Russian Federation.

[523] Young (2008), Circumpolar health indicators: sources, data, and maps, 21.

[524] Young (2008), Circumpolar health indicators: sources, data, and maps, 21.

[525] Federal State Statistics Service (2010d).

[526] Kozlov et al. (2007, p. 13

[527] Federal State Statistics Service (2010d).

[528] Bogoyavlensky (2012).

cally small or indigenous such as the Komi, the Komi-Permyaks, the Yakuts and the Buryats.[529] One interesting aspect is that the official policy definition for recognition of indigenous peoples does not include minorities with a population over 50,000 people which seems arbitrary and counter to the notion of rebuilding healthy, viable and economically sustainable indigenous communities.

Complete and accurate current medical and demographic data on the indigenous peoples of the Russian North are lacking.[530] The Soviet Union collected information about indigenous peoples, and this information could be accessed for professional or academic purposes. Available statistics demonstrated positive dynamics in indigenous peoples' health. However, the restructuring of the health care system in the 1990s, as well as the abolition of ethnic identity in the Russian passport in 1997, led to the gradual end of the centralized collection and systematization of statistical information on indigenous peoples of the North.[531] Countrywide reports by international organizations such as WHO, and the OECD do not pay specific information on indigenous peoples. Therefore, while specific information on indigenous peoples' health and access to health services is available from discrete research initiatives, the routine use of regular statistical methods to capture and evaluate indigenous peoples' health and health services on a large scale is no longer possible.[532] Health and demographic information about the peoples who have been recognized as indigenous only recently is particularly scarce. Therefore this report also has to rely on older data sources.

Rapid changes in the twentieth century

In the twentieth century, the indigenous peoples living in the Russian Federation faced rapid social, economic and cultural change. The inflow of migrants from Russia's central regions to the "regions of new development" quickly turned indigenous peoples into minorities in their homelands. Between 1926 and 1935, under a decade, the share of indigenous peoples in the districts with indigenous populations in the northern parts of Russia fell from 56 per cent to 35 per cent. It further decreased to 15 per cent in 1970 and 4.4 per cent in 1989.[533]

The Soviet policies focused on integrating indigenous peoples into mainstream Soviet society, combining the communist ideology with an ethnic policy corresponding to the "all-European outlook" of the epoch".[534] Traditionally, the economy of indigenous northerners was based on animal resources. They practised reindeer herding, fishing and hunting in taiga[535] and tundra. From the beginning of the twentieth century, indigenous peoples were subjected to collectivization, industrialization, forced migration to urban centres and sedentarization, all of which failed to take into consideration indigenous cultures and ways of life. Rapid industrialization led to the contamination and devastation of landscape and wildlife and decreased access to indigenous self-subsistence activities. Collectivization destroyed indigenous community-based economies.

---

[529] Kozlov et al. (2007), p. 12.

[530] Abryutina (2012), p. 212; Snodgrass (2013), p. 74.

[531] Abryutina (2012), p. 213.

[532] Abryutina (2012), p. 213.

[533] Kozlov and Lisitsyn (2008), p. 86.

[534] Cheshko (2000) in Kozlov and Lisitsyn (2008), p. 87.

[535] A sub-Arctic, evergreen coniferous forest of northern Eurasia located just south of the tundra, dominated by firs and spruces.

Forced migration to cities and towns caused indigenous peoples, who lacked the skills necessary for survival in urban settings and could not rely on their usual family and social networks, to be pushed to the bottom of the social ladder.[536]

The introduction of mandatory boarding schools had the most pronounced consequences. In the 1950s, the children of nomadic hunters and reindeer herders received education for several months a year in large settlements; a decade later, this was replaced by a system of boarding schools, which became mandatory for both nomadic and settled populations in the North and were financed by the state. Education was delivered in Russian by non-indigenous teachers. Indigenous languages were taught only as a separate subject in elementary grades. Boarding schools did not take into consideration indigenous cultures, indigenous physiology or psychology. Education in Russian and extended stays far away from family resulted in the gradual replacement of the mother tongue with Russian, created a generation gap, had a negative effect on family cohesion and led to psychological deprivation.[537] Boarding school diets did not take into account indigenous physiology: for example, indigenous children were regularly given milk, though it has been proven that 50-90 per cent of northern indigenous children are unable to digest milk sugar and should, therefore, exercise caution with the consumption of whole milk.[538]

The policies that the Soviet Union adopted vis-à-vis indigenous peoples had both negative and positive consequences. Withdrawal from family and social networks and the disruption of cultural transmission mechanisms resulted in the loss of the mother tongue, traditional skills and indigenous healing practices. The reduction in traditional nomadic migration resulted in some consanguineous marriages, a practice leading to genetic disorders. Stress and psychological deprivation contributed to alcohol abuse. On the positive side, indigenous peoples received equal rights with non-indigenous peoples, secure employment and income, literacy, access to medical care and preservation of indigenous traditional diet, as well as access to non-indigenous food.[539]

Indigenous peoples' health status

The health of indigenous peoples in northern Russia is extremely poor, and there are clear differences with Russia as a whole.[540] Rapid social transformation and transition from traditional to new occupations, as well as dietary changes, led to a high incidence of diseases that were rare in indigenous peoples in the past.[541] New health problems include myopia, myocardial infarction, ischaemic heart diseases and hypertension, the latter two problems being particularly explosive.[542] Indigenous peoples of the North have unusually high rates of oesophageal cancer: in 1976-1990, incidence in the Chukchi, Koryak[543] and Taimyr[544] autonomous districts was 4-12 times higher than

[536] Nettleton et al. (2007), p. 63.

[537] Kozlov and Lisitsyn (2008), p. 86.

[538] Abryutina (2012), p. 213.

[539] Abryutina (2012), p. 213.

[540] Snodgrass (2013) p. 79.

[541] Medvestnik (2008).

[542] Medvestnik (2008).

[543] Note that the Koryak autonomous district ceased to exist as a distinct federal subject as of 1 January 2007.

[544] Note that the Taimyr autonomous district ceased to exist as a distinct federal subject as of 1 January 2007.

the average in Siberia and the Far East.[545] Parasite infections in the North are twice as common as in the general Russian population.[546] Among the indigenous peoples of the Yamal-Nenets autonomous district, the incidence of parasitic infections was 3.5 times the average district rate.[547] Tuberculosis incidence among indigenous northerners is several times the Russian average.[548] For example, in the Koryak autonomous district, tuberculosis incidence was almost 7 times higher at a rate of 444.6 per 100,000 of population compared to 67 per 100,000 in the Russian Federation.[549] The incidence of death from infectious diseases, mainly from tuberculosis, is more than twice higher in indigenous northerners as in the general Russian population. Generally, the data available from 1998-2007 reveal the deterioration of indigenous peoples' health over this period.[550]

Table 2: Summary of the health information and key risk factors for selected indigenous peoples in northern Russia[551]

Indigenous people	Overall health and key health challenges	Main lifestyle, innate?
Evenki, Khanty, Mansi, Yakut[552]	Overall poor health; pronounced disparities compared with non-native population	Dietary change
	Life expectancy lower by approximately 10 years (but Russia is low in general)[553]	Low activity levels
		High smoking levels
	High infant mortality rate	Very high rates of alcoholism
	High cardiovascular disease burden (especially stroke) but relatively low type 2 diabetes	Psychosocial stress
		Pollution
	Moderate obesity levels and very high hypertension rates	Poor living conditions
		Climate change
	Modestly elevated infectious disease burden	Adaptive pattern that may predispose to high blood pressure
	Very high rates of alcoholism, suicide and violence	

The life expectancy of the indigenous people living in the North of Russia is considerably lower than the overall life expectancy in the Russian Federation. Indigenous northerners can expect to live 10-11 years less and non-indigenous northerners 3-4 years less than the overall average Russian population. Indigenous men live 14 years less than women,[554] which generally correspond to

---

[545] Choynzonov et al. (2004), p. 51.

[546] Abryutina (2012), p. 211

[547] Russian Federation (2002), The concept of a complex district target programme of socioeconomic development of indigenous numerically small peoples of the North of the Yamal-Nenets autonomous district for 2003-2005.

[548] Abryutina (2012), p. 211.

[549] Abryutina (2012), p. 211.

[550] Manchuk and Nadtochiy (2010), pp. 24-32.

[551] Adapted from Snodgrass (2013), p. 75.

[552] The Yakut are a Turkic minority mainly residing in the Republic of Sakha (Yakutia).

[553] According to federal statistics, the average life expectancy in Russia was 70.24 in 2012. Average male life expectancy in the same year was 64.56 and the average female life expectancy 75.86 years.

[554] Stepanovskaya et al. (1998), p. 9.

overall Russian differences between male and female life expectancy. For example, in the Berezo-vo region of the Khanty-Mansi autonomous district, in the late 1990s the average age at death was 48 for men and 60 for women.[555]

Table 3: Life expectancy at birth in 2000[556]

	Numerically small peoples of the North	All-Russian average
Male	45	61
Female	55	74

Another important indicator for access to health services is infant mortality rates, which have been consistently high. In 2003-2004 the infant mortality rate was 20 per live births among indigenous peoples in the North, compared with the Russian average of 13.3 per 1,000 live births.[557]

Table 4: Selected demographic indicators of the northern indigenous population (crude birth rate, crude death rate, and natural increase per 1,000: infant mortality rate per 1,000 live births.[558]

Period	Crude Birth Rate	Crude Death Rate	Natural increase	Infant mortality rate
1984-1988	30.2	10.5	19.7	41.1
1989-1993	25.7	10.8	14.8	30.4
1994-1998	19.8	12.6	7.2	32.5
1999-2002	17.6	11.7	5.9	27.6

Table 5: Infant mortality in the Taimyr autonomous district559 in 1990-1992 (expressed as per 1,000 livebirths)[560]

Year	Indigenous people	Non-indigenous people
1990	27.7	15.8
1991	29.2	19.9
1992	67.6	40.5

There is a strong sex-ratio imbalance: in all indigenous nations but one, the Aleuts, the number of women greatly exceeds the number of men. The Even male-female ratio is 1,000:1,469; Veps, 1,000:1,450; and Saami 1,000:1,300.[561] The urban-rural comparison of sex ratio suggests that this sex-ratio imbalance is driven by the migration of indigenous women to urban areas. The sex-ratio

---

[555] Kozlov and Lisitsyn (2008), p. 95.

[556] Based on data from Northern Practical Dictionary (2005) as quoted in Kozlov et al. (2007), p. 29.

[557] Kozlov and Lisitsyn (2008), p. 93.

[558] Estimated by Bogoyavlensky (2004). Quoted in Kozlov and Lisitsyn (2008), p. 93.

[559] Note that the Taimyr autonomous district ceased to exist as a distinct federal subject as of 1 January 2007.

[560] Kozlov et al. (2007), p. 32.

[561] Russian Population Census (2013), Press Kit, 9.

imbalance among indigenous urban dwellers is particularly striking, with male-female ratio being 1,000:1,805 among the Even; 1,000:1,690 among the Dolgan; and 1,000:1642 among the Ket people.[562] On average, the number of indigenous women in urban areas exceeds the number of indigenous men by a third.

Alcohol and its impact on mortality

Rapid social changes, poverty and uncertainty have resulted in high levels of stress, substance abuse, accidents, violence and suicide. The shift away from the typical protein-lipid diet of indigenous northerners which leads to the reduction of stress-relieving hormone corticosteroid,[563] have resulted in high levels of anxiety and higher alcohol consumption.[564] Poisonings from low-quality alcohol are also frequent. Although alcohol abuse has a major impact on the mortality pattern of northern regions in general, it has had a particularly significant impact on indigenous peoples, with levels of alcohol use atypically high among women. For instance, in the Berezovo region of the Khanty-Mansi autonomous district, in 1996-1999, out of 362 deaths among indigenous peoples excluding infants, one third were associated with alcohol, while the rate of alcohol-related deaths was 15 per cent in non-indigenous population. Alcohol-related deaths in women were five times higher among the indigenous peoples than among Russian northerners.[565] In the Chukchi autonomous district, alcohol caused 42 per cent of indigenous women's deaths, while alcohol caused 19 per cent of deaths of non-indigenous women.[566] Even when it does not end in human losses, alcohol consumption leads to economic losses which directly or indirectly decrease life quality. The rate of death resulting from external causes among indigenous northerners is more than twice the Russian average. At 100 cases per 100,000, indigenous suicide rates exceeded 2.5 times the national average and five times the critical threshold for suicide rates established by the WHO. The incidence of violent deaths is 70 per 100,000 compared to 27 per 100,000 overall in Russia.[567] In the early 1990s, 73 per cent of murders, 55 per cent of suicides, 64 per cent of accidental injuries among indigenous northerners occurred in a condition of medium or strong alcoholic intoxication.[568]

After a steady increase during Soviet times, the growth of indigenous populations in Russia slowed down during the last two decades of the twentieth century due to the decline in the birth rate and an increase in the death rate.[569] Consequently, the average age of indigenous northerners remains considerably lower than that of the general population of the Russian Federation, with the median age of most indigenous peoples of the North between 21 and 29 years.[570] The median age of the general population of the Russian Federation is 38 years. The overall number

---

[562] Russian Population Census (2013), Press Kit, 9.

[563] Panin (1987)

[564] Borinskaya et al. (2009) pp. 126-127

[565] Data from Kozlov and Vershubsky (1999) as quoted in Kozlov and Lisitsyn (2008), p. 98.

[566] Data from Kozlov and Vershubsky (1999) as quoted in Kozlov and Lisitsyn (2008), p. 98.

[567] Bogoyavlensky (2012).

[568] Data from Kozlov and Vershubsky (1999) as quoted in Kozlov and Lisitsyn (2008), p. 98.

[569] Kozlov and Lisitsyn (2008), pp. 92-93.

[570] Russian Population Census (2013), Press Kit, 9.

of indigenous peoples in the Russian Federation increased by 9,567 between the 2002 and 2010 censuses. However, population increase occurred only in 16 out of 47 indigenous groups.[571]

Organization of health care provision in the North of the Russian Federation

Russia's North has the same formal structure of health care services as the rest of the country and, in addition, it practises the use of mobile health teams. Small rural villages are serviced by medical aid stations equipped with a few beds. These stations are staffed by medical assistants and midwives and report to local hospitals. The latter are equipped with clinical laboratory and radiology units and have one or more physicians, a surgeon and a gynaecologist. The closer to administrative centres, the more specialized is the level of facilities and staff. The system includes specialized medical dispensaries for certain diseases, such as tuberculosis, cancer, sexually trans-mitted infections, psychiatric disorders and skin diseases. Emergency evacuation from remote villages is usually conducted by regular light planes and helicopters at the request of hospitals.[572]

Russian federal legislation guarantees indigenous peoples' access to free medical care in state and municipal health care facilities within the framework of the programme of state guarantees for mandatory health insurance.[573] Regional programmes of state guarantees of provision of free health services may exceed federal standards set at the national level. This allows regional programmes to take into consideration the climate and geography of the region and other specific features.[574]

Thus, a distinctive feature of health care provision in the Russian North are mobile health care teams. The decision to create such teams rests with the health authorities at the district level. There are no set standards regarding these teams' size, personnel, functions or equipment. Whereas some mobile teams are staffed with one medical assistant and nurse, other mobile teams may be staffed with medical specialists providing more complex diagnostic and treatment services, such as, for example, lung examinations by fluoroscopy.[575] While many medical assistants and nurses in pre-dominantly indigenous areas are indigenous, most doctors are not. Although indigenous peoples rarely face language problems in their communication with doctors, there is a need for doctors to have better knowledge of the indigenous cultures.[576] Physicians training at medical universities are neither exposed to course on "northern medicine" nor trained to work with indigenous peoples.[577]

Key factors influencing indigenous peoples' access to health services

Environmental factor: pollution and degradation

It is necessary to bear in mind that the simple provision of health services, while essential, will not solve indigenous peoples' health problems; there is an urgent need for action to protect the environment in which indigenous peoples live. Environmental pollution is one crucial factor that

---

[571] Russian Population Census (2013), Press Kit, 8.

[572] Kozlov and Lisitsyn (2008), p. 99.

[573] The Russian Federation (1999), On Guarantees of Rights for Indigenous Numerically Small Peoples of the Russian Federation. Article 8.9.

[574] The Russian Federation (2011), On fundamental principles of health care in the Russian Federation.

[575] Kozlov and Lisitsyn (2008), p. 99.

[576] Kozlov and Lisitsyn (2008), p. 99.

[577] Kozlov and Lisitsyn (2008), p. 99.

undermines indigenous peoples' health. Indigenous northerners in the Russian Federation live in regions with rich natural resources, among them oil, gas and gold, and extractive industries contribute to ecological destruction. The environment is contaminated with petroleum products, radioactive fallout from nuclear testing and fallen rocket debris. About 40 per cent of reindeer pastures are no longer usable.[578] Lack of sewage facilities in the North adds to water pollution.

Toxic chemicals are a major source of environmental pollution and causal factor in poor health. Among the most dangerous of these toxins are persistent organic pollutants (POPs)—pesticides, industrial chemicals and by-products—that have a particular combination of physical and chemical properties that, when released into the environment, remain intact for years. They become widely distributed as a result of natural processes involving soil, water and air. POPs accumulate in the fatty tissue of living organisms are more concentrated higher in the food chain and are toxic to both humans and wildlife. POPs end up in the Arctic through the "grasshopper effect", a process by which pollutants released in one area are transported to far-removed regions by way of continuous evaporation and condensation in the atmosphere. POPs also concentrate in living organisms through bioaccumulation process through which pollutants are absorbed and stored in fatty tissue. Fish, predatory birds, mammals and humans, all of which are high in the food chain, absorb the greatest concentrations of pollutants. As a result, POPs are found in people and animals living in the Arctic, thousands of kilometres from any major POPs source.[579]

Today, then, indigenous northerners' diet consists of either expensive commercial processed foods high in sugar and salt or cheaper traditional foods containing dangerous contaminants. The effects of POPs on human health can include allergies, immune system disruption, damage to the nervous system, reproductive disorders and cancer.[580] POPs are transferred from mother to foetus in utero, which can lead to the development of new pathologies.[581] One of the most dangerous POPs is DDT, widely used in the past for pest and disease control. DDT remains in the soil 10-15 years after application and long-term exposure is associated with chronic illnesses.[582] Indigenous northerners also used DDT for cleaning, treating their homes and even washing.[583] Empty DDT containers were used for storing water, making dough and brewing alcohol. In addition, indigenous peoples used DDT for processing reindeer hides and meat, and often did so on the banks of rivers and lakes from which they took drinking water.[584]

Among other toxic substances present in Russia's North are heavy metals such as mercury, lead and cadmium. The quantity of mercury released into the environment in the Yamal-Nenets and Taimyr autonomous districts[585] reaches 15 tons a year; polychlorinated biphenyls, 3.2 tons. In a number of coastal regions of the Russian Arctic, the blood of the indigenous residents has con-

---

[578] Novikova (2008), p. 283.

[579] Stockholm Convention on Persistent Organic Pollutants.

[580] WHO Glossary: Persistent Organic Pollutants (POPs).

[581] Abryutina (2012), p. 217.

[582] The 12 initial POPs under the Stockholm Convention. Stockholm Convention on Persistent Organic Pollutants (POPs).

[583] Abryutina (2012), p. 217.

[584] Abryutina (2012), p. 217.

[585] Note that the Taimyr autonomous district ceased to exist as a distinct federal subject as of 1 January 2007.

centrations of polychlorinated biphenyls, hexachlorocyclohexane, DDT, lead and mercury 10 times higher than that of the residents of Russia's large urban centres.[586]

Indigenous peoples are highly dependent on natural foods, in part out of necessity due to poverty but also for biological and cultural reasons. Today, however, the consumption of meat and fat from certain species of birds, fish and animals can present danger, particularly to pregnant and nursing women and to children. Indigenous northerners have a tradition of breastfeeding for up to seven years,[587] but this can be harmful under current conditions, as milk is rich in fats containing toxic chemicals.[588] Research shows that 75 per cent of infant mortality of indigenous peoples is caused by genetic diseases or diseases that cause foetal changes in infants.[589] The level of environmental pollution correlates positively with rates of stillbirths, mental disorders and cataracts.[590]

Some adaptive mechanisms acquired over centuries of exposure to harsh climatic conditions may have adverse effects in current environmental conditions. Indigenous northerners have developed a peculiar breathing pattern which protects them from extremely cold air: a very brief inhalation is followed by a long exhalation. This breathing pattern may, however, be harmful with the current state of environmental pollution, as toxic substances are held longer in the lungs, leading to a whole range of respiratory and pulmonary diseases, including lung cancer.[591]

Geographic factor: remote and rural locations, vast territories and low population density

Many indigenous peoples in the North of Russia continue to lead rural and nomadic lifestyles in their traditional environments. Harsh climatic conditions, vast territories, extremely low population density and remote locations hinder access to health services. "In the 2002 Census, only 28 per cent of indigenous peoples within the territories of their primary residence were classified as urban, a proportion similar to that of the total USSR population in the 1930s, compared with 73 per cent in the Russian Federation in 2002".[592] Although an increase in energy prices on world markets resulted in greater macroeconomic stability and better living standards across Russia, there is a clear urban-rural divide throughout the country. Poverty is now a predominantly rural phenomenon, and indigenous northerners experience particularly severe hardship. As previously mentioned, there has been a sharp drop in the number of rural hospitals since the collapse of the Soviet Union. Both indigenous and non-indigenous rural populations have poorer health and less access to health services than urban residents. Rural indigenous northerners tend to demonstrate lower satisfaction with their ethnic origin than their urban counterparts.[593]

Population density in indigenous territories is extremely low: it is 0.07 per 1 square kilometres in the Chukchi autonomous district, 0.31 in the Republic of Sakha and 0.7 in the Yamal-Nenets autonomous district. Russia's northern regions occupy 53.4 per cent of the country's territory but only

---

[586] Institute of Professional Environmental Practice.

[587] Abryutina (2012), p. 217.

[588] Abryutina (2012), p. 217.

[589] Naroditsky et al. (1995), pp. 62-7.

[590] Naroditsky et al. (1995), pp. 62-7.

[591] Sedov (1988), pp. 12-23.

[592] Kozlov and Lisitsyn (2008), p. 95.

[593] Kozlov and Lisitsyn (2008), p. 95.

5.7 per cent of the country's total population.[594] Even if, as Table 1 shows, the number of medical personnel per 10,000 population in indigenous areas is close to the Russian average, reaching small, widely scattered communities in remote areas with harsh climate is a challenge, and more resources are required for the provision of health services under such conditions in comparison to areas with higher population densities and milder climates. According to the OECD, northern districts have some of the highest public health expenditures per capita.[595]

Although the government launched a number of federal-level health programmes to improve primary-care provision in rural areas, indigenous nomads' access to timely and comprehensive health services, particularly prevention services, remains limited. The dissolution of the Soviet Union in 1991, lead to an exodus of professionals, including doctors, from Russia's Arctic regions.[596] The practice of mobile health teams has declined since the collapse of the Soviet Union and is irregular. Reindeer-herding communities depend on unreliable communications networks and air ambulance not only for emergencies but also for primary care services. In some areas, radio communication is possible only a couple of times a day, and even this depends on the weather. Thus, even if air ambulance is located in the same district, uses the shortest flying routes and runs around the clock, access to health services is undermined by limited communication networks. The difficulty of obtaining health care pushes elder nomads to move into villages.

Socioeconomic factor: level of education, employment and occupation, income

The social fabric of the Soviet Union provided indigenous peoples with a certain safety net that guaranteed employment and income. The reforms of the 1990s led to massive abandonment of reindeer herding, fishing, hunting and other traditional activities. Few communities worldwide experienced such a rapid shift from stability to a complete economic breakdown. To this day unemployment rates are high among indigenous northerners, particularly men, and official numbers are likely conservative, as data reflect only the number of people who voluntarily register as unemployed. Few indigenous peoples are employed in the formal sector, which means that few have access to the potential health benefits that work in the formal sector provides.

In 10 of the 15 northern regions of the Russian Federation, GRP per capita is higher than the national average. However, there is a marked gap in income levels between indigenous and non-indigenous populations. "According to local surveys carried out among the Khanty-Mansi population in 1999, the per capita monetary income for rural Khanty and Mansi ... amounted to only 15 per cent of the regional average. All the surveyed indigenous peoples lived below the officially established monthly subsistence wage for this region".[597] Low income forces indigenous peoples to turn to a subsistence economy, which has a negative effect on nutrition and health.[598] Additionally, low income may lead to decreased health care access in situations where out-of-pocket payments are required, for example, if they travel to larger residential areas. According to the global corruption watchdog Transparency International, the Russian health care system suffers from corruption, and those who cannot afford to pay or bribe may not receive proper care.

---

[594] Akopov and Gadzhiev (2008), p. 481.

[595] OECD (2012), p. 37.

[596] Kozlov and Lisitsyn (2008), p. 100.

[597] Kozlov and Lisitsyn (2008), p. 88.

[598] Kozlov and Lisitsyn (2008), p. 89.

"According to a summer 2006 study commissioned by the group, 13 per cent of 1,502 respondents who had sought medical help during the previous year had to pay an average of $90 under the table, out of wages averaging $480 a month".[599] Rural residents bear a double burden as they not only lack access to health care services, but are less able to afford the costs of illness, including the loss of work days and, if they have to travel to obtain health care services, out-of-pocket payments for transportation, accommodation and food.

Another important factor increasing indigenous peoples' chances of achieving better health is education. The level of education among indigenous people is generally lower than that of non-indigenous populations.[600] Lower education levels have a negative impact on health and contribute to a cycle of poor health. Education increases access to health care and successful education relies on adequate health. Health is a crucial factor in school attendance and performance. Healthier individuals learn more efficiently and they are more able to productively use education at any point in life.[601] Improved education and health help to break cycles of poverty and have multiplied effects for subsequent generations. Education is a precondition for training as a nurse or doctor (as mentioned above, while there are indigenous mid-level medical staff, there are few indigenous doctors). Educated parents are better able to attend to their children's health and nutritional needs and educated people are better able to come up with innovations that benefit their communities.[602] While education and income levels have an impact on health, health also has a significant impact on education and income levels.

The study comparing health indicators of nomadic indigenous, sedentary indigenous and non-indigenous women in the Far North of the Krasnoyarsk Krai showed that nomadic indigenous women living in the tundra are in better health than sedentary indigenous women in small towns and settlements, which demonstrates two things. On one hand, having left their traditional lifestyle in the tundra for urban settlements, they may not have been able to adapt well to the new living conditions.[603] It may be that with no family support the urban based sedentary indigenous women have higher levels of smoking and alcohol consumption and abuse.[604] On the other hand, the fact that nomadic indigenous women are in better health but their infant- and child-mortality rates are higher can be accounted to lower living standards in the tundra, lack of sanitation, delays in seeking medical care as well as access to health services due to remote locations and a lack of means of communication.[605]

---

[599] New York Times (2007).

[600] Russian Population Census (2013), Press Kit, 13.

[601] Todaro and Smith (2006), p. 366.

[602] Todaro and Smith (2006), p. 369.

[603] Zakharova et al. (2012) p. 50.

[604] Zakharova et al. (2012) p. 50.

[605] Zakharova et al. (2012) p. 50.

Table 6: Comparison of health indicators of nomadic indigenous sedentary indigenous and non-indigenous women in the Far North of the Krasnoyarsk Krai[606] (per cent)

Pathologies	Indigenous nomadic	Indigenous sedentary	Non-indigenous
Diseases of the circulatory system	2.0	7.3	7.3
Diseases of the respiratory system	6.7	13.3	8.7
Diseases of renal and urinary systems	10.0	20.0	26.0
Disorders of fat metabolism	4.0	5.3	9.4
Thyroid disease	4.0	17.3	12.7
Diseases of the digestive system	2.0	3.3	5.3
Gynaecological diseases	64.0	67.3	74.7
Harmful habits			
Smoking	32.7	58.0	46.0
Alcohol consumption	8.0	10.0	7.3
Alcohol abuse	0.7	2.0	1.3
Child mortality			
Women who lost one infant	7.3	6.0	2.7
Women who lost two infants	1.3	0.7	0.0
Women who lost three infants	0.7	0.0	0.0
Women who had one stillbirth	2.7	2.0	0.0
Women who had two stillbirths	1.3	0.0	0.0

This finding underlines the importance of ensuring indigenous peoples have access to health care in their natural environment and of supporting them in attaining the highest possible health standards wherever they live.

Interventions to alleviate access barriers to health services can be both demand-side and supply-side oriented, with the most effective interventions being those that address the two simultaneously, e.g., provision of services combined with raising awareness and social marketing. Some of the priority areas for targeting improvements are primary care, prevention, psychological counselling services, and the identification of environmental risks.

The mobile health teams have been a successful model in bringing health care to indigenous northerners, whether they are nomadic reindeer herders and fishermen or simply live in remote villages. Sufficiently outfitted, the teams have proven that they can provide direct health services and raise awareness about prevention.

---

[606] Adapted from Zakharova et al. (2012), pp. 47-48.

Such interventions in remote northern areas require financial commitments that take into account geographic characteristics and can make a real contribution to the health status of indigenous peoples. When planning the allocation of resources, the social justice goals of preserving unique ethnic groups collective identities and ancient ways of knowing—rather than purely economic considerations—should be taken into account. Described below are some of the most successful models of health service provision to northern indigenous communities.

Delivery of health services in the tundra: Red Tent[607]

In 2008, the Yasavey Association of the Nenets peoples and medical specialists from Arkhangelsk implemented a project called "Kanin Red Tent", a revival of an old practice used by the Soviet authorities in the 1930s. A doctor and a cultural worker travelled for nine weeks around the settlements in the Kanin tundra, working with the families of nomadic reindeer herders of the Kanin peninsula. They covered 10 groups of nomadic reindeer herders of a total of approximately 250 individuals, a third of them children. The work of the mobile health team was divided into four parts. First, in order to fill existing information gaps, they took a medical and social inventory of the nomadic population covered by the project. Second, using special equipment allowing assessment of 40 different parameters, they tried to get a picture of how indigenous nomads cope with infections, climatic and meteorological conditions and changes in daily rhythms. Third, they taught reindeer herders basic first-aid techniques to be used in cases of high fever, food poisoning, etc., and provided each group of herders with a first-aid manual. Finally, having taken stock of the most frequent health problems, they prescribed medications and selected patients to receive in-depth specialized health care services at hospitals of different levels. With hypertension being a major health problem among indigenous nomads, the doctor provided herders with blood pressure monitors and trained them to use them. The "red tent" provided emergency aid, including emergency dental care, physiotherapy services and medications, and provided supervision to two pregnant women. In addition, medical staff provided veterinary services to over 50 reindeer. Finally, the health team devised policy recommendations for preventing disease and promoting health in the conditions of the tundra. In the future, "red tents" could include nurses to deliver primary health care including vaccination. This project appears to be one of the most successful approaches to bringing health care services to indigenous northerners.

---

[607] Zubov and Sovershayev (2008).

Awareness Raising: Persistent toxic substances (PTS), food security and indigenous peoples of the Russian North.[608]

The project Persistent Toxic Substances, Food Security and Indigenous Peoples of the Russian North was a joint project established by the Association of Indigenous Peoples of the North, Siberia and Far East of the Russian Federation (RAIPON), the Arctic Monitoring and Assessment Programme (AMAP) and the Global Environmental Facility (GEF). The project was implemented in 2001-2005 in four Arctic regions: Murmansk oblast and the Nenets, Taimyr and Chukchi autonomous districts. AMAP Assessments had documented how PTS have a tendency to be transported to, and accumulate in, the Arctic region. Arctic indigenous communities have some of the highest exposures to PTS of any populations on Earth due to cold Arctic climate, lipid-rich food chains, and lifestyles of indigenous people and their reliance on traditional food. The economic changes of the 1990s resulted in increased consumption by indigenous people of traditional food rich in PTS. The project aimed at assisting indigenous peoples of the Russian north in developing appropriate remedial actions to reduce the health risks associated with contamination of their environment and traditional food sources. The project distributed accessible information materials about PTS and ways to reduce health risks through modified cooking practices for traditional foods and use of imported, "European" foods, as well as the disposal of hazardous materials. The project also attempted to address root causes and advocated for the Russian Federation to join existing international agreements concerning measures to reduce the use of PTS, and to increase its involvement in the work of the Arctic Council to reduce emissions of PTS. The project put special emphasis on empowering indigenous peoples to participate in these negotiations.

Conclusion

This chapter has highlighted the health challenges faced by the indigenous peoples living in the North of the Russian Federation and drawing on analytical frameworks, identified the most relevant factors affecting indigenous peoples' access to health services in the North of the Russian Federation. Rural poverty, lack of economic opportunity, environmental degradation, adverse geography and insufficient allocation of resources for health care in rural and remote locations significantly affect indigenous peoples' access to health services and put their health at risk.

The available data suggest that indigenous peoples' health status merits special attention, and there is a need for the development of specific health care concepts and targeted interventions tailored to the needs of northern indigenous populations. A comprehensive strategy is needed and should be developed in partnership and consultation with indigenous peoples and draw on the experience of other Arctic countries in enhancing access of indigenous peoples to health services. The strategy could include 1) prioritizing the collection and analysis of disaggregated demographic and health data, 2) providing resources to ensure affordable, culturally capable health care access where people live, e.g., through mobile health teams with knowledge of indigenous culture and health, 3) implementing awareness and prevention programs and (iv) ensuring access to specialised care and treatments including emergency care, e.g. through evacuations, when needed. These specific mea-

---

[608] GEF, UNEP, AMAP, RAIPON (2004).

[609] Note that the Taimyr autonomous district ceased to exist as a distinct federal subject as of 1 January 2007.

sures need to be accompanied by urgent local, national and international action to address the root economic, social and environmental causes impacting on indigenous peoples' health.

List of references

Abryutina, L.I. (2012). Mezhdu dvux ognei. Vliyanie sotsialnykh iekologicheskikh faktorov na zdorovye korennykh malochislennykh narodov Severa. In Sovremennoe sostoyanie I puti razvitiya korennykh malochislennykh narodov Severa, Sibiri I Dal'nego Vostoka Rossiiskoi Federatsii, V.A. Shtyrov (Ed.) (The current status and the development of indigenous minorities of the North, Siberia and Far East of the Russian Federation). Moscow: Sovet Federatsii Federalnogo Sobraniya Rossiiskoi Federatsii (Russian Federation Council), pp. 210-221. Available from http://council.gov.ru/media/files/41d44f244940b60fdf20.pdf/.

Ainana, A.I., and others (2002). A feasibility study for the harvest of grey and bowhead whales to meet the cultural, traditional and nutritional requirements of the indigenous peoples of Chukotka for the years 2003-2007. Department of Agriculture, Food and Trade, Chukchi Autonomous Region, Anadyr.

Arctic Council Sustainable Development Working Group (2005). Analysis of Arctic children and youth health indicators. Future of children and youth of the Arctic initiative: report of the health programme. Available from http://portal.sdwg.org/.

Arctic Monitoring and Assessment Programme (2009). Arctic Monitoring and Assessment Programme assessment 2009: human health in the Arctic. Oslo. Available from http://www.amap.no/documents/index.cfm.

Barlow, Jim (2013). Climate and health pose big risks to Arctic natives. Eugene, Oregon: University of Oregon. Available from http://www.futurity.org/climate-and-health-pose-big-risks-to-arctic-natives/.

Bogoyavlensky (2012). Poslednie dannye o chislennosti narodov Severa (The latest data on the peoples of the North). Available from http://www.raipon.info/dokumenty/1-novosti/2637-2011-12-27-11-54-03.html.

Bristow, F., Stephens, C., and Nettleton, C. (2003). UtzW'achil: health and wellbeing among indigenous peoples. London: Health Unlimited/London School of Hygiene and Tropical Medicine.

Carino, J. (2009). Poverty and well-being. In United Nations Permanent Forum on Indigenous Issues. The state of the world's indigenous peoples. New York: United Nations Department of Economic and Social Affairs, Secretariat of the Permanent Forum on Indigenous Issues, pp. 13-45. Available from http://www.un.org/esa/socdev/unpfii/documents/sowip_web.pdf.

Cheshko, S.V.. (2000). Raspad Sovetskogo Soyuza: etnopoliticheskii analiz. (The collapse of the Soviet Union: ethnopolitical analysis). Moscow, 2nd ed.

Choynozov, E.L., and others (2004). Onkologicheskaya zabolevaemost' narodov Severa v regione Sibiri i Dal'nego Vostoka. Bulleten' SO RAMN, vol.1, No.111. Tomsk: GU NII onkologii TNTs SO RAMN. Available from http://old.soramn.ru/Journal/2004/N1/Chapter2_art2.pdf.

Committee on Indigenous Health (2002). Indigenous peoples and health. United Nations Economic and Social Council Permanent Forum on Indigenous Issues, First Session, 13-24 May 2002. New York. Available from http://www.dialoguebetweennations.com/n2n/pfii/english/HealthAnnex1.htm.

Convention on Biological Diversity (1992). The Convention on Biological Diversity. Available from http://www.biodiv.org/convention/.

Convention on Biological Diversity (2010). Article 8(j): traditional knowledge, innovations and practices. Available from http://www.cbd.int/traditional/.

Co-operation on Health and Biodiversity Initiative (2008). Second international conference on health and biodiversity. Available from http://www.cohabnet.org/cohab2008/index.htm.

Cunningham, M. (2009). Health. In United Nations Permanent Forum on Indigenous Issues. State of the world's indigenous peoples. New York: United Nations Department of Economic and Social Affairs, Secretariat of the Permanent Forum on Indigenous Issues, pp. 155-187. Available from http://www.un.org/esa/socdev/unpfii/documents/sowip_web.pdf.

Dallmann, Winfried K. (2004a). Perestroika's legacy and indigenous peoples in Magadan. In ANSIPRA's bulletin (Arctic Network for the Support of the Indigenous Peoples of the Russian Arctic), No.11-12. Available from http://npolar.no/ansipra/english/Index/html.

_____ (2004b). Social and economic problems of the indigenous population of the Magadanskaya Oblast, with the example of the Ola village. In ANSIPRA's bulletin (Arctic Network for the Support of the Indigenous Peoples of the Russian Arctic), No.11-12. Available from http://npolar.no/ansipra/english/Index/html.

Dallmann, Winfried K., Norwegian Polar Institute, Vladislav Peskov (2003). The oil adventure and indigenous people in the Nenets Autonomous Okrug. In ANSIPRA's bulletin (Arctic Network for the Support of the Indigenous Peoples of the Russian Arctic), No.10. Available from http://npolar.no/ansipra/english/Index/html.

Damman, S. (2007). Indigenous vulnerability and the process towards the Millennium Development Goals. Will a human rights-based approach help? International Journal on Minority and Group Rights, vol.14, No.4, pp. 489-539.

Danishevski K., Gilmore A., and M. McKee (2007). Public attitudes towards smoking and tobacco control policy in Russia. Tobacco Control, vol. 17, pp. 276-283.

Declaration of Alma-Ata (n.d.). International conference on primary health care, Alma-Ata, USSR, 6-12 September 1978. Available from http://www.who.int/publications/almaata_declaration_en.pdf. Accessed 25 October 2013.

Drobniewski, F., and others (2004). Bear trap: the colliding epidemics of multidrug resistant tuberculosis and HIV in Russia. International Journal of STD & AIDS, vol. 15, pp. 641-646.

Dudarev, A. (2006). DDT and DDE in the Russian Arctic and reproductive health of indigenous peoples International POPs Elimination Project — IPEP, 2005. Available from http:// www.ipen.org.

Durie, M. (2003). The health of indigenous peoples. British Medical Journal, vol. 326, No. 7388 (March 8), pp. 510-511. Available from http://www.ncbi.nlm.nih.gov/pmc/articles/PMC1125408/pdf/510.pdf.

Egeland, G.M., and G.G. Harrison (2013). Health disparities: promoting Indigenous Peoples' health through traditional food systems and self-determination. In Indigenous Peoples' food systems and well-being: interventions and policies for healthy communities, H.V. Kuhnlein, and others. Chapter 2. Rome: Food and Agriculture Organization of the United Nations.

Ensor, T., and S. Cooper (2004). Overcoming barriers to health service access: influencing the demand side. Health Policy Planning, vol. 17, pp. 246-56.

Environmental Change Institute (2007). Indigenous peoples and climate change. Symposium organized by J. Salick and A. Byg, University of Oxford, 12-13 April 2007. Oxford, UK. Available from http://www.eci.ox.ac.uk/news/events/070412conference.php.

Federal State Statistics Service (2008). Zdravookhranenie v Rossii, 2007. (Healthcare in Russia, 2007). Moscow: Federal'naya sluzhba gosudarstvennoi statistiki.

Federal State Statistics Service (2010a). Demograficheskii ezhegodnik Rossii, 2009. (Demographic yearbook of Russia, 2009). Moscow: Federal'naya sluzhba gosudarstvennoi statistiki.

_____ (2010b). Demograficheskii ezhegodnik Rossii. Statisticheskii sbornik (The demographic yearbook of Russia. Statistical handbook, 2010). Moscow: Federalnaya sluzhba gosudarstvennoi statistiki. Available from http://www.arcticstat.org/TableViewer.aspx?S=1&ID=15081.

_____ (2010c). Ekonomicheskii i sotsialnye pokazateli rayonov prozhivaniya korennykh malochislennyh narodov Severa. Moscow: Federal'naya sluzhba gosudarstvennoi statistiki. Available from http://www.gks.ru/wps/wcm/connect/rosstat_main/rosstat/ru/statistics/publications/catalog/doc_1140095345328.

_____ (2010d). Perechen narodov prozhivaniya korennyh i malochislennyh narodov Severa po sostoyaniyu na 01.01.2010. Moscow: Federalnaya sluzhba gosudarstvennoi statistiki. Available from http://www.gks.ru/bgd/regl/b10_23/Main.htm.

_____ (2010e). Regiony Rossii: sotsial'no-ekonomicheskie pokazateli 2010. (Regions of Russia: social and economic indicators, 2010). Moscow: Federal'naya sluzhba gosudarstvennoi statistiki.

_____ (2010f). Rossiiskii statisticheskii ezhegodnik, 2009. (Russian statistical yearbook, 2009). Moscow: Federal'naya sluzhba gosudarstvennoi statistiki.

Fink, S. (2002) International efforts spotlight traditional, complementary, and alternative medicine. American Journal of Public Health, vol. 92, pp. 1734-1739.

Food and Agriculture Organization of the United Nations (1996). Declaration on world food security. World Food Summit. Rome.

Food and Agriculture Organization of the United Nations (2009). Indigenous peoples' food systems: the many dimensions of culture, diversity and environment for nutrition and health, H.V. Kuhnlein, B. Erasmus and D. Spigelski, eds. Rome.

Global Environmental Facility, United Nations Environment Programme, Arctic Monitoring and Assessment Programme, Russian Association of the Indigenous Peoples of the North, Siberia and Far East (2004). Persistent toxic substances, food security and indigenous peoples of the Russian North. Final report. Oslo. Available from http://www.amap.no/.

Gracey, Michael, and Malcolm King (2009). Indigenous health. Part 1. Determinants and disease patterns. The Lancet, vol. 374. No. 9683, pp. 65-75.

Graham, Holly, and Lynnette Leeseberg Stamler (2010). Contemporary perceptions of health from an indigenous (plains cree) perspective. Journal de la santé autochthone (January). National Aboriginal Health Organisation. Available from http://www.naho.ca/jah/english/jah06_01/v6_I1_Contemporary_Perceptions.pdf.

Gruskin, Sofia, and Daniel Tarantola (2002). Health and human rights. In Oxford textbook of public health, 4th ed., Detels, R., and others, eds. Oxford, UK: Oxford University Press, pp. 311-336.

Gwatkin, D.R. (2000). Health inequalities and health of the poor. What do we know? What can we do? Bulletin of the World Health Organization, vol. 78, pp. 3-18.

Haines, A., and A.J. McMichael (1997). Climate change and health: implications for research, monitoring and policy. British Medical Journal, vol. 315. No. 7112, pp. 870-874.

Institute of Professional Environmental Practice (n.d.) Mery po snizheniyu riska vrednogo vozdeistviya stoikikh toksichnykh veschestv na zdorovye korennykh zhitelei arkticheskix rayonov Rossii. Project report. Severo-zapadniy nauchniy zentr gigieny i obshestvennogo zdorov'ya. Available from http://www.ecoaccord.org/pop/ipep/arctic2.htm. Accessed 25 October 2013.

Islam, R., and M. A. Sheikh (2010). Cultural and socioeconomic factors in health, health services and prevention for indigenous people. Antrocom Online Journal of Anthropology, vol 6, No. 2, pp. 263-273.

Jacobs, Bart, and others (2011). Addressing access barriers to health services: an analytical framework for selecting appropriate interventions in low-income Asian countries. Health Policy and Planning Advance Access (May 12). Available from http://www.who.int/alliance-hpsr/resources/alliancehpsr_jacobs_ir_barriershealth2011.pdf.

James C.D., Hanson K., McPake B. and others. To retain or remove user fees? Reflections on the current debate in low- and middle-income countries. Applied Health Economic and Health Policy, vol. 5, pp. 147-53.

Kapustina, Tatiana A. (2010). Epidemiologiya khronicheskikh zabolevanii ukha, gorla i nosa u korennykh zhitelei Severa i optimizatsiya lor-pomoschi. (Epidemiology of chronic diseases of ear, throat and nose in native people of the North. Optimization of otorhinolaringological assistance). Bulleten' SO RAMN, vol. 30, No. 3, pp. 45-51. NII meditsinskikh problem Severa SO RAMN. (Research Institute for Medical Problems of Northern Regions of SB RAMS). Available from http://old.soramn.ru/Journal/2010/N3/p45-51.pdf.

King, M., A. Smith, and M. Gracey (2009). Indigenous health. Part 2. The underlying causes of the health gap. The Lancet, vol. 374, No. 9683, pp. 76-85.

King, S. R. and M. S. Tempesta (1994). From shaman to human clinical trials: the role of industry in ethnobotany, conservation and community reciprocity. Ciba Foundation Symposium, vol. 185, pp. 197-206.

Kozlov, Andrew I. (2004). Impact of economic changes on the diet of Chukotka natives. International journal on circumpolar health, vol .63, No.3, pp. 235-242. Available from http://www.circumpolarhealthjournal.net/index.php/ijch/article/view/17717/20188.

Kozlov, Andrew I., and D. Lisitsyn (2008). Arctic Russia. In Health Transitions in Arctic Populations, Young T.Kue, P. Bjerregaard, eds. Toronto, Buffalo, London: University of Toronto Press, pp. 71-102.

Kozlov Andrew I. and Galina Vershubsky (1999). Meditsinskaya antropologiya korennogo naseleniya Severa Rossii. (Medical anthropology of indigenous population of the Russian North). Moscow: MNEPU.

Kozlov, Andrew I., Galina Vershubsky, and Maria Kozlova (2003). Stress under modernizing indigenous population of Siberia. International Journal of Circumpolar Health, vol.62, No.2, pp. 158-166.

_____ (2007). Indigenous peoples of Northern Russia: anthropology and health. Circumpolar Health Supplements, No.1.Oulu, Finland. Available from: http://www.circumpolarhealthjournal.net/public/journals/32/chs/CHS_2007_1.pdf.

Kuhnlein, H.V., and H.M. Chan (2000). Environment and contaminants in traditional food systems of northern indigenous peoples. Annual Review of Nutrition, vol. 20, pp. 595-626.

Kuhnlein, H.V., and others (2006). Indigenous peoples' food systems for health: finding interventions that work. Public Health Nutrition, vol.9, No.8, pp. 1013-1019. The Lancet, vol.374, No. 9683, pp. 76-85.

Kunnas, N. (2003). Revitalization of minority languages as a way to promote well-being in the North. International Journal of Circumpolar Health, vol.62, No. 4, pp. 410-22.

Leon, D.A., and V.M. Shkolnikov (1998). Social stress and the Russian mortality crisis. The Journal of the American Medical Association, vol.279, pp. 790-1.

Manchuk V.T., and L.A. Nadtochiy (2010). Sostoyanie I formirovanie zdorovya korennykh malochislennykh narodov Severa i Sibiri. (The health status and development of indigenous numerically small peoples of the North and Siberia). Bulletin of RAMN, vol. 3, pp. 24-32.

Marmot, M. (2005). Social determinants of health inequalities. The Lancet, vol. 365, pp. 1099-1104.

Mowbray, M. and World Health Organization Commission on Social Determinants of Health (2007). Social determinants and indigenous health: the international experience and its policy implications. International Symposium on the Social Determinants of Indigenous Health (April). Adelaide. Geneva: World Health Organization. Available from http://www.who.int/social_determinants/resources/indigenous_health_adelaide_report_07.pdf. Accessed 3 October 2013.

Murashko, O. (2006a). Development assistance plan for the indigenous peoples of Sakhalin continuing the discussion on the situation in Sakhalin. In ANSIPRA's bulletin (indigenous peoples of Russia), vol.15. Available from http://www. npolar.no/ansipra/english/Index/html.

_____ (2006b). Who is to blame for the tragedy of the Amur Evenks? In ANSIPRA's bulletin (indigenous peoples of Russia), vol.15. Available from http://www. npolar.no/ansipra/english/Index/html.

Naroditsky, V.I., Astakhova T.I., Denisova D.V., and M.N. Dyomina (1995). Analiz smertnosti detskogo naseleniya Chukotki v aspekte sotsialnyx i ekologicheskikh faktorov riska. (Analysis of child mortality in Chukotka and the social and ecological risk factors). In Problemy zdorovya naseleniya Krainego Severa v novykh ekonomicheskikh usloviyakh. (Health problems of Far North under new economic conditions). Novosibirsk: Nauka, pp. 62-67.

Nettleton, C., D.A. Napolitano, and C. Stephens (2007). An overview or current knowledge of the social determinants of indigenous health. Symposium on the social determinants of Indigenous health (April). Adelaide. Geneva: World Health Organization.

New York Times (2007). Despite oil wealth, Russia faces huge health care problems, 28 June 2007. Available from http://www.nytimes.com/2007/06/28/business/worldbusiness/28iht-russhealth.4.6394606.html?_r=0.

Novikova, M., ed. (2008) Ludi Severa: prava na resursy i ekspertiza. (The right to resources and expertise). Issledovaniya po antropologii prava. Moscow: Strategiya. Available from http://www.jurant.ru/materials/peoples_North.pdf.

Nussbaum, Martha C. (2000). Women and Human Development: The Capabilities Approach. Cambridge: Cambridge University Press.

O demokraticheskikh i sotsialno-ekonomicheskikh kharakteristikakh naseleniya korennykh malochislennykh narodov Rossii (po itogam Vserossiiskoi perepisi naseleniya 2010 goda) (On demographic and socioeconomic features of indigenous peoples of the Russian Federation (results of the Russian Federal Census 2010) (2013). Russian Population Census. Press kit. Available from http://www.perepis-2010.ru/smi/detail.php?ID=7715.

O'Donnell, Owen (2007). Access to health care in developing countries: breaking down demand side barriers. Cadernos de Saude Publica, vol. 23, No. 12, pp. 2820-2834.

Official web site of the Federal Consumer Right Protection and Human Wellbeing Surveillance Service (Rospotrebnadzor): http://rospotrebnadzor.ru/news (Russian with some English pages).

Official web site of the Federal Medical and Biological Agency: http://www.fmbaros.ru/ (Russian only).

Official web site of the Federal MHI Fund: http://portal.ffoms.ru/ (Russian only).

Official web site of the Federal Service on Surveillance in Healthcare and Social Development (Roszdravnadzor): http://www.roszdravnadzor.ru/ (Russian only).

Official web site of the Ministry of Health and Social Development: http://www.minzdravsoc.ru/ (Russian with some English pages).

Official web site of the President of the Russian Federation: http://kremlin.ru/ (Russian and English versions).

Official web site of the Russian Federal State Statistics Service (Rosstat): http://www.gks.ru/ (Russian with some English pages).

Official web site of the Russian Parliament (Duma): http://www.duma.gov.ru/ (Russian only).

Oliver A., and E. Mossialos (2004). Equity of access to health care: outlining the foundations for action. Journal of Epidemiology and Community Health, vol. 58: pp. 655-658.

Organisation for Economic Co-operation and Development (2012). Organisation for Economic Co-operation and Development reviews of health systems: Russian Federation. Available from http://www.keepeek.com/Digital-Asset-Management/oecd/social-issues-migration-health/oecd-reviews-of-health-systems-russian-federation-2012_9789264168091-en#page1.

Organisation for Economic Co-operation and Development (2012). Recent health policy developments in the Russian Federation. In Organisation for Economic Co-operation and Development reviews of health systems: Russian Federation 2012.

Parkinson, Alan J., and Birgitta Evengård (2009). Climate change, its impact on human health in the Arctic and the public health response to threats of emerging infectious diseases. Global Health Action, vol. 2. DOI: 10.3402/gha.v2i0.2075.

Peters, D.H., Garg, A., Bloom, G., and others (2008). Poverty and access to health care in developing countries. Annals of the New York Academy of Sciences, vol. 1136, pp. 161-71.

Popovich, L. (2011). Russian Federation. Health system review. Health Systems in Transition, vol. 13, No. 7.

Revich, Boris A. (2008). Vliyanie globalnykh klimaticheskikh izmenenii na zdorovye naseleniya rossiiskoi Arktiki. (The effect of climate change on the health of the population of the Russian Arctic.) Available from http://www.ecfor.ru/pdf.php?id=books/revich01/oon.

Ring, I., and N. Brown (2003). The health status of indigenous peoples and others. The gap is narrowing in the United States, Canada, and New Zealand, but a lot more is needed. British Medical Journal, vol. 327, No. 7412, pp. 404-405.

Russian Federation, Federalnii zakon ob osnovakh okhrany zdorov'ya grazhdan v Rossiiskoi Federatsii, No.323-F3 (of 21 November 2011). (Federal law On fundamental principles of health care in the Russian Federation). Chapter 10. Available from http://www.consultant.ru/document/cons_doc_LAW_152447/?frame=9.

Russian Federation (2002). O kontseptsii kompleksnoi okruzhnoi tselevoi programmy sotsial-no-ekonomicheskogo razvitiya korennykh malochislennykh narodov Severa Yamalo-Nenetskogo avtonomnogo okruga na 2003-2005 gody. (The concept of a complex district target programme of socioeconomic development of indigenous numerically small peoples of the North of the Yamal-Nenets autonomous district for 2003-2005). Available from http://yamal-nenets.narod.ru/data03/tex15528.htm.

Russian Medical Association: http://www.rmass.ru/ (Russian only).

Secretariat of the Stockholm Convention (2001). The Stockholm Convention on Persistent Organic Pollutants. Available from http://chm.pops.int/TheConvention/Overview/TextoftheConvention/tabid/2232/Default.aspx.

Sedov, K.R. Nekotorye itogi i perspektivy razvitiya nauchnykh issledovanii po izucheniyu pitaniya naseleniya Sibiri. (Some results and perspectives on development of scientific research on nutrition of Siberian populations.) Bulleten' SO RAMN, vol.2, pp. 12-23.

Sen, Amartya K. (1985). Commodities and Capabilities. Amsterdam: Elsevier.

Sen, Amartya K. (1999). Development as freedom. New York: Knopf.

Shkolnikov, Vladimir M., and others (2004). Russian mortality beyond vital statistics. Effects of social status and behaviours on deaths from circulatory disease and external causes - a case-control study of men aged 20-55 years in Udmurtia, 1998-1999. Demogr Res (Special Collection), vol. 2, pp. 71-103.

Shtyrov, V.A., ed. (2012) Sovremennoe sostoyanie i puti razvitiya korennykh malochislennykh narodov Severa, Sibiri i Dal'nego Vostoka Rossiiskoi Federatsii. (The current status and the development of indigenous minorities of the North, Siberia and Far East of the Russian Federation). Moscow: Sovet Federatsii Federalnogo Sobraniya Rossiiskoi Federatsii (Russian Federation Council). Available from http://council.gov.ru/media/files/41d44f244940b60fdf20.pdf/.

Sims, J., and H.V. Kuhnlein (2003). Indigenous peoples' participatory health research, planning and management. Preparing research agreements. Geneva: World Health Organization and Centre for Indigenous Peoples' Nutrition and Environment. Available from http://www.who.int/ethics/indigenous_peoples/en/index1.html.

Snodgrass, Josh J. (2013). Health of Indigenous Circumpolar Populations. Annual Review of Anthropology, vol. 42.

Snodgrass, Josh J., and others (2006). Emergence of obesity in indigenous Siberians. Journal of Physiological Anthropology, vol. 25, pp. 75-84. Available from http://www.bonesandbehavior.org/snodgrass2006jpa.pdf.

Snodgrass, Josh J., and others (2010). Rapid changes in cardiovascular risk factors associated with economic development and lifestyle change in an indigenous circumpolar population from Siberia. Abstract. Available from http://www.bonesandbehavior.org/snodgrass2010aapa.pdf.

Sorensen, Mark V., and others (2005). Health consequences of post socialist transition: dietary and lifestyle determinants of plasma lipids in Yakutia. American Journal of Human Biology, vol. 17, pp. 576-592. Available from http://www.bonesandbehavior.org/sorensen2005ajhb.pdf.

Sorensen, Mark V., and others (2009). Lifestyle incongruity, stress and immune function in Indigenous Siberians: The health impacts of rapid social and economic change. American Journal of Physical Anthropology, vol. 138, pp. 62-69. Available from http://www.bonesandbehavior.org/sorensen2009ajpa.pdf.

Stepanovskaya, I.A., Dorzhinkevich, S.I. and Borisov V.G. (1998). Problemy sotsialnogo razvitiya korennykh malochislennykh narodov Severa. (Social development problems of indigenous numerically small peoples of the North). IPU RAN.

Stephens, Carolyn, and others (2005). Indigenous peoples' health—why are they behind everyone, everywhere? The Lancet, vol. 366, No. 9479, pp. 10-13.

Stephens, Carolyn, and others (2006). Disappearing, displaced, and undervalued: a call to action for Indigenous health worldwide. The Lancet, vol. 367, No. 9527, pp. 2019-2028.

Tkachenko, E., and others (2000). Public health in Russia: the view from the inside. Health Policy and Planning, vol.15, No.2, pp. 164-169.

Todaro, Michael P., and Stephen C. Smith (2006). Economic development, 9th ed. Upper Saddle River, New Jersey: Prentice Hall.

United Nations (2000). United Nations Millennium Declaration.

United Nations Development Programme (2004). Human development reports. Cultural liberty in today's diverse world. New York.

United Nations Economic and Social Council (2004). Report of the workshop on data collection and disaggregation for indigenous peoples. In Workshop on data collection and disaggregation for indigenous peoples, 19-21 January. New York: United Nations Educational, Scientific and Cultural Organization.

United Nations Educational, Scientific and Cultural Organization (2005). Best practices on indigenous knowledge. Available from http://www.unesco.org/most/bpikpub.htm.

United Nations General Assembly (2005). Draft programme of action for the Second International decade of the World's Indigenous People. Report of the Secretary General.

United Nations General Assembly (2007). Declaration on the rights of indigenous peoples. 13 September. Available from http://daccess-dds-ny.un.org/doc/UNDOC/GEN/N06/512/07/PDF/N0651207.pdf?OpenElement. Accessed 3 October 2013.

United Nations Permanent Forum on Indigenous Issues (2005). Fourth session: the MDGs and indigenous peoples. New York.

United Nations Permanent Forum on Indigenous Issues (2006). Millennium development goals and indigenous peoples. Report on the Second Session of the UNPFII. Para. 26. United Nations. E/C.19/2003/22.

United Nations Permanent Forum on Indigenous Issues (2009). The state of the world's indigenous peoples. New York: United Nations Department of Economic and Social Affairs, Secretariat of the Permanent Forum on Indigenous Issues. Available from http://www.un.org/esa/socdev/unpfii/documents/sowip_web.pdf.

United Nations Population Fund UNFPA (2005). State of world population, the promise of equality: gender equity, reproductive health and the MDGs. Available from https://www.unfpa.org/swp/2005/pdf/en_swp05.pdf. Accessed 3 October 2013.

Vozoris, N.T., and V.S. Tarasuk (2003). Household food insufficiency is associated with poorer health. Journal of Nutrition, vol. 133, pp. 120-126.

Walberg, P., and others (1998). Economic change, crime and mortality crisis in Russia: regional analysis. British Medical Journal, vol.317, pp. 312-318.

Wigle, Don T. (2005). Analysis of Arctic children and youth health indicators: future of children and youth of the Arctic initiative report of the health programme. Ottawa: Health Canada. Available from http://www.sdwg.org.

World Bank (2010). Indigenous peoples. Available from http://web.worldbank.org/wbsite/external/topics/extsocialdevelopment/extindpeople/0,,menupk:407808~pagepk:149018~pipk:149093~thesitepk:407802,00.html.

World Health Organization (1948). Constitution of the World Health Organization. Available from http://www.who.int/governance/eb/who_constitution_en.pdf.

World Health Organization (1999). The Geneva declaration on the health and survival of indigenous peoples. Available from http://www.dialoguebetweennations.com/n2n/pfii/english/HealthAnnex1.htm. Accessed 3 October 2013.

World Health Organization (2010). The health and human rights of indigenous peoples. Available from http://www.who.int/hhr/activities/indigenous/en/.

World Health Organization (2012). The right to health. Fact sheet N°323. Available from http://www.who.int/mediacentre/factsheets/fs323/en/.

Young, Kue T., and Peter Bjerregaard, eds. (2008). Health transitions in Arctic populations. Toronto: University of Toronto Press.

Young, Kue T. (2008). Circumpolar health indicators: sources, data, and maps. Circumpolar Health Supplements, vol. 3. Oulu, Finland: International Association of Circumpolar Health Publishers. Available from http://www.circumpolarhealthjournal.net/public/journals/32/chs/CHS_2008_3.pdf.

Zakharova, T.G., Kashina M.A., and G.N. Zakharov (2012). Zavisimost reproduktivnogo zdorov'ya zhenshinkorennyh narodov krainego severa ot uklada zhizni. Zemskii vrach, vol.3, pp.47-50. Available from http://cyberleninka.ru/article/n/zavisimost-reproduktivnogo-zdorovya-zhenschin-korennyh-narodov-kraynego-severa-ot-uklada-zhizni.

Zubov, L.A., and A.L. Sovershayev (2008). "Kaninskii Krasnii chum" kak forma organizatsii meditsinskoi pomoshi i resheniya mediko-sotsialnyh problem kochuyushyh olenevodov Nenetskogo avtonomnogo okruga . "KKCh" medical report. Arkhangelsk: Northern State Medical University. Available from http://www.nsmu.ru/science/nii_pol_med/korennoe_nasel/krasniy_chum.php.

www.ingramcontent.com/pod-product-compliance
Lightning Source LLC
Chambersburg PA
CBHW082355270326
41935CB00013B/1626